GOLF LIST
MANIA!

The Most Authoritative and Opinionated Rankings of the Best and Worst of the Game

Leonard Shapiro and Ed Sherman

RUNNING PRESS
PHILADELPHIA · LONDON

Library of Congress Control Number: 2010937314

ISBN 978-0-7624-4069-6

Cover and Interior Designed by Jason Kayser
Photo Research by Susan Oyama
Edited by Greg Jones

Running Press Book Publishers
2300 Chestnut Street
Philadelphia, PA 19103-4371

Visit us on the web!
www.runningpress.com

CONTENTS

Leonard Shapiro:
To Vicky, Jennifer, Emily, and Taylor, aces and
albatrosses all, for everything.

Ed Sherman:
To my parents, Jerry and Susan, for
introducing me to golf. And to Ilene, Matthew, and
Sam for filling out my dream foursome.

FOREWORD

► BY JIM NANTZ

I got a phone call from two of my favorite friends in the media, Ed Sherman and Len Shapiro. They said they were writing a book on golf. Having been familiar with their games (not pretty), I knew they weren't collaborating on a golf instruction book. They are more "Lunge and Duck" than "Stack and Tilt."

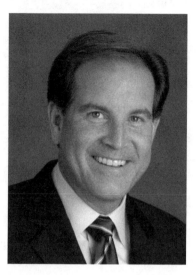

Although they may not be great golfers, they are great chroniclers of the game. They asked me to do the foreword for their new book, *Golf List Mania!* I figured there only was one way to approach it: I decided to come up with a series of lists.

Let's start from the beginning . . .

Why Would I Want to Write a Foreword for Such a Book?

5. Why not?

4. It might be kind of cool.

3. It will be high quality.

2. It gets me thinking about golf.

1. I've always been into lists myself.

★ ★ ★ ★

Then I got to thinking about the authors of this book. Let me tell you about them.

What You Should Know about Ed Sherman

5. He is among the best left-handed golfers in the media. Of course, there aren't many lefties.

9

4. He's living for the day when he hears me on the call for his beloved University of Illinois basketball team winning the NCAA title. So close in 2005.

3. He was a longtime writer for the *Chicago Tribune*, one of my favorite papers, and still writes for several publications, including Crain's *Chicago Business*.

2. He has won several Golf Writers Association of America awards.

1. He knows golf.

What You Should Know about Len Shapiro

5. He did a really nice review of my book, *Always by My Side*, for the *Washington Post* in 2007, writing that I was "proof positive that nice guys can finish first, at least on the national bestseller list."

4. He's waiting for that one shining moment when his alma mater, the University of Wisconsin, wins the NCAA, preferably beating Sherman's Illinois team in the title game.

3. He was a longtime writer for the *Washington Post*, also one of my favorite papers, and still writes a popular media column for the paper's Web site.

2. He's a former president of the Golf Writers Association and also has won several writing awards in addition to being honored by the Pro Football Hall of Fame for a long and distinguished career covering the NFL.

1. A former caddy who started looping at age 14, he knows golf, too.

★ ★ ★ ★

Then I thought about their concept.

Why Lists Work for Golf

5. It'll be a good challenge for those golfers who can't count past five.

4. It's a heck of a lot easier to come up with a list of the ten greatest courses than it is to break 90 on any of them.

3. Each list is like a hole on a course—different and distinct.

2. Golf is a thinking man's game. It requires a mindset and appreciation for strategy. There's strategy involved in making a list.

1. Golfers aren't that much into numbers, but they're into lists. Lists provide context.

★ ★ ★ ★

Could the authors back it up? Of course.

Here Are Some of My Favorite Lists in the Book

10. "Greatest Shots of All Time." I was fortunate to be on hand for a few of them.

9. "The Perfect Golfer." The authors select the attributes to create a player who would break 60 on a regular basis.

8. "Ten Free-Spirited Favorites." A terrific account of the players who added some spice to the game.

7. "Fantasy Foursomes." An eclectic mix full of all sorts of possibilities.

6. "Beyond the Green Jacket." Only one player gets the Green Jacket, but the Masters offers an array of other prizes for the players.

5. "The Funny Irishman: David Feherty's Best Lines." A list of hilarious quotes from my colleague, who fortunately for him is making a better living with his mouth than he did with his clubs.

4. "Tuning in to Better Golf on Television" by CBS golf producer Lance Barrow. The best in the business writes about how technology has changed how golf is covered on television.

3. "Top Ten Golf Movies." Several of my CBS colleagues and I appeared on the No. 2 movie on the list. Unfortunately, no Oscar nominations.

2. "Favorite Moments." My most memorable moments. I weigh in on the great tournaments that I'll never forget.

1. "My Five Most Important Victories" by Arnold Palmer. You'll be surprised which championship "The King" selects for No. 1.

★ ★ ★ ★

And there's plenty more. It all leads to my final list.

Why You'll Enjoy This Book

5. Contributions from famous golf writers. You'll get the perspective from some of the best in the business.

4. Original lists contributed by the greats, including golf's "Big 3": Jack Nicklaus, Arnold Palmer, and Gary Player. It doesn't get much better than that.

3. A walk through golf history from Young and Old Tom Morris to Tiger Woods. You'll learn a thing or two along the way.

2. There are no right answers. The fun part of this book is the debates that the lists spark. I'm sure there will be lists that make you think, "That guy is a complete idiot." Isn't that the essence of golf and sports?

1. The next best thing to playing golf is reading about golf. You also make fewer bogeys that way. My good friends Ed and Len have compiled more than 100 juicy and interesting lists that are sure to entertain.

I hope you enjoy this unique look at the game we all love.

INTRODUCTION

Here's betting that your high school football uniform now would be two sizes too small.

Your last nine-on-nine baseball game probably occurred before you received your driver's license. And for most of us, if you tried to play full-court basketball now, you'd pull or rip muscles that you didn't know you had.

That's what separates golf from everything else. Unlike the other sports, the game can be experienced on so many different levels and for an entire lifetime.

We can watch Tiger, Phil, Sergio, Ernie, and the best players in the world on a Sunday afternoon. Then we can go out the following day and play the same sport as the pros. And if you're extremely lucky, perhaps even on the same course.

This is a book that tries to capture that essence of golf. Everyone is a player, whether you're 9 or 99.

The authors' ages are somewhere in between (unfortunately pushing closer to 99). We've played a lot of bad golf as players. Let's just put it this way: If the over-the-top move was the key to a successful swing, they'd be writing about us.

Also, as longtime chroniclers of the game, we've had the privilege of witnessing a lot of good and bad golf. We have been on hand for many epic moments that rank among the best in golf history.

The lists and all the information and opinions inside this book are a celebration of golf. These views are our boiled-up passion exploding on these pages. Stuff about the game that makes us glad, thrilled, irritated, frustrated, and downright ticked off (slow play!)—it's all in here.

These are many of the same lists that golfers argue about at the 19th hole throughout the world. We've also recruited some of the game's biggest names and personalities to contribute to the debate with their own lists.

For those keeping score, Ed's lists are noted with "ES" by the title, and Len's have "LS." Our esteemed contributors' lists are given complete bylines.

Ultimately, the lists are just our opinions and observations about golf. Do we think we're right on everything? Hardly! Is there a possibility we failed to include somebody or something here and there? Perhaps. We don't claim to be perfect.

The idea is to spark some debate. Feel to free to disagree. Believe us, it happens all the time.

However, just know that we all have one thing in common: We love golf. The good, the bad, and the snowmans.

Now move to the first tee to join Arnold Palmer.

MY FIVE MOST MEMORABLE GOLF SHOTS

►BY ARNOLD PALMER

Just call him The King, because Arnold Palmer truly is golf royalty, the winner of 62 PGA Tour events and seven major championships as well as a man many believe is singularly responsible for popularizing golf in the United States over the course of his brilliant career. Now an octogenarian who regularly shoots his age or lower and plays or practices virtually every day, Arnie took a few minutes to provide us with two very telling lists.

5. 1968 PGA Championship. A 3-wood out of heavy rough to the 18th green in the final round was a career best shot that didn't produce a victory. I missed an eight-foot birdie putt and lost the championship by a single stroke to Julius Boros at Pecan Valley Country Club in San Antonio.

4. 1958 Masters. A 3-wood to the 13th green in the final round set up an eagle with a ruling that waited on an embedded ball drop at No. 12. The drop eventually was allowed and I won the first of my four Masters by a shot over Doug Ford and Fred Hawkins.

3. 1961 British Open. A hit with a 6-iron to the green from a very difficult lie at the 15th hole in the final round at Royal Birkdale. I made a critical par there and beat Dai Rees by a stroke, the first of my two British Open titles.

2. 1960 Masters. I made a 30-foot birdie putt at No. 17 in the final round and won the tournament by a shot over Ken Venturi.

1. 1960 U. S. Open. Just as everyone had written me off when I trailed the lead by seven shots after three rounds at Cherry Hills in Denver, I drove the green on my tee shot at the 346-yard first hole in the final round. I made a 2-putt birdie there—the first of six birdies on the opening seven holes—and beat Jack Nicklaus by two shots for my only Open title.

MY FIVE MOST IMPORTANT VICTORIES

►BY ARNOLD PALMER

5. 1955 Canadian Open. It was my first of 62 career victories on the PGA Tour. I beat Jackie Burke, Jr. by four shots at the Weston Golf Club in Toronto.

4. 1961 British Open. Held at Royal Birkdale, it was the first of my two British Open championships in a year when I won six events.

3. 1958 Masters. The first of my four Masters championships.

2. 1960 U.S. Open. My only Open championship during a year when I was named *Sports Illustrated*'s Sportsman of the Year. The tournament at Cherry Hills in Denver is considered one of the greatest Opens in history.

1. 1954 U.S. Amateur. I was 24 years old and seven months out of the Coast Guard. I defeated Robert Sweeny, a 43-year-old businessman and a very fine player, 1-up over 36 holes at the Country Club of Detroit. I've always considered winning the Amateur the turning point of my career and my life.

A is for Albatross, a double eagle, or an ace, a hole in one.

B is for Birdie and Bogey. Nine of each on your scorecard is par for the course.

C is for Caddy, a bag man of a very special kind.

D is for Dormie, a match-play advantage—2-up with two to play, for example— that means the man with the lead has earned at least a tie.

E is for Eldrick, now more Cheetah than Tiger.

F is for Flagstick, the bulls-eye target of golf.

G is for Gimme, but only inside the leather.

H is for Handicap, the ultimate equalizer for the recreational player.

I is for Irons, hybrids or the real deal.

J is for Jack, no Nicklaus necessary.

K is for The King, or Arnie if you insist.

L is for Lefty, which sounds far classier than Philly Mick.

M is for Majors, 18 is the record owned by J as in Jack.

N is for Nassau, not the Long Island county but the sport's most popular gambling game.

O is for The Old Course at St. Andrews, the golf heaven hard by the sea.

P is for Pimiento Cheese Sandwich, Augusta National's haute cuisine.

Q is for Qualifying School, where grown men in spiked shoes have been known to puke in the woods.

R is for Samuel Ryder, a tea mogul responsible for the most coveted Cup of all.

S is for the dreaded Shank, or better yet "shankapotamus," our favorite new word describing a shank-master who always walks sideways to find his ball.

T is for Toom, what they call five-time British Open champion Tom Watson in Scotland.

U is for U.S. Open, boys and girls, America's national championship.

V is for Frenchman Jean Van de Velde, the modern definition of a golf choke.

W is for Wind, as in writer Herbert Warren Wind, the poet laureate of Amen Corner.

X is for Score Unknown when you stopped counting at ten.

Y is for Yips, often a reason for X.

Z is for Zinger, or Paul Azinger, the best American Ryder Cup captain of the twenty-first century.

★ ★ ★ ★

"I'll shoot my age if I have to live to be 105."

—Bob Hope

WHY WE (OCCASIONALLY) HATE GOLF

Admit it, there are times on the golf course when you want to pull your hair out, bay at the moon, and throw those fancy-schmancy Ping irons in the closest available pond. Anyone who has ever played the game knows it's a mostly love/sometimes hate sort of relationship. Len Shapiro, who broke his maiden in the game in 1960 as a 13-year-old caddy earning $5 a bag, a free Coke at the turn, but definitely no tip, offers a few of his least favorite things about a sport often referred to as the devil's game.

10. Where have all the caddies gone? Oh sure, they're always available at Augusta National, Winged Foot, and Seminole, but why don't more courses take the time and effort to develop a caddy program for the local kids looking to make a few bucks on weekends and summer vacations? Wouldn't you and your buddy pony up $25 each to have a super looper lug your bag, rake your traps, clean your sticks, find your golf balls, help with club selection, tend the pins, and actually offer up reliable yardage? Park that cart and go take a walk.

9. Cheating hearts. We've all been there. Your opponent in that hotly contested $2 Nassau is in danger of going three down with four to play. He slices it off the tee into the deep dark woods, probably over the fence or OB. And yet, just as all seems lost, he bellows "GOT IT!!" You go over to check out his next shot, and a shiny new Titleist is sitting up on a perfect tuft of grass, with a yawning opening between the trees, giving him a clear path to the green. Have you no shame, sir? Not really.

8. Practice does not make perfect. Not on a Saturday afternoon, with foursomes going out every eight minutes and your favorite course jammed to the max. And then you notice that guy in the middle of the fairway just up ahead take a practice swing, and then another, and a third and fourth. Then comes the waggle, the Sergio Garcia grips it and regrips it, and the ball skitters 60 yards into the second cut. Before every shot, it's the same maddening routine, often with similar results. Suddenly, your pleasant four-hour round turns into a six-hour ordeal.

7. Pushy parents. Ever been to a junior golf tournament and walked a few holes with little Roscoe Hilton Armbrister IV, with his proud parents watching from the sidelines? Then he misses a three-foot putt, and here comes Roscoe Hilton Armbrister III, the boy's fire-breathing old man, smack in his face, berating the poor kid as

18

he skulks from the green to the next tee, dreading the reaction if he somehow misses the fairway on his next drive. Do your kids a favor when you come out to watch them play: Show up, then shut up.

6. Restricted tee times. Yes, they still exist. At some clubs and even a few public facilities, on weekends ladies can't tee off before noon so all those hard-working bread-winners who spent the whole week toiling in the office can play in the morning and get back home by cocktail hour. Of course, many of those same ladies have also been stuck in rush-hour traffic, grinding in the next office and often doing the work of the four men who just teed off, probably for lower pay. It's the twenty-first century fellas—time to change those sexist rules.

5. Island greens. Okay, Pete Dye can get away with it, especially when his wife Alice gives him the idea in the first place for the 17th at Sawgrass. But now, why does it seem as if every new high-end course in America just has to have a green located in the middle of a pond, no bailout available left or right, front or back, in a place where grass is not supposed to grow? Of course, thousands of golf balls manage to find all those new watery graves. Maybe you've seen them for sale in your pro shop, a 75-cent special that's all pure profit. To the moon Alice, to the moon.

4. Television swing replays. Every network does it—that super slow motion shot of a golfer from backswing to contact to follow-through, accompanied by a breathless description from the resident golf analyst (who last won a tournament in 1987) of what the golfer did right and wrong in an attempt to tell you why the ball hooked into the rough or split the fairway. I've been watching these replays for years and, heavens to Peter Kostis, still have no clue whatsoever about what they're talking about. And if Johnny Miller utters the word "supination" one more time, the flat screen may not survive. Google supination and one entry reads, "Shop FoodSmart for supination relief products, including insoles, ankle supports, comfortable shoes and more."

3. Weather or not. Larry David had it right on *Curb Your Enthusiasm*. The 6-handicapper weatherman goes on the air at 6 and 11 Friday night and predicts severe thunderstorms the very same next Saturday morning that you have a highly antici-pated tee time with your best buds. Everyone watches the weather, and then they all cancel by tweet, text, or talk on the phone. Next morning, the sun shines, not a cloud in the sky, and guess who has your tee time? The 6-handicap weatherman, dummy, who else? And there's no one on the course because they're all Doppler dummies and canceled, too.

2. The money pit. Otherwise known as your love affair with golf. The $1,200 set of forged irons, the $600 state-of-the-art driver, golf balls at $36 a dozen, the $150 greens fees (maybe $100 because they aerated the greens last week) and the $125 Bobby Jones golf shirt you just had to have. It started out as an XL, at least until you threw it in the wash a few times and watched it shrink to an S before your very eyes— a faded, wrinkled *shmata* you wouldn't be caught dead wearing to change the oil in your lawn mower, if you still could afford a lawn mower, or squeeze into the shriveled shirt.

1. First tee shakes. It never fails. You're a little late, don't have time to warm up at the range, so you arrive cold at the first tee, with three groups lined up behind you waiting their turn and watching from their carts to see how long you'll be holding them up for the next six or seven hours. You stretch, you take a practice swing, and then you step up and . . . squirt a top/dribbled/near-whiff worm-burner that carries all of 25 ugly yards and doesn't even make it to the ladies tees. Mulligan? Not with the steamed starter glaring at you a few feet away. And then you can't find your ball. You're so ashamed, you just keep walking, a dreaded snowman right from the get-go. The devil's game, indeed.

★ ★ ★ ★

"If I can hit a curveball, why can't I hit a ball that is standing still on a course?"

—Larry Nelson

Yes, there are plenty of moments when I wonder if my quality of life would be better if I didn't spend so much time playing golf. I'd probably have an advanced degree in something. Frustration can make the game feel like endless torture. But those moments are fleeting. I can't give it up. It's my obsession. And I'm guessing it is yours, too. We return because we love the game. There are countless reasons. Here are a few.

8. Integrity. Golf truly is a game of honor. In other sports, players and coaches will do whatever it takes to gain an edge. If an umpire or referee blows a call in your favor, so much the better. In golf, the player is the referee. It is his or her duty to uphold the rules of the game. Golf repeatedly gets lauded when top players call rules infractions on themselves, often when nobody else saw it. It ultimately costs them thousands of dollars and perhaps a chance to win a tournament. Said legendary sportswriter Grantland Rice: "Eighteen holes of match or medal play will teach you more about your foe than will 18 years of dealing with him across a desk."

7. Playing the same courses as the pros. You'll never be able to hit a ball over the Green Monster in Fenway Park or run out of the tunnel at Notre Dame Stadium. But if you're fortunate enough, you can play on the same courses used for tournaments, big and small. You need an inside connection to get on Augusta National, but plenty of other elite venues (Pebble Beach, St. Andrews, Pinehurst, etc.) are available for those willing to part with some cash. It gives you the opportunity to play some of the shots the pros play. It also provides you with greater appreciation for their round of 65 after you posted a sterling 96.

6. The great outdoors. I live in Chicago, and that means we get about 15 nice days per year. Our short golf season weather goes from 40s and raining straight to 90s and steaming. Not much in between. So perhaps it allows us to appreciate the opportunity golf gives us to be outdoors. Regardless of the weather, there's nothing like being in nature for four hours. Green grass and trees. And for us up north, on the rare days when it is 75 and sunny, golf is, shall we say, priceless.

5. Shooting your age. Really, how much cooler does it get than being able to shoot your age—especially when you're only 63. It speaks to golf being a game for a lifetime. People play to 100 and beyond. Of course, at that age, you're just happy to post any kind of score.

4. Generations. Sticking with the game for a lifetime theme, one of the great things about golf is that it binds generations of families. A grandson can play 18 holes with his father, grandfather, and, if you're lucky, great-grandfather. Talk about a dream foursome. Name me another sport that affords you those kinds of special moments. It truly doesn't get any better than that.

3. Variety. Specific boundaries restrict tennis courts and football fields. That's obviously not the case in golf. Courses are determined by the land and the architect's imagination. No two courses are the same, and most are widely different. Flat, hilly, trees, wide open, lakes, high grass, and on and on.

Often, I find myself driving past a course and start imagining what it would be like to play that course. I never do that when I go by a tennis court or football field.

2. Camaraderie. Most of us (as in 99.9 percent) never will attempt to make a living off of golf. For us, the game is a chance to hang with our buddies and enjoy a few laughs, perhaps at your friend's expense. Golf is a communal game. That Saturday tee time with your regular foursome is about more than golf: It's about friendship.

1. That one shot. If you're like me, most of your rounds are full of futility. An endless repetition on chunks, banana balls, duck hooks, worm-burners, and countless other disasters. All those poor shots push us to the brink of throwing the clubs in the lake, vowing to never play again.

But then comes that one brief moment of perfection. The clean contact off the clubface like they talk about in *Golf Digest*. The ball flight that makes you imagine David Feherty saying, "It's going right for the flag." Then you watch with your mouth open as the ball kisses the green, setting up your birdie putt.

It's almost like that famous scene from *Godfather III* when Al Pacino says, "Just when I thought that I was out, they pull me back in." That's what that one shot does for you. It brings you back. Again, and again, and again.

Truthfully, is there anything better?

Thank heavens for the occasional golfer marching to a slightly different drum-beat, players who took a slightly different approach to the game than so many of their grinding-to-the-max, eyes-only-on-the-prize peers. The following char-acters offered up so much more on and off the course with their colorful quotes, celebratory antics, offbeat attire, and, yes, even the occasional terrible tantrum.

10. Boo Weekley. This self-proclaimed redneck from the Florida panhandle will forever be known for gleefully riding his "driver horse" after hitting his opening tee shot in a 2008 Ryder Cup match. Asked at his first British Open in 2007 what he thought about the cuisine in Scotland that week, he said, "It's been rough on the food. Ain't got no sweet tea and ain't got no fried chicken."

9. Rich Beem. The Beemer was selling car stereos and speakers in a Seattle elec-tronics store before finally making it big with a breakthrough win at the old Kemper Open in Bethesda, Maryland. The title of Alan Shipnuck's book recounting that tri-umph and his eventful rookie season should tell you all you need to know: *Bud, Sweat and Tees: A Walk on the Wild Side of the PGA Tour.*

8. Tommy Bolt. His angry eruptions on the golf course earned the 1958 U.S. Open champion monikers like "Terrible-Tempered Tommy" and "Thunder Bolt." He once asked a caddy for advice on what club to hit and was handed a 2-iron, the only undamaged stick left in his bag. Bolt told the old *Saturday Evening Post* that fans in his gallery "come out for one reason and one reason only. They want to see me blow my top. And I'm sorry to say I obliged them."

7. Doug Sanders. He once was named one of the country's top ten sexiest athletes and was known as a stylish dresser, with colorful shoes a trademark for a man known as "The Peacock of the Fairways." *Life* magazine wrote that Sanders was all about "golf, girls and living," and, especially, living it up. He was known to favor the occa-sional cocktail or six and said during one tournament, "I had girls all over the course bringing me vodka tonics."

6. Sam Snead. One of the all-time great players also was a folksy Virginian who occasionally played barefoot, won countless bets demonstrating that he could kick the top of a door frame, and once said, "Keep close count of your nickels and dimes, stay away from whiskey and never concede a putt." During one interview at Augusta National after hitting a ceremonial first drive to open the Masters, he complained that his teeth were bothering him. Asked what was wrong, he immediately removed a full set of false choppers to point out exactly where it hurt.

5. Fuzzy Zoeller. He likes to whistle his way around a golf course, tossing quips left and right. Once, while playing a newly designed course, he wondered, "Where are the windmills and the animals?" Paired with Craig Stadler, he asked the Walrus about his new shoes: "Nice clogs. Did you get them at a Buster Brown fire sale?" He used a towel as a mock white flag of surrender from the 18th fairway at the 1984 U.S. Open, and his loose lips got him in a heap of trouble when Tiger Woods won the '97 Masters: "Tell him not to serve fried chicken next year" at the champions dinner, adding, "or collard greens or whatever the hell they serve." Zoeller later apologized, but it may be best remembered as his most infamous quip.

4. Christina Kim. The Korean American from Southern California is among the most colorful players in the history of the LPGA, known for her exuberant on-course celebrations and form-fitting wardrobe. She often wears a trademark Kangol beret; favors tight pants, shorts, and tops; and was born to eat and Tweet. She once said she went shopping with her father, and when he suggested a more traditional outfit, she told him, "The only way I'm wearing that is if I die and you get to dress me for the funeral."

3. Mac O'Grady. He was born Phil McGleno but has legally changed his name several times and also reinvented himself from an ambidextrous player who won twice on the PGA Tour to a widely respected swing coach. He once asked the U.S. Golf Association if he could be considered a pro as a righthander but be eligible to play amateur events as a lefthander. He said his goal in life was someday to have a large enough lead in a PGA Tour event in which he had played righty to finish the 72nd hole as a lefty. "There's a certain reputation I have," he once said. "They [the PGA Tour] think I'm beyond the *Twilight Zone*. I like that."

2. Chi Chi Rodriguez. The native of Puerto Rico has always thought of himself as an entertainer on the golf course. He used to drop his trademark straw hat on top of the hole after a birdie or an eagle to bottle up the good karma and was best known for his colorful matador routine, using his putter as a sword after sinking a long putt. He took the name Chi Chi from one of his idols, Puerto Rican baseball player Chi Chi Flores, and once said that he was so poor growing up, he would drink milk with a fork to make it last longer and that his house was so small there wasn't enough room to change his mind.

1. Lee Trevino. He will always be known as "The Merry Mex," a former caddy who hustled bets as a young man hitting golf balls with shovels and 32-ounce Dr. Pepper bottles. At the start of his 1971 U.S. Open playoff against Jack Nicklaus, he threw a rubber snake at his opponent on the first tee and then beat him to win the title. After being struck by lightning at the 1975 Western Open, a reporter asked him what he would do the next time a storm approached while he was on the course. Trevino said he'd pull out a 1-iron and point to the sky because "not even God can hit a 1-iron."

BEST U.S. OPENS

The U.S. Open is the toughest tournament in golf, and many times the most maddening. The diabolical set-ups make the pros look like 15-handicappers. Watching the best in the world struggle makes for compelling theater and often produces some of the game's biggest moments. Here are the ten (plus one) top U.S. Opens.

11. 1974: Massacre. Coming off Johnny Miller shooting a 63 the year before at Oakmont, the USGA was determined to avoid a repeat at Winged Foot. Talk about going to the other extreme. The course was virtually unplayable. Hale Irwin won, but the most memorable part was his winning score: 7-over. This Open would be forever known as "The Massacre at Winged Foot."

10. 1922: An era begins. The start of an epic era for golf took place at Skokie Country Club. A young Bobby Jones came in as the favorite to win his first U.S. Open. Instead, he met his match in Gene Sarazen, a relatively unknown 22-year-old assistant pro. Jones played exceptional golf, but Sarazen was one stroke better. It would be the first of many memorable showdowns between Jones and Sarazen.

9. 1964: Heated. Like Ben Hogan in 1950, this tournament is best remembered for perseverance. Playing in searing heat at Congressional Country Club outside of D.C., a sweat-soaked Ken Venturi wobbled down the fairways, looking as if he should be immediately hooked to an IV. Venturi, though, trudged on through a sweltering 36 holes on the final day and somehow found the strength to post a 4-shot victory over Tommy Jacobs.

8. 1999: Payne's day. For pure emotion and drama, it is hard to beat the 1999 Open at Pinehurst. After Tiger Woods faded, it came down to Payne Stewart and Phil Mickelson down the stretch. Mickelson, going for his first major, carried a beeper with him because his wife, Amy, was due to have the couple's first child at any moment. But it was Stewart who stole the show. Needing a 15-footer to save par on the final hole and win outright, he promptly sank the putt for his second U.S. Open title. In a memorable scene, he grabbed Mickelson and said, "You're going to be a father." Indeed, Phil and Amy welcomed a daughter the next day. The tournament then took on added significance when Stewart died in a plane crash that fall. A statue of Stewart's leg-in-the-air pose following his winning putt now sits in front of Pinehurst's clubhouse, a permanent tribute to what happened on that day.

7. 1962: Spoiler. Oakmont hosted the first of many epic battles between Arnold Palmer and Jack Nicklaus. Oakmont was a home game for Palmer, a Pittsburgh-area native. But the 22-year-old Nicklaus, playing in his first year as a pro, was up to the challenge. With the crowd against him, he stared down Palmer in an 18-hole playoff, beating him by three shots.

6. 1930: Third leg. The whole sporting world was focused on Interlachen Country Club as Bobby Jones went for the third leg of his Grand Slam bid. A third-round 68 gave him a 5-stroke lead. Jones faltered a bit down the stretch, but he still had enough for a 2-shot victory over Macdonald Smith. It was three-down-and-one-to-go for Jones's historic Grand Slam.

5. 2008: Wounded knee. Tiger Woods did his version of "Ben Hogan at Merion" at Torrey Pines. Hobbled by a bad knee that eventually required major reconstructive surgery, you could almost feel his pain as Woods limped off the tee. Doctors even told him not to play, but there was no way he was going to miss an Open at Torrey Pines. Rocco Mediate proved to be an unlikely rival, pushing Woods to the limit. But Woods matched him, sinking a dramatic birdie putt on 18 to force a playoff. Then he eventually won on the 19th hole the next day. Considering what he overcame, Woods called it his greatest victory.

4. 1913: Stunning upset. This is the legendary tournament in which Francis Ouimet, a former caddy and unsung amateur, outdueled Harry Vardon to win at Brookline Country Club. Ouimet's unlikely victory thrilled Americans, making him the game's first national hero. Nothing beats this Open for historical impact. The country's love affair with golf began here.

3. 1982: The chip. The tournament had everything: the aura of Pebble Beach; an epic battle between Tom Watson and Jack Nicklaus; and a shot for the ages. Tied for the final-round lead on the 17th, Watson was in trouble, with his ball embedded in the deep rough. Surely, Watson was looking at a bogey, putting Nicklaus in charge. Instead, Watson canned a miracle chip for birdie. He danced around the green en route to his only U.S. Open title.

2. 1950: The comeback. Merion was the site of Ben Hogan's crowning moment. A year earlier, he had almost died in a car accident. Still recovering from terrible injuries, Hogan practically willed himself to victory. To make the test even more demanding, he had to endure an 18-hole playoff on his battered leg. Hogan survived, beating George Fazio and Lloyd Mangrum. His triumph truly was inspiring and always stood as a symbol of Hogan's greatness.

Ben Hogan holds his trophy cup after winning the 1950 U.S. Open.

1. 1960: Past, present, future. Never in the history of golf did the generations collide as they did at Cherry Hills in 1960. The contenders included Arnold Palmer, the game's brash young star; an aging Ben Hogan, trying to grab one last moment of glory; and a 20-year old amateur named Jack Nicklaus. Ultimately, it was Palmer who stepped up to produce the defining moment of his career. Trailing by seven shots going into the final round, he boldly predicted a 65 would win the tournament. Then Palmer drove the first green (a 346-yard par 4), shot a 65, and claimed a 2-shot victory over Nicklaus.

THE FUNNY IRISHMAN: DAVID FEHERTY'S BEST LINES

David Feherty will be the first to admit that his mouth has been far more valuable to him than his golf swing. Feherty was only a journeyman player in Europe, but he is a Hall of Famer in terms of wit and one-liners as a commentator. CBS was astute enough to pick up on those traits and make him into a star with the microphone. The following is a sample of Feherty's humor and unique insights into life. Believe us when we say that there is much, much more where this stuff came from.

16. On picking a favorite to win: "It's hard to tell who's going to win this week, but it probably won't be a big, fat guy."

15. On John Daly's hair: "Worst haircut I've ever seen in my life. And I've had a few bad ones. It looks like he has a divot over each ear."

14. On Ireland: "Where I come from we have nine to ten months of bad weather, then winter sets in. That's why we're so angry with each other but love everyone else."

13. On his swing: "I was swinging like a toilet door on a prawn trawler."

12. After winning a European Tour event in 1987: "I really don't enjoy playing this game at all anymore. You would have to be a pervert to enjoy the sort of feelings that I went through out there."

11. On his decision to give up his playing career in favor of broadcasting: "When CBS came to me and asked me to do on-course commentary, I said, 'You know, I'm only 37, I still have hopes of [playing] a little better.' So they told me what they were going to pay me, and I said, 'You want to buy a set of clubs?'"

10. When asked why he was moving to the United States to work as a golf analyst: "Because I've already insulted everyone in Europe."

9. On the PGA Tour's elite: "We're back to where if Tiger plays well, he wins. And if he plays really well, he wins by eight. It's not the Big Five. It never was. It's a Big Four and a Giant, Humongous One."

8. On seeing Tiger Woods for the first time: "I just stood there watching him walk past and thinking, 'I don't know what that is, but I know there weren't two of them on Noah's Ark.'"

7. On his esteem for Tiger Woods: "People have accused me of being so far up Tiger's arse that he can barely make a full swing, but I maintain that he is a special person. There's no one else on the planet who can do what he does or even thinks of doing what he does. I've often thought, instead of showing Tiger's reaction to a shot he's hit, we really should show the reaction of those around him."

6. On the Masters: "They don't do comedy at the Masters. The Masters, for me, is like holding onto a really big collection of gas for a week. It's like having my buttocks surgically clenched at Augusta General Hospital on Wednesday, and surgically unclenched on Monday on the way to Hilton Head."

5. The title of one of his books: *Somewhere in Ireland a Village is Missing an Idiot.*

4. On giving up drinking: "I didn't quit drinking because I was a bad drunk. I quit because I was a spectacular drunk. It got to be like a video game, where you get to the highest level and it's not even a challenge."

3. On failing: "It's how you deal with failure that determines how you achieve success."

2. On God: "If God wanted people to believe in him, why'd he invent logic then?"

1. On his mission in life: "I want to entertain people. If I can't make them laugh, I want to make them smile."

Mission accomplished, David.

The rules of golf are not made to be broken, but they certainly are subject to some interesting interpretations. The following is a common-sense primer on a rule book that can be terribly obtuse.

11. Oops on the tee. If you accidentally knock the ball off the tee, there is no penalty. If you tee off in front of the tee markers, there is no penalty in match play, though your opponent has the right to ask you to replay the shot.

10. Damaged ball. If your ball becomes damaged and is unfit for further play, you may replace it without a penalty in the presence of your opponent or a marker.

9. Provisional ball. You're allowed to play a provisional ball if you believe your shot has gone out of bounds or is lost outside a water hazard (or a hazard if the local rules permit) after announcing your intention. You may keep playing the ball as a provisional until you reach the area of the original ball.

8. Opponent's strokes. In match play, you are allowed during the course of play on a hole to ask your opponent how many strokes he's taken. If he gives you the wrong information, you win the hole.

7. Relief from loose impediments. Unless you're in a hazard, you are allowed to move natural objects that are not fixed or growing, as in pebbles, leaves, twigs. On greens, you also may remove dirt and sand.

6. Casual water. If your ball is in casual water or you have to stand in casual water to hit your shot, you get a free drop within two club lengths from a point that provides complete relief from the nearest margin of the area but not nearer to the hole. Same thing applies for ground under repair.

5. Relief from obstruction. You're entitled to relief without a penalty from anything artificial, whether it's erected, placed, or left on the course. This includes pipes, paper, rakes, glass, buildings, shelters, hoses, benches, and even ball washers. If an obstruction is moveable, you may move it with no penalty. If it's fixed and interferes with your stance or swing, you may drop two club lengths from the impediment, but no closer to the hole.

4. Playing out of turn. If you do it in match play, your opponent has the right to ask you to replay the shot.

3. Hit by ball. In match play, if your ball hits you, your partner, your caddies, or your equipment, you lose the hole. If your ball strikes your opponent, his caddy, or equipment, he loses the hole.

2. Ball on ball. If your shot strikes an opponent's ball on the green, he has the option, if his ball is moved, to leave it where it lies or replace it to the original spot.

1. Dispute resolution. In any dispute or doubt about your rights or how to proceed in a match play situation, you must make a claim before teeing off on the next hole. You don't have the option to play an alternate ball.

★ ★ ★ ★

"If profanity had an influence on the flight of the ball, the game of golf would be far better than it is."

—Horace G. Hutchinson

BEST BODIES

Let's get this clear here: We're not talking about the sexiest players in golf. Sorry ladies, Adam Scott doesn't make this list. Sorry guys, Natalie Gulbis doesn't make this list either. We're talking about golfers who could beat your butts on and off the course. Players who toned their bodies to the point at which they had less body fat than one of Craig Stadler's steaks for dinner. And if they happened to also look sexy? All the better.

9. Vijay Singh. There's a reason Singh became the most successful player ever after the age of 40. He defied time by turning himself into a rock. Singh's dedication to fitness saw him overtake Tiger Woods for the No. 1 world ranking in 2005 at the age of 42. And he kept on rolling, and working out. He changed the perception of what golfers are capable of doing in their 40s.

8. Frank Stranahan. You probably never heard of "The Toledo Strongman." Stranahan was a unique character in golf. Born into a wealthy family, he never turned pro, winning more than 70 amateur tournaments. He had quite a game, as evidenced by runner-up finishes in the Masters and British Open. He also was a power lifter, winning several titles. Nobody messed with Frank.

7. Steve Williams. Speaking about not messing around with somebody. You're in trouble if you get in Williams's way, especially if you're a camera. "Stevie" may be a caddy, but few people in golf look more intimidating on the course. He learned early on he needed to be in top shape to keep up with Tiger Woods.

6. Lorena Ochoa. Ochoa didn't become one of the best woman golfers of all time by accident. She dedicated herself to a vigorous workout routine, incorporating weights and distance running. Don't be surprised if you see her pop up in a triathlon one day.

5. Camilo Villegas. Villegas makes the young girls swoon with his rippled muscles bulging out of his tight shirts. But it wasn't always that way for him. He arrived in Florida carrying only 139 pounds on his 5-9 frame. Villegas dedicated himself to getting strong. The end result saw him add more than 20 pounds of strength, making him a force in golf.

4. Greg Norman. Few golfers ever cut a more physically imposing presence than "The Shark." His wide shoulders and ridiculously narrow hips gave him the perfect V frame. Norman was a fitness fiend during his career. He once said, "I'm appalled by people who don't look after their bodies. When I was a kid, we were told that exercising was bad for your golf swing. I was the one who first changed all that."

3. Annika Sorenstam. Sorenstam was having a nice career as she neared 30, but she still lagged behind Karrie Webb. So she embarked on an all-out workout program. She turned herself into a muscle machine, and in the process added more than 20 yards off the tee. The results speak for themselves. The powerful version of Sorenstam might have been the best women's player of all time.

2. Tiger Woods. It was Woods who redefined the notion of fitness and golf. His aggressive workout routine gave him the body of a free safety in football. His combination of strength, power, and agility had everyone else running to the weight room in a futile effort to catch up.

1. Gary Player. To overcome all the obstacles that Player faced, you have to work harder. That's exactly what Player did. During an era in which golfers shunned anything to do with exercise, Player made it his passion. His workouts transformed him into a legend and a role model. While in his 70s, he boasted that he still could beat most golfers in their 30s in a fitness contest.

Player said, "I was determined to become as strong and fit as I could possibly be. When I first competed against the likes of Palmer and Nicklaus, I realized that due to my small stature, my only hope of gaining an edge was to outwork them. So I became obsessed with exercise and diet. I was going to be sure that my body would not let me down."

★ ★ ★ ★

"Bob Hope's swing? I've seen better swings on a condemned playground."

—Bing Crosby

WORST BODIES/BEST GOLFERS

Long before Tiger Woods and Annika Sorenstam made fitness an in-thing, the workout for golfers usually consisted of doing 16-ounce curls, as in tipping a few beers at the 19th hole. It helps to be in a great shape, but as golf has shown, it isn't a requirement. There have been plenty of top players who, instead of sporting six-pack abs, looked like they downed plenty of six-packs. Here are the best of the worst . . . or worst of the best. Take your choice.

8. Duffy Waldorf. He always has been a favorite. Just start with the name. How could you not love a man named Duffy Waldorf? At six-foot with a listed weight of 225 pounds, he goes out of his way to showcase his large frame by wearing loud shirts and caps. A four-time PGA Tour winner, Waldorf is a wine connoisseur. You've got to figure he had a few 48-ounce steaks to go along with those vintage Cabernets.

7. Billy Casper. If you look at some old photos of Casper, you'll see several chins and an ample paunch. However, a few extra pounds didn't prevent him from winning 51 titles and three majors.

6. Craig Parry. The native of Australia looks like a bowling ball rolling down the fairways. Standing at 5-6, his weight is listed at 180 pounds. That must have been from high school. Besides his belly, the other thing that stands out for Parry is his massive forearms. Hence his nickname: "Popeye."

5. Colin Montgomerie. It's been struggle for "Monty" to stay in shape. During most of his reign as Europe's best golfer, he looked like he was carrying around a sack of potatoes under his shirt. He suffered from having the dreaded "man boobs." And it led to a nickname he surely hates: "Mrs. Doubtfire."

4. Tim Herron. Herron's nickname says it all: "Lumpy." At 5-10, 210 pounds (Ha!), Herron's picture usually is referred to by people who think golf isn't a sport. A native of Minnesota, he is an avid ice fisherman. You'd have to figure he pounded a few beers to stay warm. Of his weight he once said, "You can't really feel sorry for me because I have a choice, in a way, of how I want to look. It's just time and effort, and I know I could put it in to get into better shape, but I just don't."

3. John Daly. Prior to getting lap-band surgery, which caused him to slim down, Daly was the poster child for the fat, out-of-shape golfer. He devoured M&Ms by the barrel and, despite battles with alcoholism, downed beer by the keg. After winning the 1995 British Open, he refused to partake in the British Open Champions Dinner because "You can't get this fat boy into a suit."

2. Craig Stadler. The combination of his portly stature (5-10, 250 pounds) and a thick, bushy mustache led to Stadler having one of the greatest nicknames of all time: "The Walrus." He always is a sight to behold waddling down the fairways. In 1999 he lost a bunch of weight and then promptly missed the cut in the 2000 Masters. He decided he played better as a fat man. He once said, "I'm fat and happy. When I go to the fitness trailer, it's to watch guys work out with a beer in my hand."

1. Jack Nicklaus. "The Golden Bear" is the nickname best associated with Nicklaus. However, early in his career, he had another nickname: "Fat Jack." Nicklaus carried a considerable gut as a young man. It stood out even more when he was shown in pictures with Arnold Palmer, who was trim and dashing. It's a good thing "Fat Jack" didn't want to stay that way. He eventually took off the weight and became a leading man in his own right.

★ ★ ★ ★

"I'd play every day if I could. It's cheaper than a shrink and there are no telephones on my golf cart."

—Brent Musburger

CHARLES AND TIGER

Anybody who has watched Charles Barkley on the Golf Channel knows that he has one of the worst swings in golf. It is full of lurches and stops as well as general ineptness. However, Barkley's horrid swing didn't prevent him from making a connection with Tiger Woods. They became close friends, and Barkley remained loyal to Woods when he went through his personal problems.

Here is Sir Charles's assessment of Tiger as a golfer from an interview Ed had with him in 2006.

8. On when he first met Woods: "[As member of the Phoenix Suns] I played with Phil Mickelson who is a great player. I played with Tom Lehman who is a great player."

"I played with Tiger when he was getting ready to turn pro. I knew it. I called all my boys. He hadn't started yet, but I knew I played with the best golfer who ever lived.

"It was the same situation when I first played with Michael Jordan. When we were at the Olympic trials [in 1984], I knew it then about Michael. I saw that one first hand. He better than everybody else. You could see the talent.

"Same thing with Tiger. He better than everyone else."

7. On Tiger vs. Charles: "He gives me a shot a hole. I can't ask for more than a shot a hole. I've got to have some pride. Never beaten him, but I would like to."

6. On Tiger on the basketball court: "He thinks he can play basketball. I tell him as a basketball player, he's a great golfer."

5. On the grinder: "I respect him so much for never giving up. He never gets enough credit for that. He never wants to miss a cut. When he hits a bad shot, he's [upset]. When he's close to making a cut, he's grinding. He don't have to do any of that stuff. That's what I respect. He never quits. I love that."

4. On the mental edge: "I think that's overrated. He just better than everybody else. You know, he don't want to win more than Retief Goosen or Vijay Singh. Michael Jordan didn't want to win more than me. He was just better than me.

"Trust me, I played against Michael. If there was anybody I wanted to beat, it was MJ. But he was just better."

"When I'm watching Tiger on TV, I love when they say [about Woods], 'He does this, he does that.' I'm like, 'He only does that because he's better than everybody else.'"

3. On the work ethic: "There's never been an athlete who works harder than Tiger. I thought Michael was the hardest working athlete I've ever seen until I met Tiger.

"There are few times that superior talent and hard work come together. Tiger works so hard, and he has the talent that goes with it. That's a deadly combination.

"He's been changing his swing. We never had this conversation, but is he doing that to keep himself motivated? He was kicking [butt] with the other swing. The swing wasn't broken the first time, was it?

"Just go out and try to hit balls for four to five hours. That takes an amazing amount of energy and effort. We're hackers. If you don't play on tour, you're a hacker. How many hackers have the ability to go out there to hit balls for four to five hours after they lifted weights and did cardio?

"You could have talent, but if you don't work on it, it won't come together."

2. On the 1997 Masters: "My favorite memory is him winning the Masters the first time. To see a black man win the Masters. I remember where I was. I was in the locker room [prior to a basketball game]. He had a 25-shot lead, but I just had to be in there to watch it.

"Growing up in Alabama, it was a big deal to fight racism. To see all those blacks who work at the Masters. To see it finally happening. He told me about Lee Elder driving eight hours overnight just to be there. That's the kind of stuff, man, that's off the charts."

1. One wish: "I wouldn't want any of the other [junk]. I would just love to be able to play golf like he does."

★ ★ ★ ★

"Of all the hazards, fear is the worst."

—Sam Snead

FANTASY FOURSOMES

We've all played this game before. What would be your fantasy foursome? We decided to have a little fun with it and create some variations on the theme.

All-Babe foursome. Babe Ruth, Babe Didrikson Zaharis, Babe Herman, Babe Winkelman. Ruth and Herman may provide the power, but Zaharis would beat both by 15 strokes. Winkelman, meanwhile, could fish for lost balls. Okay, bad joke.

Real Babe foursome. Kathy Ireland, Cheryl Ladd, Katherine Hepburn, Dinah Shore. Not only would these women provide nice scenery, Hepburn was quite a player. She used to give boyfriend Howard Hughes a run for his money on the course.

Beat-your-head-in foursome. Ty Cobb, Michael Jordan, Steve Spurrier, Cal Ripken, Jr. These guys didn't give an inch in their respective sports, and they are just as competitive on the course. You might want to wear a helmet and bring some extra cash.

Quarterback foursome. John Elway, Dan Marino, Drew Brees, Tony Romo. Two of them are Hall of Famers and Brees also could get to Canton one day. But the best of this bunch is Romo, who has made bids to qualify for the U.S. Open.

Funny guy foursome. Bob Hope, Jackie Gleason, Bill Murray, George Lopez. Perhaps Gleason could bring Art "Ed Norton" Carney as his caddy. Carney then could reprise his classic line at address, "Hellllooooo ball."

Singer foursome. Bing Crosby, Frank Sinatra, Andy Williams, Celine Dion. This group always hits the sweet spot with their voices.

Bad player/good company foursome. Charles Barkley, Jack Lemmon, Ray Romano, Larry David. These guys don't have much game; Lemmon never made the cut in Crosby's Pebble Beach tournament. But you would have a lot of fun being out there with them.

Good player/bad company foursome. Vijay Singh, Tommy Armour III, Leonard Thompson, Tommy Bolt. This bunch is going to be extremely cranky. Best keep quiet and be ready to duck from flying clubs.

Analyst foursome. David Feherty, Roger Maltbie, Dave Marr, Peter Allis. The golf will be terrific and the conversation will be even better. Feherty also could fit into the "Funny guy" foursome.

Announcer foursome. Jim McKay, Jack Whitaker, Jim Nantz, Dan Hicks, Verne Lundquist. As an added bonus, you could get these guys to do play-by-play of your game. We added Lundquist to the group so he could yell, "YEES SIRR!" when you make a putt.

Actor foursome. Jack Nicholson, Clint Eastwood, Humphrey Bogart, Kevin Costner. As you're standing over that 3-footer on the last hole to win the match, Eastwood will say, "Do you feel lucky? Well, do ya', Punk?" That'll add some pressure.

Bad guy foursome. Al Capone, O. J. Simpson, Bernie Madoff, Richard Nixon. If Madoff says he has a great investment opportunity for you, better take a pass.

Rocker foursome. Alice Cooper, Justin Timberlake, Huey Lewis, Darius Rucker. Cooper traded his addiction to drugs and alcohol for an addiction to golf. Good move.

Presidential foursome. Bill Clinton, George H. W. Bush, Dwight Eisenhower, John Kennedy. No mulligans, Bill!

Best-there-ever-was foursome. Bobby Jones, Ben Hogan, Jack Nicklaus, Tiger Woods. Nothing more needs to be said.

★ ★ ★ ★

"The only time my prayers are never answered is on the golf course."

—Billy Graham

Greg Norman ended the year as the No. 1 player five times in his career and won 88 titles worldwide. But ultimately, his Hall of Fame career will be best remembered for the majors that got away. With eight runner-up finishes, he didn't just lose: He lost spectacularly. Either somebody broke his heart with a miracle shot or he inflicted the damage on himself with an epic final round meltdown.

Here are the best, or worst, of Norman's near-misses.

9. 2008 British Open. The tournament at Royal Birkdale was a chance for Norman to write a different ending to his legacy. At age 53, he went into the final round holding the lead. It was a remarkable, stunning turn of events. Perhaps after all his heartbreaks in the majors, the golf gods were going to make it up to him? Alas, it wasn't to be, as the familiar story got played out one more time. Norman stumbled on Sunday and finished third.

8. 1995 U.S. Open. Norman vaulted back to No. 1 in 1995, posting three victories and $1.64 million in earnings. But he couldn't seal the deal in the majors. He battled Corey Pavin down the stretch at the U.S. Open at Shinnecock. However, a final round 73 left him two shots short.

7. 1984 U.S. Open. He was an emerging young star at Winged Foot. Norman thrilled the large galleries when he sank a 40-foot putt for par on 18. The scene produced the memorable shot of Fuzzy Zoeller waving the white flag in the fairway, thinking he had lost the tournament to Norman. Instead, they ended in a tie, and Zoeller easily defeated Norman in a playoff on Monday. It would be the first of four playoff losses in the majors for Norman.

6. 1993 PGA Championship. Both Paul Azinger and Greg Norman played solid golf at Inverness in Toledo, finishing tied at 12-under through 72 holes. Norman, though, blinked in the playoff, giving Azinger the title when he missed a 4-footer for par on the second extra hole. Norman was no stranger to finishing second at Inverness in a PGA. He also did it in 1986.

5. 1989 British Open. The final round was a good Greg, bad Greg. He blitzed through Royal Troon with a record 64. His terrific play got him into a three-way playoff with Wayne Grady and Mark Calcavecchia. It was the first year they instituted a 4-hole playoff, and Calcavecchia and Norman were tied going into 18. Then Norman had one of his patented meltdowns. He hit his drive into a bunker and his second also found sand. It was over when Norman hit his third shot out of bounds. He picked up from there. Suddenly, his 64 was a distant memory.

4. 1986 Masters. Norman played a role in giving Jack Nicklaus his epic sixth Green Jacket. Norman went into the final round leading by a stroke. Despite Nicklaus's furious rally on the back nine, Norman could have negated the great story with a birdie on 18 for the victory. At the very least, a par would have produced a playoff. Instead, Norman hit his approach into the bunker and then missed a 15-foot putt for par. Nicklaus had his victory for the ages; Norman, another disappointment.

3. 1986 PGA Championship. This tournament ran the entire gambit for Norman. He began the final round with a 4-shot lead but stumbled with a 76. That opened the door for Bob Tway. He stunned Norman by holing a bunker shot for birdie on 18, giving him the victory. It wouldn't be the last time Norman would be the victim of a miracle shot.

2. 1996 Masters. This tournament will forever serve as the defining moment of Norman's career. After all his heartbreaks and disasters, Norman finally was going to get the coronation that he desperately wanted at Augusta National. It was all laid out for him as he went into Sunday with a 6-shot lead. Then he imploded in a gut-wrenching final round 78. The litany of bogeys became excruciating to watch, as millions of viewers saw Norman's dream evaporate. Nick Faldo swooped in to capture the Green Jacket. Instead, Norman found himself playing a familiar role: the gracious loser.

1. 1987 Masters. Norman knew after this tournament that perhaps fate wasn't on his side when it came to the majors. At the height of his game, he seemed primed to win during the second hole of his playoff with Larry Mize. With Norman safely on in two at 11, Mize was off the green, facing a difficult up-and-down to save par. Mize then stunned himself and the golf world, chipping in for birdie to steal the Green Jacket from Norman.

Later, Norman would reflect back and say of all the heartbreaks he suffered, 1987 hurt the most:

"The one that killed me inside was Larry Mize's chip at the Masters," Norman said. "That was destiny saying, 'You aren't going to win this tournament.'"

PHIL'S RUNNER-UP BLUES

Phil Mickelson is golf's high-wire act. Win or lose, we know Mickelson isn't going to play it safe. The U.S. Open, though, isn't a tournament in which daring play is rewarded. It is a plodder's event, where par is a good score. Perhaps that's why Mickelson hasn't been able to get over the hump in a tournament he desperately wants to win. Through 2010 he had a record five runner-up finishes in the U.S. Open. Included is a meltdown of epic proportions.

Here's the rundown of runner-up Phil.

5. 2002 at Bethpage. Tiger Woods won this tournament, but Mickelson definitely was the "people's favorite." The rowdy New York crowd went crazy as Mickelson shot a 67 on Saturday to pull within five shots of Woods. Then on Sunday Mickelson had a chance when a birdie on 13 narrowed Woods's lead to two shots. But the rally ended when an errant drive on 16 led to a bogey. Mickelson may have won the hearts of the New York fans, but Woods went home with the trophy.

4. 2009 at Bethpage. The Phil love fest resumed. The New Yorkers cheered for Mickelson as if he was Derek Jeter. They had additional motivation: Prior to the tournament, it was disclosed Mickelson's wife, Amy, was suffering from breast cancer. It would make quite a story if Mickelson could win one for Amy. It was all set up for him. An eagle on 13 tied him for the lead during the final round. Alas, Mickelson couldn't bring it home, as his putter failed him down the stretch. Another runner-up finish, this time to Lucas Glover.

3. 2004 at Shinnecock. Mickelson came into his first U.S. Open as a major winner for the first time. Two months earlier he broke through at the Masters. He played beautifully at Shinnecock and looked to be in a position to make it two majors in a row. During the final round, he made birdies on 15 and 16 to take the lead over Retief Goosen. But in a classic Phil moment, he wilted with a double bogey 5 on the par-3 17th. The collapse included a 3-putt from five feet. He falls short again, this time by two shots to Goosen.

2. 1999 at Pinehurst. Mickelson's wife Amy was involved in the drama again, but this time for a much happier reason. With Amy ready to deliver the couple's first child at any moment, Mickelson wore a beeper on the course. He said he would leave immediately if it went off. Against this backdrop, Mickelson carried the lead down the stretch. Most people remember this tournament as the one Payne Stewart won by sinking the dramatic par-saving 15-footer on 18. But Mickelson had his chances. Sitting on the lead on 16, he made a bogey. Then on 17, he failed to convert an 8-footer for birdie.

Stewart made the shots in the clutch; Mickelson didn't. After Stewart won, he grabbed Mickelson and said, "You're going to have a baby." The next day, Amy delivered a girl.

Payne Stewart (L) hugs Phil Mickelson after winning the 1999 U.S. Open Championship.

1. 2006 at Winged Foot. The American version of Jean Van de Velde at Carnoustie. Despite struggling all day, Mickelson arrived at 18 with a 1-shot lead. Then, in a sequence of events that will be dissected forever, Mickelson sprayed his driver left, hitting a hospitality tent. Why did he use his driver? Then he went for a miracle shot, hitting a tree. Why didn't he play it safe and try to punch out? At worst, a bogey puts him in a playoff.

Taking the safe route, though, isn't part of Mickelson's game. Ultimately, it cost him a double-bogey, handing the title to Geoff Oglivy. Afterward, Mickelson uttered his immortal line, "I am such an idiot."

He knew he blew it. But he also knew he couldn't play it any other way.

TOP LEFTIES

Naturally, I had to do this list. As a lefty who has endured a lifetime of people saying, "You're standing on the wrong side of the ball (Ha! Ha!)," I had to write about my true golf heroes. They showed that you can succeed from the wrong side. It's a short list, but a proud one.

8. Ernie Gonzalez. Gonzalez played on the PGA Tour in the late '80s, winning the 1986 Pensacola Open. It was Gonzalez's lone claim to fame. However, given the shortage of lefties, the title was good enough to put him on the list.

7. Sam Adams. Like Gonzalez, Adams was another one-timer, winning the 1973 Quad Cities Open. However, he's got a distinction that Phil Mickelson can't match: Adams was the first American lefty to win on the PGA Tour.

6. Russ Cochran. Cochran provided me with one of my most memorable moments as a lefty. I was on hand to watch Cochran overcome a 5-stroke deficit to Greg Norman in the final eight holes to win the 1991 Western Open. Okay, Norman folded like a cheap tent. No matter, Cochran took advantage for his lone PGA Tour victory. All told, Cochran had 60 top-ten finishes in his career.

5. Bubba Watson. He is the left-handers' big power hitter. Born in Baghdad, Florida (not Iraq), Watson unleashes missiles off the tee. Early in his career, he hit a 398-yard drive at the Sony Open in Hawaii. Even right-handers are in awe of Watson.

4. Steve Flesch. Flesch worked his way up through the Asian and Nationwide Tours before finally achieving success on the PGA Tour. He was the Tour's Rookie of the Year in 1998 and broke through with his first victory at New Orleans in 2003. He's also one of the game's good guys. That shouldn't be a surprise: He's a lefty.

3. Mike Weir. Weir isn't just a hero for lefties. The Canadians also revere him. He's in the icon team photo with Wayne Gretzky. Weir's victory in the 2003 Masters sparked a national celebration up north. Lefties rejoiced, too.

2. Bob Charles. The New Zealand native was the patron saint of lefties for more than a generation. When you named top lefties in golf, the list began and ended with Charles. He became the first lefty to win a major, claiming the 1963 British Open.

All told, he won 67 tournaments worldwide, including 23 on the Champions Tour. In 2008 he recorded another first by becoming the first lefty inducted into the Golf Hall of Fame.

1. Phil Mickelson. Mickelson actually is a righty (so is Charles for that matter), but he found true happiness swinging from the left side in golf. Mickelson has had many ups and downs in his career, and several of his biggest screw-ups are documented elsewhere in this book. But when it comes to the Babe Ruth of lefties in golf, there is only one: Phil Mickelson.

★ ★ ★ ★

"Golf gives you an insight into human nature, your own as well as your opponent's."

—Grantland Rice

WORST WORDS IN GOLF

We've all heard them up close and personal any time we head to the first tee and drive ourselves crazy for the next four hours (make that five-and-a-half hours at any muni in the world). Forget about those Tiger-esque F-bombs— we're talking about all the other dirty words the game has engendered over the years, words you just never want to hear. Ever. A sampling:

10. Snapper. As in snap-hook, an affliction that often leaves you lost in the left woods and on your way to a big number. Also synonymous with duck hook, only uglier.

9. Worm-burner. That screamed drive that never gets more than three inches off the ground, scaring the bejeezus out of any wiggly worm just down below. If you're lucky, you'll get a kick off the cart path and find yourself a hundred yards closer to the hole. If not, say hello double bogey. Or worse.

8. Fried egg. We're not talking about what you just gulped down in the snack bar while you waited for your tee time. It's what your ball looks like when you hit a towering wedge into soft sand. The ball is the yolk, sunny-side up and surrounded by sunken sand. Good luck knocking that rotten egg stiff to the pin.

7. Chunk. It's the sound you really never expected until you grounded your club about an inch too far behind the ball and took a healthy chunk of topsoil/turf along with your gawd-awful chip, leaving you 70 feet away in 3-putt city.

6. Dreaded snowman. You just wrote down an ugly 8 on your scorecard. Doesn't that numeral look like a not-so-cuddly snowman, minus the carrot nose and eyes made out of coal? So much for breaking 100.

5. Yips. Also very much dreaded, particularly by aging professional golfers who start getting the shakes and rattles as they're about to roll their golf ball toward the cup. Cure unknown. Tennis anyone?

4. Elephant's ass. A towering fly ball off the tee that's going nowhere, as in high as an elephant's ass, and just as stinkin'.

3. Topped it. You just took a mighty swing at that little dimpled spheroid and barely made contact with the tippy-top of the ball. With a little bit of top-spin good fortune, you might have reached the Ladies Tee.

2. Shank. You wouldn't wish a case of the shanks on your worst enemy, unless he's got you three down with four to play. Out of nowhere, the ball skids sideways. Then it happens again, and again. Maybe you'll figure out why. If so, let us know. Soon.

1. You're still away. That's right, Alice, you just left your 25-footer 10 feet short of the hole. Everyone else is inside three feet, so go ahead, Myrtle, hitch up your skirt and try again, and make sure you get it to the hole this time.

★ ★ ★ ★

"You can't call it a sport. You don't run, jump, you don't shoot, you don't pass. All you have to do is buy some clothes that don't match."

—Steve Sax

So many movies have teed up great golf scenes over the years, going all the way back to the Bob Hope and Bing Crosby road movies/romantic comedies of the 1940s and even the Three Stooges' goofy short comedy sketches shown on the big screen in the build-up to the main feature. Then came *Goldfinger*, with Odd Job trying to decapitate James Bond with his derby hat near the 18th hole, and *M*A*S*H*, which showed the twosome of Elliott Gould and Donald Sutherland hitting golf balls off a helicopter landing zone. For this list, we put aside all the fine films that only included a golfing scene or two and stuck to movies that featured golf as their main focus.

10. *Pat and Mike* (1952). Katherine Hepburn and Spencer Tracey star in the story of a female golf and tennis professional (Hepburn) who hooks up with a new manager (Tracy). Hepburn really was quite a golfer, and as usual, she and Tracy fall in love, with all the usual romantic comedy routines these two performed so well, no matter the setting.

9. *Happy Gilmore* (1996). Adam Sandler plays a failed hockey player who uses a wacky slapshot swing to rise through the ranks and make a name for himself in professional golf as he tries to earn enough money to save his grandmother's home. There's a classic scene when Sandler gets into a rowdy fight with Bob Barker, arguably the funniest bit in a funny movie.

8. *The Legend of Bagger Vance* (2000). Will Smith is cast as an angelic caddy who helps a shell-shocked and alcoholic war veteran (Matt Damon) find his game and eventually get the girl, who just happens to be the radiant Charlize Theron, always worth the price of a movie admission or rental.

7. *Follow The Sun* (1951). The Ben Hogan story, from car crash to U.S. Open glory, with Glenn Ford playing The Hawk in a true and typically moving biopic that Hollywood script writers couldn't have made up the plot for if they tried.

6. *The Caddy* (1953). One of the great comedy teams of all time, Dean Martin and Jerry Lewis play two losers—Lewis a caddy and Martin the pro employing him—making their way around the pro circuit. Lewis, as usual, drives everyone crazy, including Byron Nelson, Sam Snead, and Ben Hogan, who all have cameos in the production.

5. *The Greatest Game Ever Played* (2005). The film adaptation of Mark Frost's fabulous book depicts Francis Ouimet's dramatic upset victory in the 1913 U.S. Open over Englishman Harry Vardon, with Eddy, his cute, pudgy, ten-year-old caddy, leading the way.

4. *Bobby Jones: Stroke of Genius* (2004). Jim Caviezel went from playing Jesus Christ in one movie to Bobby Jones in the next, and some cynics might say he pretty much just stayed in character for this biopic on the world's greatest amateur player, a golfing god, though one in the habit of throwing up before big matches.

3. *Dead Solid Perfect* (1988). A made-for-TV movie based on the bawdy and hilarious Dan Jenkins novel of the same name about a journeyman golf pro, played by Randy Quaid, trying to find his game in the crucible of the professional tour. Keith Olbermann makes a cameo, but you can't tell if he's a righty or a lefty.

2. *Tin Cup* (1996). Kevin Costner became a pretty good player just getting ready to make this comedy about an alcoholic driving range owner who sobers up in time to contend for the U.S. Open title, with Cheech Marin caddying for him. Rene Russo provides the ultimate incentive as a psychologist dating Costner's rival, an obnoxious pro (played by Don Johnson).

1. *Caddyshack* (1980). Bill Murray, Chevy Chase, and Rodney Dangerfield romp through the funniest golf movie of all time at Bushwood Country Club (now known as Grande Oaks in Ft. Lauderdale, Florida). But a greens-seeking gopher steals lot of scenes and chows down on far too much grass. By the way, the psychedelic pants favored by John Daly in recent years are made by a company called Loudmouth, whose clothing pays homage to the outlandish threads worn by Dangerfield's character in the movie.

GREAT CADDYSHACK PICK-UP LINES

Caddyshack, made in 1980, is by far our choice as greatest golf movie of all time, and when you look at some of the dialogue, you'll immediately understand why. We particularly enjoyed some classic pick-up lines you might think twice about ever using, particularly if you're fond of your teeth.

10. "You're a lot of woman, you know that? You want to make $14 the hard way?" —Al Czervik

9. "I tell you, I never saw dead people smoke before."—Al Czervik

8. "Will you come and loofah my stretch marks?"—Mrs. Smails

7. "How about a Fresca?"—Judge Smails

6. "The last time I saw a mouth like that, it had a hook in it."—Al Czervik

5. "I bet you've got a lot of nice ties . . . You want to tie me up with some of your ties, Ty?"—Lacy Underall

4. "I'm having a little party at the Yacht Club next Sunday. Christening my new sloop. Do you have any plans? How would you like to mow my lawn?"—Judge Smails

3. "This is the worst looking hat I ever saw. You buy a hat like this, I bet you get a free bowl of soup with it."—Al Czervik

2. "I was born to love you. I was born to lick your face. I was born to rub you. But you were born to rub me first."—Ty Webb

1. "Hey baby, you're all right. You must have been something before electricity." —Al Czervik.

TUNING IN TO BETTER GOLF
ON TELEVISION

▶ BY LANCE BARROW

Lance Barrow has been working on CBS golf broadcasts since 1976, when he served as a spotter and researcher for play-by-play giant Pat Summerall. He worked side-by-side in the production truck for many years with Frank Chirkinian, the network's pioneering major domo of all things golf, and when The Ayatollah retired in 1996, Barrow replaced him as CBS's coordinating producer for golf. He's also the network's main man on NFL production, but this is a golf book, so we asked him, in his own words, to pick out some of the most significant technological breakthroughs in the coverage of a game he also plays to a single-digit handicap.

6. Swing vision. This has been a great help in analyzing a player's swings in super slow motion. The technology had previously been used in more of a sterile, indoor environment, like showing crash testing in cars or commercials in which they shot bullets through locks. We have great teachers on our staff, and everyone who covers golf for us is a professional who knows an awful lot about the swing. Every golfer watching at home is looking for an edge, how to hit it better, and this is a great teaching tool. I believe some people watch it on our broadcast and then go out into the garage or the backyard and try to practice hitting that same shot they just saw.

5. The blimp. We all take it for granted now at major sporting events, but in golf, it's really become a valuable tool, especially in showing aerial shots of holes. From the ground, it's tough to cover the flight of the ball, and the blimp lets you do that. Unlike football or baseball, with one field and one ball, golf has 18 different playing fields and lots of balls in the air. A camera up in the blimp gives us a chance to cover the whole area. From the ground, you might not be able to see that ball bounce on the bank next to a pond and go down to the water, but you see it all from the camera up in the air.

4. Mini-cams. Frank Chirkinian was a big believer in having mini-cams, but when they first came out, they were big and bulky and you needed a lot of cable to get around. Now, there's no cable, they're lighter, and they're wireless with RF (radio frequency), so they can literally be used all over the golf course. You can go anywhere with them, and it makes the whole process so much easier. We're now on the air much longer than we used to be, and with the minis, you don't miss anything.

3. RF microphones. Again, because they're wireless, you can take them everywhere and they give you sound that puts you right in the middle of the action. You can point the camera at someone and also hear what they're saying—a player talking to his caddy, saying something to the gallery, a discussion with a rules official, that kind of thing. We try to get as close as possible without being intrusive, and it really adds to the quality of what you're seeing at home.

2. High definition. HD is one of the greatest things ever to happen to televised golf. It just brings out so much more of the beauty of the game as well as letting people watching actually see the contours of the course and especially the greens. It also lets you cover the ball and travel with the ball in the air so much better. We can now stand behind the golfer with a camera and show you the flight of the ball much longer than we ever could before. We used to cut away much sooner. Now we'll stay with it so you can see how players actually work the ball right and left.

1. Color. We all take color television for granted, but going from black and white to color in golf changed the game forever. Think about watching those old reruns of black-and-white golf, and it just isn't the same. I can't imagine watching Augusta National in black and white, or Pebble Beach or any of the places we go. I see pictures of old tournaments in black and white and I think to myself when they started saying "this show is in living color," it was like Dorothy getting to Oz. All of a sudden, everything becomes beautiful.

★ ★ ★ ★

"Swinging at daisies is like playing electric guitar with a tennis racket: if it were that easy, we could all be Jerry Garcia. The ball changes everything."

—Golf writer Michael Bamberger

THEY HAVE STYLE

The stereotype for golf attire usually is various shades of beige and dull slacks. A few golfers, though, broke the mold with bold fashion statements. In many cases they are or were defined as much by their clothes as their games. There are many candidates here, so excuse us if we left out your favorite.

10. Ben Hogan. Hogan was all business on the course and wasn't interested in making a fashion statement. But he sported a distinctive white ivy flat cap that became his trademark. Because Hogan wore the nineteenth-century-style cap, others had to follow. If you couldn't swing like Hogan, at least you could look like him.

9. Michelle McGann. Speaking of hats, Michelle McGann also has been easy to spot during her career thanks to what she wears on her head. Her colorful large hats make her stand even taller than her height, listed at six-foot.

8. Gary Player. The Black Knight. It could 105 degrees in the shade and Player would be dressed in black from head to toe. It was his signature, making the 5-7 golfer stand out for more than just his game. The attire also helped him make a political statement. He had a period when he wore slacks with one leg black and the other white. He did it to protest Apartheid in his native South Africa. All hail The Black Knight.

7. Camilo Villegas. With his Hollywood/model looks, Villegas could look good in anything. Villegas, though, decided to turn up the volume with tight-fitting J. Lindeberg outfits, featuring a variety of colorful shirts, slacks, and belts. Little wonder why all the young girls swoon.

6. Greg Norman. Norman did more than cut a dashing figure wearing his straw hats and stylish shirts and slacks. He created a signature "Shark" clothing line that made him millions. Norman may have fallen short in the majors, but nobody sold more apparel than Norman.

5. Ian Poulter. He won the 2010 World Match Play wearing all pink in the final against Paul Casey. And nobody thought twice about it because Poulter had long conditioned us to expect to see him in unique outfits. Still, he did pull a stunner one year when he played a round in the British Open clad in slacks featuring Great Britain's Union Jack. That's one way to show you love your country.

Ian Poulter.

4. Walter Hagen. Golf's first and perhaps ultimate showman, Hagen had to make sure he looked the part. He arrived at a tournament (at times in a limo) with his hair perfectly slicked back and sporting colorful plus-fours and two-toned shoes. "The Haig" was a trendsetter when it came to style on the golf course.

3. Payne Stewart. Stewart was the modern version of Hagen, wearing his signature plus-fours in the '80s and '90s. Early on, Stewart decided he wanted to be different, and the old-style classic look fit him perfectly. He also figured out a way to turn it into an endorsement deal when he signed with the NFL to wear team-inspired attire. If it was a final round Sunday in Chicago, you could count on Stewart being decked out in Bears logos. Not only did the endorsement make him some cash, it also made him a favorite with the hometown fans.

2. Jesper Parnevik. Parnevik brought cutting-edge style to golf in the 1990s. He was the first to sport the J. Lindeberg European look on the course. But he took it one step further, turning up the bill of his cap. He never deviated, even wearing his cap up for the Ryder Cup when all the players were supposed to look the same. Parnevik once said, "If you look good, it's easier to play good golf." Parnevik always got the look-good part right.

1. Doug Sanders. He was called "The Peacock of the Fairways." He was a veritable rainbow on the course, showing up in various eye-popping colors—orange, pink, green—you name it, Sanders wore it. And that included his shoes. He dyed them to keep the entire outfit color coordinated. He once said, "My clothes were beautiful. Still are."

History sometimes doesn't allow everyone to receive the proper credit for their accomplishments. Several notable players had exceptional careers. Yet they somehow got obscured by greater stars. We're going to correct that wrong by identifying some of the most underrated players of all time. And if we left somebody off this list, then you know he's really underrated.

9. Larry Nelson. A Vietnam veteran, he didn't even take up the game until he was 21. Obviously, he was a quick learner, as he won ten titles and three majors (a U.S. Open and two PGAs). Yet despite that résumé, he got bypassed for being a U.S. Ryder Cup captain and didn't gain entry into the World Golf Hall of Fame until 2006.

8. Jimmy Demaret. Demaret won 31 PGA Tour events, including three majors. Yet he often got overshadowed playing in the same era as Ben Hogan, Sam Snead, and Byron Nelson. "He was the most underrated golfer in history," said Hogan. "This man played shots I hadn't dreamed of. I learned them. But it was Jimmy who showed them to me first. He was the best wind player I've ever seen in my life."

However, Demaret is credited with saying one of the best lines of all time: "Golf and sex are about the only things you can enjoy without being good at them."

7. Bernhard Langer. The German's low-key demeanor probably cost him some accolades. He definitely was one of the best ever to come out of Europe. He had 79 victories worldwide and won two Masters. Plus, he was the captain for Europe's Ryder Cup–winning team in 2004.

6. Doug Ford. His career has gone largely unnoticed. He had 19 PGA Tour victories and two majors (Masters and PGA). He was the Player of the Year in 1957.

5. Craig Wood. Wood died in 1968. So he wasn't around to wonder why it took him until 2008 to get elected into the World Golf Hall of Fame. All he did was win 21 PGA Tour titles, including two majors. Players were elected into the Hall with much less on their résumés.

4. Denny Shute. The same holds true for Shute, who was inducted into the Hall with Wood in 2008. His 16 titles included two PGAs and a British Open during the 1930s. History wasn't always kind to Wood and Shute, but at least a wrong has been rectified.

3. Hubert Green. Green was an exceptional player who probably never received all the proper recognition. The numbers speak for themselves: 19 titles and two majors. He won the 1977 U.S. Open at Southern Hills despite knowing in the final round that somebody had made a death threat against him.

2. Lloyd Mangrum. Mangrum earns distinction on another list: best player to win only one major. He won 36 times, but his failure to win more than one major title probably held him back from a historical perspective. Nevertheless, the players who competed against him in the '30s and '40s knew he had plenty of game.

At the 1996 Masters, Byron Nelson said, "I asked three young pros if they ever heard of Lloyd Mangrum, and they never had. Lloyd's the best player who's been forgotten since I've been playing golf."

1. Billy Casper. In the 1960s the "Big 3" were Jack Nicklaus, Arnold Palmer, and Gary Player. Casper should have been the fourth. His career featured a staggering 51 PGA Tour victories and three majors, including two U.S. Opens. From 1964 through 1970, Casper won 27 times on the PGA Tour—four more times than Nicklaus and eight more than Palmer and Player combined. Johnny Miller once said of Casper: "He has the greatest pair of hands God ever gave to a human being."

★ ★ ★ ★

"Playing the game I have learned the meaning of humility. It has given me an understanding of futility of the human effort."

—Abba Eban

TEN MOST OVERRATED PLAYERS

Overrated is a term no athlete ever wants associated with their good name, but golf has plenty of them—players who showed great promise at an early age but never fulfilled all those great expectations of youth. For most of the players on this list, there's still plenty of time to erase that label, but for now, it's sad but true. By the way, if any of the following ten wins a major or two from the time this was written until the book's official publication date, all is forgiven, and cross their name off the list.

10. Natalie Gulbis. The LPGA glamour girl looks lovely in her bikini calendar and is always a fan favorite (in the male division) wherever she goes. But the runner-up as the tour's Rookie of the Year in 2002 who had a dozen top-ten finishes in 2005 with over $1 million in earnings still has only one career victory on her résumé, and she's hardly ever been in Sunday contention over the last three years.

9. Luke Donald. The Englishman won the State Farm event in his rookie season of 2002 and became only the 11th tour rookie to earn $1 million his first season. But he's only won once since, at the 2006 Honda. Though he's been as high as No. 7 in the world rankings, Donald only has four top-ten finishes in major championships and is no longer considered the brightest shining light in British golf.

8. Davis Love III. Tough to put a PGA Championship winner (1997) with 20 tour victories in this category, but Love had so much going for him in his late 20s and 30s, when he was considered a lock by many as a likely candidate to win multiple major titles. The son of a widely respected teaching professional, Love has always had one of the sweetest swings, and dispositions, in golf. But he never seemed to have that killer instinct down the stretch of a major Sunday on the back nine, with two runner-up finishes in the Masters and two more in the U.S. Open.

7. Chris DiMarco. The Long Island native and University of Florida graduate had six straight years as a top-20 money earner on the PGA Tour, but he has only three career victories to his credit. He was runner-up to Tiger Woods in the 2005 Masters after losing in a playoff and was second, two shots behind Woods, at the 2006 British Open, but he hasn't had a top ten in a major since. Injuries have been a factor in recent years, but the hero of the U.S. victory in the 2006 Presidents Cup with a 4-0-1 record hasn't had much to celebrate lately.

6. Justin Rose. At 17, the Englishman was the youngest ever Walker Cup player in 1997. At 18, still an amateur, he pitched in for a birdie on the final hole to tie for fourth in the 1998 British Open when he was hailed as the future hope of British golf. That still remains his best performance in a major championship. Rose did win twice on the PGA Tour in 2010, but he didn't qualify to play in the Masters or U.S. Open and missed the cut in the British Open and PGA Championship.

5. Michelle Wie. She was the youngest player ever to qualify for a USGA event at the age of ten, then the youngest ever to win the women's Publinx amateur title when she prevailed in 2003 at age 13. Later that summer she became the youngest player ever to make the cut in the U.S. Women's Open. While still a teenager, she had seven top-ten finishes in major events, including a second in the 2005 LPGA Championship, and she competed in several men's tournaments on the PGA Tour, though she never made the cut. A wrist injury in 2007 sent her into something of a tailspin, and she hasn't been the same player ever since, though she finally did win on the LPGA Tour at the 2009 Lorena Ochoa Invitational in Mexico. The good news for Wie: She's on track for a degree from Stanford, she's still got plenty of game, and, born in 1989, she's only a kid still with seemingly unlimited potential.

4. Michael Campbell. In 2005 the New Zealand native won the U.S. Open and two other worldwide events and finished fifth in the British Open and sixth in the PGA Championship. After what looked to be a career-defining break-out season, he's tumbled off the face of the golfing planet and has hardly been heard from since, missing the cut in 11 of his next 17 major appearances. He plays primarily on the European Tour and has admitted very publicly that he's never really worked very hard at the game since that dreamy 2005 season.

3. Charles Howell III. As a junior at Oklahoma State, the native of Augusta, Georgia, was the 2000 NCAA individual champion and in 2001 was named the PGA Tour's Rookie of the Year. But ever since, he's won only two tour events and has only one top-ten finish in a major. His performance at the Masters has been particularly perplexing, considering how often he's played the course over so many years as an amateur and a professional. From 2005 to 2008 he missed the cut three times, then failed to make the field for the 2009 or 2010 events. He's always been a consistent money winner, but so much more was expected from one of the nicest guys in the game.

2. Adam Scott. The heartthrob Australian with so many ga-ga giggly girls in his galleries also has one of the most gorgeous swings in golf. His instructor, Butch Harmon, once said that Scott had more than enough ability to contend consistently in major championships and win a few along the way as well, but it's never happened. Since 2000 he's had only four top-ten finishes in major events, with his best result a tie for third in the 2006 PGA Championship. Scott, ranked as high as No. 3 in the world in 2007, ended a two-year victory drought in 2010 when he prevailed in the Texas Open, his seventh triumph on the PGA Tour. He was 30 at the time, an age when many thought he'd easily have surpassed his childhood hero, Greg Norman, in major victories. So far, it's Norman 2, Scott 0—a great disappointment for both of them.

1. Sergio Garcia. We'll never forget his youthful enthusiasm, that leaping dash down the fairway to see the result of a brilliant Sunday shot at the 16th hole at Medinah in the 1999 PGA Championship. The 19-year-old Spaniard lost by a stroke to Tiger Woods that day and also seemed destined to become the heir apparent to countryman Seve Ballesteros as one of the greatest players in his nation's history. Garcia has been plenty good ever since, with seven PGA Tour wins, including the 2008 Players Championship. And although he's had 16 top-ten finishes in majors, he just can't seem to close the deal, often whining woe is me along the way. Until he breaks through on the grandest stages of golf, overrated will always be his middle name.

BEST PLAYERS NEVER TO WIN A MAJOR

This is one list nobody wanted to be on during their careers. It was the proverbial double-edged sword. It meant you were good, but not good enough to get it done when the game's spotlight shined the brightest: in the majors. Something was lacking, and we'll leave it at that.

For the purposes of this list, we're only going to list players who have completed their careers or are at the tail end and not likely to win a major. That's why you won't see Sergio Garcia's name here, assuming he still is majorless by the time you read this.

9. John Cook. Cook won 11 PGA Tour titles, including three in 1992. However, Cook probably has more vivid and painful memories of the two near-misses in 1992. He was runner-up in both the British Open and PGA Championship.

8. Scott Hoch. He isn't on this list if he makes that two-foot putt during his play-off with Nick Faldo in the 1989 Masters. Of course, Hoch missed, and he never got another opportunity to win another major. Even though he won 11 times on the PGA Tour, Hoch will always be remembered for the one that got away.

7. Bill Mehlhorn. Playing in the same era as Walter Hagen and Gene Sarazan, "Wild Bill" was a colorful character, wearing cowboy hats on the course. He also had some game, recording 20 PGA Tour victories. However, not one of those titles came in a major. He finished second to Hagen in the 1925 PGA Championship. Mehlhorn's problem was said to be the yips with his putter. "Wild Bill" might have won a major or two if he had been able to conquer his problem on the greens.

6. Bobby Cruickshank. The native of Scotland was a terrific player, winning 17 times on the PGA Tour during the '20s and '30s. In 1927 he was the tour's leading money winner. But Cruickshank never could get over the top in a major. He recorded four top-four finishes in the majors, including being the runner-up in the 1923 and 1932 U.S. Opens.

5. Mike Souchak. At 5-11, 215 pounds, Souchak looked more suited for football compared to the other golfers during the 1950s. He used that strength to win 15 times on the PGA Tour. His shining moment came when he recorded the first 60 in history at the 1955 Texas Open. Souchak, though, couldn't summon that greatness in a major. His best showing was a couple of third-place showings in the 1959 and 1960 U.S. Opens.

4. Kenny Perry. Considering a lack of fanfare, you might be surprised to learn he had an impressive 14 PGA Tour victories. Twice he had a chance to get the major monkey off his back, and both times he came up short in playoffs. During the 1996 PGA Championship, he was criticized for sitting in the CBS announcing booth instead of warming up for an eventual playoff with Mark Brooks, which he lost. Then at the 2009 Masters he blew a 2-shot lead with two holes to play. But back-to-back bogeys thrust him into a playoff. He then had to watch Angel Cabrera wear the Green Jacket. He still could take his name off this list by winning a major. But now that he has passed 50, it's unlikely.

3. Doug Sanders. Sanders probably will go down as golf's most flamboyant dresser. But he could have been known for much more. As it was, Sanders won 20 PGA Tour events. But like Hoch, his legacy involves a missed putt. He failed to convert a 3-footer that would have given him the 1970 British Open. Instead, he lost a playoff to Jack Nicklaus the next day, permanently sealing his status as one of the best players never to win a major.

2. Harry Cooper. Nicknamed "Lighthorse," Cooper holds the dubious mark of winning the most PGA Tour events, 31, without capturing a major. Some will make the argument that Cooper did win a major when he won the 1934 Western Open. Back then, the Western was viewed as one of the year's biggest events. But for our purposes, Cooper didn't win one of the big four. A four-time runner-up in the majors, "Lighthorse" never was able to ride it home.

1. Colin Montgomerie. Nobody wore the "Best player never to win a major" label more than Monty. Unlike his predecessors from the distant past, he played in an era when there was far more attention, if not obsession, paid to players who had the gaping hole in their résumé. An eight-time Order of Merit winner in Europe, Montgomerie suffered one heartbreak after another in the majors. Twice he lost in playoffs: 1994 U.S. Open and 1995 PGA. All told, Monty had five runner-ups in the majors. Just when you thought opportunity had passed him by, Montgomerie, at age 43, was in the perfect position to win the 2006 U.S. Open at Winged Foot. But in true Monty fashion, sitting on a 1-shot lead going into 18, he promptly recorded a double-bogey, ultimately losing by a shot. Unless a miracle occurs, Monty will head this list for a long time.

BEST PLAYERS TO WIN ONLY A SINGLE MAJOR

The golfers on this list escaped inclusion on the "Best Players Never to Win a Major" list. But just barely. They got the monkey off their backs by winning that first coveted major. But all of these players had the talent to win multiple majors. In fact, you expected them to. Even these players would admit that, although they are glad to have one in the bank, they are disappointed that they don't have more. For the purposes of this list, we're featuring players who either are done with their playing careers or we feel are highly unlikely to win another major.

12. Craig Stadler. "The Walrus" won the Masters in 1982 at the age of 28. He went on to have a solid career, winning 13 PGA Tour titles. But he never finished higher than a tie for eighth in another major.

11. Hal Sutton. He got off to a quick start in the majors when, at the age of 25, he captured the 1983 PGA Championship. Sutton, though, was never able to follow it up. Despite collecting 14 PGA Tour victories, he posted only two other top-ten finishes in majors the rest of his career.

10. Paul Azinger. He won 12 PGA Tour events, including a thrilling victory over Greg Norman in the 1993 PGA Championship. Azinger, though, was at the height of his career when he was confronted with a life-changing obstacle: cancer. He overcame the disease, but he never was the same player. This is a case of what-might-have-been for Azinger.

9. Corey Pavin. He won 15 PGA Tour titles, getting every ounce from a game that relied on guile and finesse rather than power. He joined the majors club when he won the 1995 U.S. Open, beating Greg Norman. However, his game went south shortly thereafter and he never seriously challenged in another major.

8. David Duval. Duval was another case of what-might-have-been. From 1997 to 2001 he was playing in the same stratosphere as Tiger Woods, collecting 13 PGA Tour victories. He had two runner-up finishes in the Masters before finally breaking through with a victory in the 2001 British Open. Then the door slammed shut. A series of injuries caused him to lose his swing. The enigmatic Duval went spiraling into golf oblivion, reappearing only for a stunning second-place finish in the 2009 U.S. Open. I could regret saying this, but he isn't likely to be heard from again at a major.

7. Tommy Bolt. "Terrible Tommy" was a terrific player with a terrific temper. He won 15 times on the PGA Tour, with his big moment coming in a victory at the 1958 U.S. Open. He had four other top-three finishes in majors. Who knows? He might have won more if he had been able to control his temper.

6. Lanny Wadkins. Despite bagging an impressive 21 PGA Tour titles, Wadkins had to wait until 2009 to be elected into the Golf Hall of Fame. The reason: He won only one major. After claiming the 1977 PGA Championship, he endured a series of near-misses, with four runner-up finishes in majors. Clearly, Wadkins's inability to win just one more major was held against him all those years when he was denied admission into the Hall.

5. Tom Weiskopf. Weiskopf was an immense talent with one of the best swings in golf. He won 15 PGA Tour titles and the 1973 British Open. Still, it could have been more. Perhaps he, like other golfers, was a victim of playing in the Jack Nicklaus era. Weiskopf finished second four times in the Masters. Two of those were to Nicklaus, including their memorable three-way duel with Johnny Miller at Augusta in 1975.

4. Davis Love III. We'll never forget the rainbow that appeared over the horizon when Love won the 1997 PGA Championship. Too bad it was his only crowning moment in a major. Love had several notable near-misses, including a runner-up to Ben Crenshaw in the 1995 Masters and a second-place in the 1996 U.S. Open. The possibility exists, but it would be an upset if Love added another major.

3. Tom Kite. He was among the best players of his generation. Twice the Tour's leading money winner and an eventual 19-time tournament winner, Kite had only one thing lacking on his résumé: a major. Four times he finished second in the Masters and once in the British Open. Finally, at the age of 42, Kite came through, winning the 1992 U.S. Open in brutal conditions at Pebble Beach. With Kite's ability, you would have expected him to win a few majors before that. But in his case, it was better late than never.

2. Gene Littler. Nicknamed "Gene the Machine," Littler had one of the smoothest swings in golf. It carried him a long way, producing 29 PGA Tour victories. However, he triumphed in only one major, the 1961 U.S. Open. Littler came close to winning a second, losing in playoffs at the 1970 Masters to Billy Casper and in the 1977 PGA Championship to Lanny Wadkins.

1. Lloyd Mangrum. He played in the same era as fellow native Texans Byron Nelson and Ben Hogan, and he occasionally got the best of them. Mangrum distinguished himself by winning 36 PGA Tour events. However, he only won one biggie: the 1946 U.S. Open. Twice he lost in playoffs in majors, including getting victimized by Hogan during his famous victory in the 1950 U.S. Open. Mangrum was a great player. But he also holds the dubious distinction of being the player with the most PGA Tour victories to win only one major.

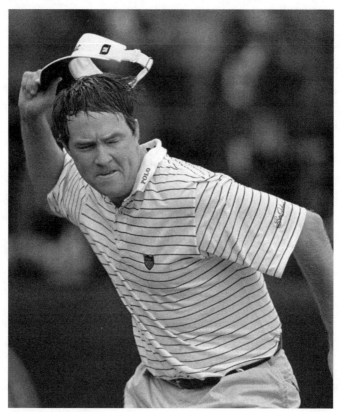

Davis Love III.

WANT TO BET?

Back in the 1920s, a world-class hustler named Titanic Thompson cleaned up on the golf course in a variety of ways. Our favorite: betting a sucker that he could make a 40-foot putt, with one condition. The attempt had to be made first thing in the morning, before anyone else played. Meanwhile, Titanic would pay off a greenskeeper to lay a 40-foot piece of hose from ball to cup overnight, guaranteeing just enough of an indentation in the short grass for the ball to track straight into the hole. We hardly recommend that sort of chicanery when you show up on the first tee with your regular weekend foursome, but it certainly can get even more interesting employing some of our favorite gambling games.

8. Side bets. Bring a wad of cash and go to it on longest drive, closest to the pin, yes or no on that knee-knocking eight-foot putt, up and down from the sand, and pay off immediately. It provides lots of incentive for the next hole when you lose a few bucks on the side.

7. Bingo bango bongo. You get a point if you hit the green first. You get a point for being closest to the hole once all four shots are on the green. You get a point if you hole out first. That's the basic concept, and you can add any or all of the options from our side bets up above. Add up every player's points and scores and, figuring $1 a point, Gamblers Anonymous likely won't be in your future.

6. Stableford. They used this system at the old PGA Tour event at Castle Pines, just for a change of pace from low-strokes wins. Employing handicaps, it's a point for a net bogey, two for a net par, three for a net birdie, and five for a net eagle. High point man wins. Again, save the rent money and make it a buck a point.

5. Skins. Pick a set amount for every hole, and the winner of the hole collects. If no one wins the hole, it carries over to the next hole and on and on, until someone wins a hole, and all those precious skins/bucks.

4. Wolf. Macho individuals love this game. Your foursome decides on a batting order off the tee. First player to hit then has a choice after seeing where the others have hit their drives. You may be down the middle, one partner is behind a tree, and the other two are in the deep rough. You have a choice of picking a partner to complete the hole or go lone wolf and take the other three on yourself. If you lose as a wolf, the bet is doubled. After 16 holes, low man in the standings gets to recoup his losses by teeing off first on the final two holes. You'll howl all the way to the clubhouse.

3. Snake. First man to 3-putt a green carries the snake until someone else in the group three putts. The last man in the group in possession of the snake at the end of 18 holes pays off the other three—brewskis in the clubhouse eases any pain from the venomous fangs of the winners.

2. Whacking. Lots of laughs on this one. A player has a 60-foot putt over the ridge and across the downhill slope, often a recipe for a 3-putt at any level of the sport. Each of his playing partners has the option to "whack" him, making the putt that much more trying. If the whackee 3-putts, he pays whoever wacked him $1. If he 2-putts, each whacker pays the putter $2. If he sinks that 60-footer, he collects $5 from the fools who whacked him. True whackers pay up on the spot, no bookkeeping necessary.

1. Nassau. Golfers worldwide have been using this format since the early 1900s, courtesy of John B. Coles Tappan, the club captain at the Nassau Country Club on Long Island. It remains the most popular of all gambling games and can easily be combined with other contests as well, depending on how deep your pockets may be that day. Let's take the $2 Nassau. Pick your partner in a foursome and play the other two. If you win the front nine, you win $2. If you win the back nine, it's $2 more. The winner over 18 holes also collects $2. Worst case scenario, you lose $6. It also can get far more interesting on "presses." Let's say you're 3-down on the front after four holes, so you press, setting up another $2 bet for the remaining five holes. If action is your goal, you can add an automatic press any time you get two down. We've known degenerate gamblers who will even press the press on the press. If you're not playing with friends, this could get ugly.

★ ★ ★ ★

"The ardent golfer would play Mount Everest if somebody put a flagstick on top."

—Pete Dye

MY ALL-TIME FAVORITE GOLF COURSES

▶BY JACK NICKLAUS

Jack Nicklaus remains the greatest golfer of all time, with a record 18 major championships in a playing career spanning more than fifty years. His golf design and architecture company also has been responsible for producing more than 275 Nicklaus signature courses around the world, and we asked him to pick out the five courses he likes to play more than any other. Diplomatic Golden Bear that he is, Nicklaus preferred not to put them in any particular order, just as he chose not to rank his five favorite career victories, saying they all held a special place in his heart. No matter. It's probably more fun to guess.

St. Andrews. The Old Course, the home of golf, where he won his second British Open in 1970, beating Doug Sanders in a playoff, and won his third and last Open title in 1978, a 2-shot victory over Tom Kite, Ben Crenshaw, Raymond Floyd, and Simon Owen.

Augusta National. Nicklaus is an honorary member of the club and the winner of a record six Masters titles, including a four-year stretch between 1963 and 1966, when he won three times with one runner-up finish. He also won his final major there at age 46 in 1986 and became the oldest Masters champion.

Pebble Beach. On one of the most beautiful seaside golf courses in the world, Nicklaus won the third of his four U.S. Open titles there in 1972, defeating Bruce Crampton by three shots. He also won the old Bing Crosby pro-am at Pebble in 1972 and 1973 and twice was runner-up in that event.

Muirfield Village. The centerpiece golf course in a Dublin, Ohio, community that Nicklaus developed, it's been the venue for the Memorial tournament, his signature event on the PGA Tour, since 1976. Nicklaus won his own tournament in 1977 and 1984, and tinkers with the course virtually every year to account for changes in club and ball technology. The course has hosted a Ryder Cup, Solheim Cup, and U.S. Amateur, and it is annually listed among the top 100 in the United States.

The Bear's Club. Nicklaus's home course in Jupiter, Florida, not far from his home and office. He designed the course, opening it in 1999, over a 400-acre piece of lush real estate with a 40,000-foot Tuscan clubhouse and arguably the finest golfing amenities in the state.

Jack Nicklaus at Augusta National.

MY FIVE FAVORITE VICTORIES ▶BY JACK NICKLAUS

With 73 PGA wins and a record 18 majors, Jack Nicklaus has won a ton. We asked him about his favorite or most significant victories, and here's what he told us, in no particular order.

1959 U.S. Amateur. At the Broadmoor in Colorado Springs, Colorado, Nicklaus, only 19 and a student at Ohio State, won the first of his two Amateur titles, beating Charles Coe, 1-up in the 36-hole final. Nicklaus has always said the victory was a springboard for launching his career.

1962 U.S. Open. As a rookie on the PGA Tour, his first professional victory came at Oakmont Country Club in the Pittsburgh suburbs, where he beat Arnold Palmer in an 18-hole playoff after both tied for the lead after 72 holes. It was the beginning of a fierce rivalry and, ultimately, a great friendship between the two titans of the game.

1966 British Open. After winning the '66 Masters and finishing third at the U.S. Open, Nicklaus won his first Open title at Muirfield, completing a career Grand Slam of winning each of the four major championships. He went on to name Muirfield Village after the venerable Scottish venue where he defeated Doug Sanders and Dave Thomas by a shot.

1973 PGA Championship. Nicklaus won his 14th major title at Canterbury Golf Club in his native Ohio, defeating Bruce Crampton by four shots to surpass Bob Jones's previous record of 13 career major championships.

1986 Masters. In the week before the tournament, *Atlanta Constitution* golf writer Tom McCollister wrote that the 46-year-old Nicklaus was "done, washed up, through." Nicklaus used those words to motivate himself all week, ultimately beating Tom Kite and Greg Norman by a shot for his 18th and final major title. The great Herbert Warren Wind described that victory as "nothing less than the most important accomplishment in golf since Bobby Jones' Grand Slam in 1930."

RUNNER-UP JACK

One of Jack Nicklaus's records figures to stand for a long time: 19 second-place finishes in majors. Imagine how much greater Nicklaus's legacy would be if he converted a few of them into victories. As great as he was, even he came up short or had his heart broken. Here are his most memorable runner-ups.

9. 1983 PGA Championship. Hal Sutton, the 1982 Rookie of the Year, opened with a 65-66 and held the lead going into the final round. Nicklaus, though, charged hard on the last day, shooting a 66. It wasn't good enough, as Sutton held on for a wire-to-wire, 1-shot victory.

8. 1968 British Open. As usual, Carnoustie got the best of the field, including Nicklaus. He opened with a 76. Even though he bounced back with a 69 during the second round, the damage was done. He wound up finishing second by two shots to Gary Player, who won the tournament at 1-over.

7. 1974 PGA Championship. Ever the character, Lee Trevino decided to go with an old putter he found in the attic of his rented home. It worked, as he went into the final round with a 1-shot lead over Nicklaus. Nicklaus was flawless on Sunday, shooting a 69. Trevino, though, matched him with his own 69 for a 1-shot victory.

6. 1977 Masters. Trailing Tom Watson by three shots going into the final round, Nicklaus mounted one of his classic Sunday charges at Augusta. He came to 18 needing a birdie for a 64 to force a playoff with Watson. This time, though, Nicklaus didn't come through in the clutch, recording a bogey to lose by two shots. It was the first time Nicklaus finished second to Watson in a major; it wouldn't be the last.

5. 1960 U.S. Open. Still an amateur, Nicklaus served notice to the golf world by placing second at Cherry Hills. He recorded a 71 in the final round, which would have been good enough to win under most circumstances. Arnold Palmer, though, shot an epic 65 to walk away with a 2-shot triumph.

4. 1971 U.S. Open. This tournament featured the famous playoff between Trevino and Nicklaus. Once again, Trevino's antics stole the show. Just before the start of their playoff, Trevino pulled a toy snake out of his bag and tossed it at Nicklaus. A lady in the gallery screamed. Nicklaus laughed. Trevino certainly broke the tension. Then he proceeded to shoot a 68, beating Nicklaus by three strokes.

3. 1972 British Open. As this list shows, if not for Watson and Trevino, Nicklaus would have won more majors. Nicklaus went into the '72 British Open eyeing the Grand Slam after winning the Masters and U.S. Open. It didn't look good as he trailed Trevino by six shots going into the final round. Nicklaus then mounted a stunning rally, shooting a 66 at Carnoustie on Sunday. Trevino, though, held on by chipping in for par at 17, good enough for a 1-shot victory.

2. 1982 U.S. Open. Watson handed Nicklaus his two most memorable defeats. Nicklaus looked to be on the verge of his fifth U.S. Open title at Pebble Beach. Tied for the lead in the clubhouse, he watched Watson's tee shot dive into the deep rough off the green on the par-3 17th. He thinks Watson is looking at a probable bogey. Instead, Watson does the impossible and chips in for birdie. He then hangs on to win by a stroke. Nicklaus said Watson's "1,000-to-1" shot resulted in Nicklaus's toughest defeat.

Tom Watson at 1982 U.S. Open.

1. 1977 British Open. The epic "Duel in the Sun" at Turnberry was the greatest showdown in golf history. Nicklaus and Watson threw their best at each other for the final 18 holes. Normally, Nicklaus's 66 would have been good enough for the victory. But Watson bested him with a 65 for the 1-shot victory. Nicklaus was disappointed, but he couldn't complain. He gave it his best shot.

GOLF'S GREATEST TRADITIONS

Golf is a game that revels in its rituals and traditions, from tossing a tee in the air on the opening hole to determine who hits first to the doffing of the cap and firm handshake on the 18th green when play has concluded. The Masters may be the clubhouse leader in perpetuating its own tournament traditions, even if it is the newest of the four majors. And there are plenty more traditions to celebrate all around the wide world of golf.

10. Sheer madness. That's the scene around the 16th hole at the TPC at Scottsdale, where thousands gather annually at the Phoenix Open, many with liquid refreshments in their hands, to toast the closest shots to the pin and the occasional hole-in-one. Florida-Georgia in college football calls itself the world's biggest outdoor cocktail party, but if that's No. 1, this has to be 1A.

9. Brits gone wild. It happens every Sunday at the British Open: a wild stampede by the crowd from behind the gallery ropes and into the fairway after the players in the final group smack their approach shots to the green at the 72nd hole. In recent years, metal police barriers now line both sides of the 18th fairway as a deterrent, but that still hasn't stopped the running of the fans.

8. The Man in Black. Gary Player was known as The Black Knight for his choice of colors, and other players also have been easily identified by their distinctive attire. The late Payne Stewart paid homage to the game's traditions by wearing plus-fours throughout his career. Tiger Woods cites Buddhist karma for his choice of power-red shirts on Sunday. And Paula Creamer on the LPGA Tour is always pretty in pink on Sunday, including a pink golf ball, the better to market herself as The Pink Panther.

7. Father's Day finish. The U.S. Open always ends on a Father's Day Sunday, unless of course there's an 18-hole playoff on Monday, another tradition for America's national championship of golf. The other three majors settle it right away with a play-off immediately after the round.

6. Ladies of the lake. It started in 1988, when Amy Alcott won the Kraft-Nabisco championship in Palm Springs and celebrated by taking a jump into the pond next to the 18th green. The next two winners chose to stay dry, but when Alcott won again in 1991, she took tournament host Dinah Shore into the drink with her, and every winner now swims with the fishes as well.

Lorena Ochoa celebrates in the water after the final round of the Kraft Nabisco Championship.

5. Golfer of the year. That's how the champion of the British Open is always referred to at the ceremony awarding the Claret Jug, even if someone else has won another major or two somewhere else. The Open? In the British Isles, there's only one, and it's definitely *not* the U.S. Open.

4. Swilken Bridge. It crosses the Swilken Burn that runs across the first and 18th holes at the Old Course at St. Andrews. It also may be the most photographed landmark on any course in the world, if only because golfing tourists from around the globe just have to have their picture taken as they near the finish of their round. Jack Nicklaus struck a famous pose himself when he waved goodbye as an Open competitor from atop the bridge in 2005. A streaker dashed out on the course at the same time, another recent Open phenomenon we hope never becomes a tradition.

3. Bubbly on the balcony. It happens every two years. A team wins the Ryder Cup and out comes the champagne, usually swilled and spritzed first on the 18th green and then on the nearest clubhouse balcony, with adoring fans down below happy to share the resulting spray. When he captained the winning European team in 2006 at the K Club in Ireland, Ian Woosnam made a giddy, gagging spectacle of himself chugging from a magnum, with photographs the next day showing the bubbly gushing out of his nose.

2. Honorary starters. One of our favorite Augusta National traditions, it began in 1963 when Fred McLeod and Jock Hutchinson were asked to strike the first ball at the tournament. Byron Nelson, Gene Sarazen, Ken Venturi, Sam Snead, Arnold Palmer, and Jack Nicklaus also have been honorary starters. Some hit only one shot and then retire to the clubhouse. Others have chosen to play the full 18. There are other Masters traditions: an exclusive champions' dinner on Tuesday night; the crow's nest, a 1,200-foot dormitory above the clubhouse where many amateurs spend Masters week; the champions locker room, also in the clubhouse; and the par-3 contest on Wednesday on the club's short course. No winner of the par-3 event has ever gone on to win the Masters.

1. A tradition like no other. It's the Green Jacket, the most coveted piece of apparel in golf, awarded to the Masters champion in a syrupy ceremony held in Butler Cabin, not far from the tenth tee. Made originally by the Brooks Uniform Company in New York, the jacket first was worn only by club members in 1937 so that spectators with questions about the course or the tournament could easily locate someone in the know. The jacket was awarded for the first time to the 1949 winner, Sam Snead. A player may take it home for a year, then must return it to the club, the only venue where he's allowed to wear it from then on.

★ ★ ★ ★

"What other people may find in poetry or art museums, I find in the flight of a good drive."

—Arnold Palmer

You know them when you see them: professional golfers who definitely go above and beyond. They may throw themselves into charity work, set up foundations to help the underprivileged, offer free clinics to inner-city kids, or donate money to good causes without ever letting anyone ever know. They definitely do not curse into a camera after a badly struck shot, cheat on their wives and/or mistresses, or blame the media for invading their privacy. The best of the best will sign autographs after a round until their hands ache, flip a ball to a child walking from green to tee, banter with the galleries, and linger in the press room until every question is asked and answered, maybe even rather thoughtfully. They're the good guys, women included, and the following are among the classiest of them all.

10. Tom Lehman. He got to the PGA Tour the hardest way imaginable, earning and losing his playing privileges several times, trying to scratch out a living on the mini-tour circuit, traveling to the far corners of the world to compete, and, one winter, even renting cross-country skis out of the pro shop at the University of Minnesota golf course. Maybe that's why, when he hit it big in the 1990s, actually gaining No. 1 in the world for one week, he never lost sight of where he had come from—and how many people had helped him along the way. Lehman, the 1996 British Open champion and a former Ryder Cup player and captain, remains one of the most approachable and accommodating players in the game, a man who still hears the slogan "Nice Pants" from galleries who remember he once was sponsored by Dockers.

9. Fred Funk. Maybe not making it on the PGA Tour until he was 33 convinced the former University of Maryland golf coach to enjoy the moment and figure out that nice guys really can finish first more than occasionally. In 2004 he took on the task of raising funds for J. T. Townsend, who suffered a severe spinal cord injury playing high school football in his home town of Jacksonville. Funk's no punk. He helped raise enough money for after-care expenses and building a wheelchair accessible home for a young man who he and his family virtually adopted.

8. Jay Haas. All you need to know about the mild-mannered, soft-talking Haas is that he was the recipient of the 2005 U.S. Golf Association Bob Jones Award given to a player who exemplifies great sportsmanship. A year later the Golf Writers Association of America presented him with the Jim Murray Award, honoring him for his career-long cooperation with the media. The 1975 NCAA individual champion from Wake Forest never won a major title on the PGA Tour, but his affable demeanor and never-ending accessibility marked him as one of the game's great gentlemen. His nine wins on the PGA Tour and double-digit triumphs on the Champions Tour also speak volumes about his talent as well.

7. Lorena Ochoa. The native of Guadalajara, Mexico, attained the No. 1 ranking in women's golf in 2008, but long before that success she was regarded as a hero to workers grooming golf courses all around the LPGA Tour. Early in her brilliant playing career, Ochoa made it a point to spend time behind the scenes thanking the men, many of them from her home country, who were mowing, raking, and weed-eating the course she'd be playing that week. Sometimes she even stayed and had lunch with them. Golf writers covering her events knew the first words out of her mouth before dissecting her round would always be a cheery "Hello everyone!" Hola and muchas gracias to one of the most gracious champions of any sport.

6. Kenny Perry. Perry never wept or wailed after botching two major championships in heartbreaking playoffs, one of them not far from his old Kentucky home at the 1996 PGA Championship at Valhalla in Louisville. At the age of 48, he had a 2-shot lead with two holes to play in the 2009 Masters, then he lost in a playoff to Angel Cabrera. When it was over, he said, "I may never get this opportunity ever again, but I had a lot of fun being in there. I had the tournament to win. I lost the tournament. But Angel hung in there. I'm proud of him." Be proud of Kenny Perry, too.

5. Ben Crenshaw. They call him Gentle Ben for a reason, perhaps because it was short for gentleman. One of the game's all-time great putters, a scholarly golf historian and a winning Ryder Cup captain on a team that staged the greatest comeback in the event's history, Crenshaw won twice at Augusta National. He endeared himself to golf fans around the world when he knelt down and broke into tears of joy obviously from the heart on the 72nd hole after winning the 1995 Masters by a shot over Davis Love III.

Ben Crenshaw (R) hugs his caddy, Carl Jackson, after winning the 1995 Masters Tournament.

4. Nick Price. This three-time major champion from Zimbabwe came a long way from the days when he flew helicopters in his nation's military. After that occasional life-threatening experience, no question he ever faced from the media corps ever seemed to faze him, and Price became a favorite go-to guy for every golf writer in the business. He never ducked a query no matter how controversial, and always made it a point to provide an astute, well-thought-out analysis of any subject he was ever asked about, a trend that continues as he plays the senior Champions Tour.

3. Nancy Lopez. She grew up in Roswell, New Mexico, and became one of the most beloved figures in the history of women's golf. Lopez won nine times during her rookie season in 1978 and 48 LPGA events overall, with three major titles. She also finished second four times in the U.S. Women's Open, the only major blemish on an otherwise sterling playing record. Fans loved her passion on the course and her friendly, accessible style outside the ropes, and she became a role model for young female athletes in an era just before the explosion of women's athletics. She was the approachable, smiling face of the LPGA Tour for many years, and as the doting mother of three daughters, she also demonstrated to her fellow players that you really could have it all.

2. Padraig Harrington. When the Irishman was honored at a dinner by the Golf Writers Association of America as the 2008 Player of the Year, Harrington gave an impassioned speech on the importance of a strong media presence at golf tournaments and bemoaned the shrinking newspaper business on both sides of the Atlantic. He's a gallery favorite who makes himself available to support all manner of good causes and a hero of Ireland not only for his passionate play (oh, those blazing Irish eyes) and his three major championships but also his humble demeanor both on and off the course.

1. *(tie)* Arnold Palmer. With his great gusto for the game, The King changed the face of the sport when he charged out of Latrobe, Pennsylvania, in the 1950s to lead his own Arnie's Army of followers, totally enamored with his go-for-broke, hitch-up-your-pants, and stride-with-a-swagger march up the fairways of the world. Some of Palmer's best pals were the newspaper guys who covered his almost fabled exploits, and he gave them all plenty to write about, even to this day as one of the most colorful and cooperative players of all time.

Jack Nicklaus. The year was 1993 and The Golden Bear had just made the cut at the U.S. Open at Baltusrol at the age of 53. As he chatted with reporters after his second round, a young production assistant for ABC Sports kept telling him he was wanted in the television tower to provide commentary on the round. Finally, Nicklaus looked at the pesky young fellow and shooed him away, saying, and we're paraphrasing here, "some of these guys have been covering me my entire career, and you tell them I'll be up there as soon as I answer every one of their questions." For Nicklaus and Palmer, it's been that way every step of the way over two of grandest careers in golf history, by far the two classiest acts of all.

★ ★ ★ ★

"Golf is a game that is played on a five-inch course—the distance between your ears."

—Bobby Jones

EIGHT (JERKS) IS ENOUGH

It's easy to find the nicest guys and dolls on the men's and women's tours, but any golf writer worth his laptop can also identify more than a few pluperfect horse's rear ends, at least in locker rooms, executive suites, and interview areas where the general public rarely has access. If they did, they might not appreciate the following not-so-great eight.

8. Scott Hoch. He once went into no-comment mode for several years over who knows what, declining to speak with reporters no matter how well he happened to play. Maybe he never liked his "Hoch as in choke" label after he missed a two-and-a-half-foot putt in a playoff that cost him the 1989 Masters. One year, a representative of the Golf Writers Association approached him at Riviera to tell him he would be honored at an upcoming GWAA dinner for his charitable work in supporting a local hospital. Hoch, as in mope, saw the man's press badge and simply walked away.

7. Carolyn Bivens. She never played the game as a pro nor was she particularly professional in her disastrous three-year stint as commissioner of the LPGA. Bivens began her reign of error by announcing ridiculous new media regulations for a tour that desperately needed all the coverage it could get, alienating many sponsors and tournament directors by imposing onerous new fees, and causing a huge uproar when she threatened to throw players off the tour for not speaking passable English. At her own LPGA Championship in 2009, she declined all interview requests and refused to show up in the press room. Within a month, she was fired and hasn't been heard from since. What a relief.

6. Colin Montgomerie. Although the Scotsman can be quite the charming fellow at times, Monty can sulk with the very best of them, particularly when things are not going very well on the golf course. A spectator moving in his line of sight 250 yards away has been known to distract a rabbit-eared man who surely must have eyes in the back and the side of his head, for all the distractions that seem to put him in a dither. Caddies, marshals, scorekeepers, and pesky photographers have often drawn his considerable wrath, and it's never Monty's fault when things go awry.

5. Cristie Kerr. One of her playing colleagues once said of the LPGA star and former U.S. Women's Open champion: "She was a bitch when she was fat, and she's still a bitch skinny." Since her marriage a few years ago, Kerr has mellowed somewhat, but catch her on an off day and it's every man for himself.

4. Leonard Thompson. When Thompson, now a senior golfer, said during a news conference that he'd had some injury problems over the previous few years, a reporter asked him exactly what those injuries were. "None of your goddamned business," Thompson growled. Marshalls all around the Champions Tour know it's a good idea to head for the closest available rest room or duck behind a nearby tree when Thompson is approaching their hole. His rotten disposition is known far and wide.

3. Sergio Garcia. Cried in his mama's arms when he didn't break 80 in his first British Open, constantly whines about bad breaks, and blames everyone but himself when things aren't going his way, which is usually the case in major championships. He's too good a player not to win a major championship or two, but champagne toasts in the press room are never going to happen.

2. Steve Williams. Tiger Woods's longtime caddy fancies himself as a bag-man and a bodyguard, a surly presence inside and outside the ropes who berates spectators, badgers press photographers, and once purposely knocked a camera out of one shooter's hands at a U.S. Open, bruising the poor fellow's eye in the process. Just stay out of his way or face the consequences. Talk about a bully pulpit.

1. Vijay Singh. The day he clinched the $10 million prize for winning the FedEx Cup in 2008, he never bothered to show up in the press room to talk about the accomplishment, just as he constantly refuses interview requests and media sessions, even when he's the leader at a major championship. When an Associated Press reporter quoted him as saying Annika Sorenstam shouldn't have been invited to play in the 2003 Colonial, he moaned to the world that he'd been misquoted, at least until the reporter played the tape for anyone who wanted to listen, revealing that's exactly what Singh had said.

★ ★ ★ ★

"Golf is a good walk spoiled."

—Mark Twain

UP CLOSE AND PERSONAL

►BY JIYAI SHIN

Jiyai Shin starting raising eyebrows in the golf world when she won 10 of the 19 events she entered on the Korean LPGA Tour in 2007 at the age of 18, an unprecedented feat that was a portent of grander things to come. In 2008 she won the Women's British Open for her first major championship, in 2009 she was named LPGA Player of the Year, and on May 3, 2010, she ascended to No. 1 in the women's world rankings, the first Korean to achieve that status since the system was instituted in 2006. Len Shapiro asked her to list a few things the golf public might not know about her.

Looks can be deceiving: I know it always looks like I'm smiling when I play, but all the time I am thinking about winning. I am a very happy person.

No language barrier: The LPGA Tour makes an English tutor available to anyone free of charge, and I've been working hard on learning the language because I think it's very important, especially with so many tournaments in the United States. I'm getting better all the time. It will take a while, but I want to speak perfect English.

Man watching: I attended the U.S. Open (in 2009) at Bethpage and my first Masters (in 2010). I learned so much watching them play from outside the ropes, especially about course management. It was hard for me to be a spectator because I feel like I want to go out there and play the course. Augusta National was just perfect—amazing conditions and so many people. I was intimidated by the crowds and the course, but I visualized trying to play it. Someday, I hope I can.

Junk food junkie: I like to eat, but I have to watch myself all the time. When I'm in California, I love hamburgers from In-N-Out. At the LPGA Championship (in Rochester, New York) they had pizza in the players' dining room every day. I love pepperoni pizza with lots of cheese, but I had to make myself stay away from there. All that pepperoni pizza—I might never leave.

Role model: Se Ri Pak is my idol. She was the player who made golf so popular in my country when I was growing up. I play because of her. And she has been very nice to me. I really like Tiger Woods, too. I got to meet him at the Masters at the Golf Writers dinner, and they took our picture together. Very special.

Author, author: I really like reading Dan Brown mysteries. First I read them in Korean, and then I read them in English. Same story, different language, but it helps me learn English, so I don't mind doing it twice, even if I already know who did it.

TV guide: My favorite show in America is *CSI: Miami*. They always have such interesting stories. It's all about justice, and the bad guys always get caught. I like that.

At the movies: My favorite movie of all time is *Notting Hill* with Julia Roberts and Hugh Grant. He's so cute. When I was young, I watched it over and over again. It was just a touching story to me, a big star falling in love with a nobody. I understand how that could happen.

Playing my song: I love to sing. People tell me I have a nice voice, and I made a CD in Korea with some religious songs that did very well. I enjoyed doing it and maybe the next one will be in English. I'm getting better with that every day.

Gut check: I'm a tough girl. I had surgery to remove my appendix (in June 2010), and two weeks later I played in the LPGA Championship. I was a little tired, but the pain wasn't too bad. I could swing and I played pretty well. (She tied for third that week and then tied for fifth two weeks later at the U.S. Women's Open.)

★ ★ ★ ★

"Golf is a game in which you try to put a small ball in a small hole with implements singularly unsuited for the purpose."

—Winston Churchill

THE SOUTH KOREAN (WOMEN'S) INVASION

▶BY RON SIRAK

Ron Sirak is the executive editor of *GolfWorld* magazine and a senior editor at *Golf Digest*. In recent years the former Associated Press golf writer and editor has offered readers extensive coverage of the LPGA Tour. We asked him to cull through all the Kims, Parks, Lees, and Chois among the 40-plus South Korean players now on the women's tour to help us get a tad more up close and personal with the ten best female players from that golf-crazy Asian nation.

10. Hee Kyung Seo. Born in 1986, she has dominated the Korean LPGA since joining it, winning a combined 11 times in 2008–09, including three KLPGA majors, and won the 2010 Kia Classic on the LPGA as a nonmember. Known among her fans as "The Super Model of the Fairways"—and for good reason. Likely to become an LPGA member in 2011.

9. Eun-Hee Ji. Born in 1986, Ji made her first LPGA victory a special one, sinking a 20-foot birdie putt on the final hole to win the U.S. Women's Open at Saucon Valley. She was top-15 on the LPGA money list in each of her first two years on tour. Her story is familiar: Turned professional at 18, played the Korean LPGA for three seasons, and then came to the American-based tour and was an immediate success.

8. Mi Hyun Kim. Next to Se Ri Pak, her eight LPGA victories are the most by a Korean-born player. Born in 1977, she joined the LPGA in 1999—the season after Pak's breakthrough year—and was an immediate success, winning twice in her rookie year as she claimed the Rolex Rookie of the Year award. She says she is 5-1, but at times it looks like she is going to hit the ground with her driver head on her backswing. She married Olympic gold medal karate champion Won Hee Lee in 2008.

7. Jee Young Lee. Born in 1985 and one of the longest hitters on the LPGA, she earned her way onto the LPGA Tour by winning the 2005 CJ Nine Bridges Classic at the age of 19, only the 14th non-LPGA member in history to win a tour event. Had 10 top-20 finishes in the majors her first four years on tour. She likes to cook when she is at home and amuses herself with PlayStation games while traveling the tour.

6. Seon Hwa Lee. Born in 1986, Seon Hwa is one of the "old ladies" among the Koreans. She is affectionately known as "The Terminator" because among her victories were the last ShopRite LPGA Classic, which went away after 2006 and returned in 2010, the last HSBC Women's world Match Play Championship in 2007, and the last Ginn Tribute in 2008. She won four times in her first three years as an LPGA member.

5. In-Kyung Kim. Yet another member of the Class of '88, she finished third in the U.S. Women's Open in 2008 and '09 and was eighth on the LPGA money list in 2009. Won the 2005 U.S. Girls Junior Championship. Only 5-3 but won an LPGA event in both her second and third year on tour. She is a quiet woman who unwinds by reading and listening to music.

4. Song-Hee Kim. Also born in 1988, Kim won five times on the Duramed Futures Tour in 2006 after being given an exemption to join the tour at the age of 17. After struggling her first year as an LPGA member in 2007, she was 14th and 11th on the money list the next two seasons, finishing in the top ten a total of 19 times as she won a combined $2 million. At 5-9, Song-Hee has a long graceful swing. Her scoring average has gone down in each of her years on tour.

3. Inbee Park. The 2008 U.S. Women's Open champion is another member of the Class of '88. She was a five-time Rolex Junior All-American, a semifinalist in the 2003 Women's Amateur, and she won the '02 Girls Junior and was runner-up in both '03 and '05. She was one of many Koreans who came to the United States at an early age to study golf. When she is not on the course, she heads for the ski slopes or plays piano.

2. Jiyai Shin. In Korea they call her the "Closing Queen" because of her ability to finish off a tournament. On the LPGA she is called "Chalk Line" because of how straight she hits the ball. She is part of the remarkable Class of 1988—a group of players now on tour who were 10 when Se Ri Pak won the LPGA Championship and U.S. Women's Open in 1998, triggering the Korean golf revolution. Her first LPGA victory was the 2008 Ricoh Women's British Open. She has a great voice and a best-selling CD in Korea. She is 5-1—maybe—but says, "on the golf course I am big."

1. Se Ri Pak. She's the godmother of Korean golf. Won the LPGA Championship and the U.S. Women's Open in 1998 at the age of 20, triggering the game's phenomenal growth in her homeland. A member of the World Golf Hall of Fame and the LPGA Hall of Fame, she has five major championships among her 25 LPGA victories. She is the only Korean to win multiple majors.

Because both authors are confirmed hackers, we like to play fast rounds. Why prolong the agony? There is nothing worse in golf than slow play. Five-hour-plus rounds are absolutely killing the game. Standing in the fairway and waiting, waiting, waiting for the slowest group in the world to putt out is excruciating.

In 2009 a Florida man took matters into his own hands by pulling a gun on a foursome that he thought was playing too slow. Although we don't advocate violence, here are some tips to keep the game moving for you and everyone else.

10. Cart management. We prefer walking. Carts absolutely slow down the game. Most people don't know how to use them to speed up play. Use some common sense. Drop off your partner at his ball and then go to yours. Park your cart near the green where you will have the shortest walk from the hole. And limit the chit-chat with your partner in the cart. That's why they have the 19th hole.

9. Proper intervals. Many courses bear considerable responsibility for contributing to slow play. The worst offense is packing too many golfers onto the course. The course tries to squeeze that extra foursome in per hour by going to six to seven minute intervals for tee times. The end result is five-hour-plus rounds. You should show your disgust for such a practice by going to another course.

8. No cell phones. You went to the course to play golf, not to talk with your accountant. The sight of somebody yammering away on the phone in the middle of the fairway is truly annoying. It's downright rude. There should be a local rule permitting a golfer to throw the person's cell phone into the woods or pond if it is the reason for slowing down play.

7. Be realistic. How many times have you seen a guy sitting about 250 yards out waiting for the foursome to clear the green? You've seen his weak game, and you're yelling at him, "Hit the ball, Tiger!" Know how far you hit the ball, and if you have no chance to reach the green, play away. Keep moving. Our favorite sprinkler heads are the ones that say, "Dream on."

6. Mulligans. You're not Bill Clinton. You don't get to award yourself with an unlimited amount of mullies on the golf course. I'll admit to taking a "breakfast ball" on the first tee, especially if I didn't hit balls before the round. But otherwise, accept your fate and play your bad shots. If you absolutely feel the need to hit a mulligan, please make sure you're not holding up the group behind you.

5. No Butch Harmon act. Nothing is more irritating than a husband holding up play because he's trying to give his wife a lesson in the fairway. You're not Butch Harmon! The golf course isn't the place to learn the game. That's why they have driving ranges. If you want to teach to your wife, child, or friends, buy a bucket of balls.

4. Play from the right tees. Golf isn't a game of macho. Golf is a game for having fun. Nothing ruins the enjoyment more than a guy or group deciding they are going to play Championship Tees at 7,500 yards. Unless you're a scratch handicapper, you have no business being back there. However, this goes beyond the back tees. If your game is more suited for the golds at 6,250 instead of the blues at 6,667, by all means, move up. Check your ego at the door. You'll have more fun and keep things moving.

3. Give up the search. You've hit your $3 Pro V1 into the woods, and now the manhunt begins. Short of bringing in ball-sniffing dogs, the search for a lost ball could be a time killer. Be reasonable, but not excessive. If you're worried about losing an expensive ball, here's a suggestion: Play a cheaper brand. You'll be doing everyone a favor.

2. The five-minute putt. Pros take an excessive amount of time on the greens, and it is hurting the game. But at least they can partially justify it because each putt is worth thousands of dollars. That isn't the case for your friendly $2 Nassau. Don't be like Jack Nicklaus and take forever to study each putt. Most golfers have no idea how to read a break on the green. To them, grain is something you find in bread. And if you play with somebody who goes into the Camilo Villegas "Spiderman" pose, consider getting another partner.

1. Just hit the ball. We all have seen the player who stands frozen like a statue over the ball. The seconds pass, and with the exception of a twitch or two, perhaps the hint of a waggle, the person hasn't moved. And this routine occurs 80 to 100 times during the round. Not only is it a time-killer, but the slow approach is also a game-killer. The best advice to avoiding slow play and improving your game is to commit to a concise pre-shot routine that takes only a few seconds. "Just hit the ball" should be everyone's mantra.

AMATEUR HOUR:
THE TOP ALL-TIME AMATEURS

They play for the love of the game, the thrill of the competition, the chance to represent their country in international play. Many of the greatest amateurs in history surely could have used their skills to earn a decent living playing professional golf, but they chose a different path, more satisfied with trophies and crystal bowls than a share of any purse money. This is a list of great amateurs who never turned pro.

12. Trip Kuehne. He is probably best known for losing to an 18-year-old Tiger Woods in the finals of the 1994 U.S. Amateur after going 5-up on Woods with 12 holes to play. Woods's victory is considered the greatest comeback in tournament history and was a major factor in Kuehne's decision not to turn pro, as his brother Hank and sister Kelli had. Kuehne nevertheless played on three Walker Cup teams, was low amateur in the 2003 U.S. Open at Olympia Fields, and fulfilled a lifelong goal when he qualified for the 2008 Masters by winning the 2007 Mid-Amateur title.

11. Maureen Orcutt. She lost in the finals of the 1927 and 1936 U.S. Women's Amateur but went on to win a record seven Eastern Amateur titles, three North and South Championships, and two Canadian Women's Amateur Championships. She played on four Curtis Cup teams that went 3-0-1, and better yet, she was among the first female sportswriters at the *New York Times* to cover—what else?—golf.

10. Vinny Giles. The Virginia native finished second in three straight U.S. Amateurs before he beat Ben Crenshaw and Mark Hayes by three shots at the Charlotte Country Club in 1972 when the event was still decided by stroke play. Giles also won the 1975 British Amateur and played in 11 professional major championships, winning low amateur honors at the 1968 Masters and 1973 U.S. Open. He went on to place as low amateur in three U.S. Senior Opens in 1993, 1996, and 1997.

9. Catherine Lacoste. The daughter of French tennis champion René Lacoste, she won the1967 U.S. Women's Open title at age 22 and remains the only amateur ever to win that event. In 1969 she won the U.S. Women's Amateur title and the British Ladies Amateur, the same event her mother, Simone de la Chaume, won in 1927. Lacoste has represented France in numerous international competitions.

8. Billy Joe Patton. A North Carolina lumber salesman, Patton had a chance to become the first and only amateur Masters champion in 1954, only to make a double-bogey on the 13th hole at Augusta National in the final round, hitting his second shot on the par-5 hole into Rae's Creek; he missed making the playoff with Ben Hogan and Sam Snead by a shot. Patton won the North South three times, claimed two Southern Open titles, and played on five U.S. Walker Cup teams.

7. Joe Carr. The Irishman won three British Amateur titles—in 1953, 1958, and 1960—and four Irish Amateur Close Championships. He also was low amateur in the 1956 and 1958 British Opens. Carr finished eighth overall in the 1960 British Open and in 1967 was the first Irishman invited to play in the Masters, where he made the cut. From 1947 to 1967 he played on a record 11 Walker Cup teams. In 1961 he won the Bob Jones Award, the highest honor given by the U.S. Golf Association, becoming the first non-American to win it.

6. Sir Michael Bonallack. He won the British Amateur four times between 1961 and 1970, along with nine English Amateur championships—five at match play and four at stroke play. He was low amateur in the 1968 and '71 British Opens and finished 11th in the 1958 British Open. Bonallack also played on nine Walker Cup teams and in 1983 became secretary of the Royal and Ancient, a position that made him among the most powerful administrators in the game.

5. William C. Campbell. A former president of the U.S. Golf Association (1982–83), the West Virginia native played in 37 U.S. Amateur championships (33 straight from 1941–77) and won the event in 1964. From 1951 to 1975 he played on eight Walker Cup teams, compiling an 11-4-3 match record, including a 7-0-1 mark in singles play. He won the U.S. Senior Amateur title in 1979 and 1980 and finished second in the 1980 U.S. Senior Open.

4. Chick Evans. A former caddy, in 1916 he became the first man ever to win the U.S. Open and British Amateur in the same year. He won the 1920 U.S. Amateur, a tournament in which he also finished as runner-up three times and played in a record 50 times. Evans won the 1910 Western Open, the only amateur to win that title until Scott Verplank prevailed in 1985. In 1930 he established a scholarship fund for caddies, and the Evans Scholars program now counts more than 8,000 college graduates.

3. Francis Ouimet. He started caddying at the Country Club in Brookline, Massachusetts, at the age of nine, and 11 years later stunned the world by winning the

1913 U.S. Open at the same course, beating English professionals Harry Vardon and Ted Ray in an 18-hole playoff. He won the U.S. Amateur championship in 1914 and 1931 and played on the first eight Walker Cup teams before captaining the next four. His teams were 11–1 in that competition, and in 1951 he became the first American named as a captain of the Royal and Ancient.

2. Carole Semple Thompson. Arguably the greatest women's amateur golfer of all time, Thompson won the U.S. Women's Amateur and British Ladies Amateur in 1973. She notched four straight U.S. Women's Senior Amateur titles from 1999 through 2002 and took the 1990 and 1997 U.S. Women's Mid-Amateur. She became the only golfer to play in 100 USGA championship events. Thompson competed on 12 Curtis Cup teams, and at the age of 53 in her last appearance on the team in 2002, she sank a 27-foot putt from just off the green to clinch the Cup for the U.S.

1. Bobby Jones. The greatest amateur golfer in history won 13 major championships, third on the all-time list behind only Jack Nicklaus and Tiger Woods. He completed the only single-season Grand Slam in the history of the game in 1930, when he won the U.S. Open, British Open, and the U.S. Amateur and British Amateur, earning himself a ticker tape parade down Wall Street and international adoration. The Atlanta native, revered for his great sportsmanship throughout his career, retired from competitive golf at the age of 28 and went on to a successful career as an attorney. Jones also founded and codesigned Augusta National with famed golf architect Alister MacKenzie and was the guiding force behind establishing the Masters tournament in 1934.

★ ★ ★ ★

"Baseball players quit playing and they take up golf. Basketball players quit, take up golf. Football players quit, take up golf. What are we supposed to take up when we quit?"

—George Archer

HOORAY FOR GOLF IN THE OLYMPICS

There were plenty of skeptics out there when the International Olympic Committee said it had decided to put golf back on the program for the 2016 Games in Rio, the first time the sport will be contested in the Games since 1904, when only the U.S. and Scotland fielded teams. Now, with 72-hole men's and women's stroke play competition, the sport will attract diverse worldwide fields, including many of the game's best players. Of course the Olympics will never replace the majors as the Holy Grail of the game, but try telling that to a player who wins gold, silver, or bronze in Brazil.

Here are more than enough reasons to celebrate golf's inclusion in the world's greatest sports spectacle.

10. Talking Tiger. Tiger Woods will be 40 years old when those Games begin, but he already has said he will definitely participate if he meets the criteria. That automatically guarantees six-deep crowds on every hole every day, and if Michelle Wie, also a huge Olympic supporter, joins him, at age 28 she should be right in her prime and poised for American gold.

9. Big numbers. The Beijing Olympics, without golf, attracted 4.7 billion television viewers around the world—and in some of the most remote outposts on the planet. With that kind of exposure, investments in golf equipment, apparel companies, and architectural firms should do wonders for all our 401Ks over the next few years.

8. Big government. The prospect of Olympic golf on the 2016 program surely will induce nations to begin pouring funds into beefing up existing junior programs— or developing new ones as feeder systems—and perhaps to pave the way to build more courses in places that don't have very many at the moment.

7. Women of the world. Women's golf could be the biggest beneficiary of all. The LPGA, already a worldwide tour, will get more exposure than at any time in its history, and that can only translate into more participants, more rounds played by females around the world, and more dollars spent on spiffy new outfits. Wouldn't it also be something if the repressive North Korean regime decided it was time to cut into South Korea's dominance of the women's game and started developing their own home-grown athletes for Rio? Golf Détente has a lovely Olympic ring to it, don't you know?

6. The face of the game. When Woods came out on the PGA Tour in 1996 and quickly started winning, a whole new rainbow demographic began streaming to courses wherever he played. And so perhaps we'll get a Vietnamese virtuoso, a kid from Kenya, a lassie from Laos on the medal podium, and what would that do for the game in those nations on those continents?

5. Ugly Americans. No, we're not talking about John Daly here. We're thinking more about all those American golf tourists whose personal bucket list of courses they have to play before they pass on to the great fairway in the sky will absolutely include the first Olympic golf courses in 112 years. They'll need hotels and restaurants and shops to make sure the big spenders stay in the neighborhood, which is also wonderful news for Brazil's local and national economy.

4. Jobs aplenty. Rio doesn't have a world-class golf facility capable of hosting an Olympic competition, so they're planning to start from scratch. That means hundreds of jobs for course workers, not to mention countless more for the development projects likely to spring up around the venues now and in the long-term future.

3. A word from your sponsor. Golf has traditionally attracted big-money corporate sponsors, and almost as soon as golf was announced as a 2016 Olympic sport, the jockeying among countless companies already involved in the game, or hoping to break into that orbit, began in earnest. The Lords of the IOC will have to guard against overly blatant commercialism, but don't be surprised to see Nike swooshes around every corner and Rolex clocks on every tee box.

2. South of the border. Golf has always been played in South America, but on a miniscule scale. We've had a two-time major champion from Argentina in Angel Cabrera, and by the time you read this, Colombia's Camilo Villegas may have a few majors on his résumé as well. Imagine the boom in the game in those two nations, or anywhere else on the continent, if either one of those players prevailed in Brazil.

1. It's the economy, stupid. Let's focus on China for the best example. During the Beijing Games, there were 250,000 golfers in a country of 1.4 billion, less than about .01 percent of the total population. If those numbers ever matched the participation rate in the United States of 1.3 percent, that would add 17 million new golfers in that country alone, and it would have the potential to produce a golf economy that would be four times larger than the United States. Gentlemen, start your E-Trades.

NO GOLD FOR GOLF

Golf in the Olympics doesn't work for me. Here are my reasons why golf should do without.

7. Amateurs. Golf in the Olympics would be much better if it was limited just to amateurs. Not only would you get to see the top amateurs in the world, but winning the gold medal would mean much more to one of them compared to some professional. Ernie Els and Nick Faldo supported the idea. The International Olympic Committee wasn't interested.

6. Tennis. I walked by the tennis complex almost every day while covering the 2000 Olympics in Sydney. Even though the field included big-name stars like the Williams sisters, I had no desire to go inside. Tennis has been part of the Olympics for years, but you wouldn't know it. The Olympics is about track, swimming, and gymnastics. Nobody cares about tennis. It barely receives any coverage. The same will hold true for golf. It will be relegated to secondary status.

5. Flawed format. The plan is for the men and women to play a 72-hole stroke play tournament in Rio in 2016. Boring. In order for this to work, the Olympics should have offered us something different. Perhaps a Ryder Cup–like team format with various countries playing against each other. There's nothing like the pressure of match play, and this format would be about playing for national pride, not an individual honor. Opportunity missed here.

4. False promise. The argument is that golf in the Olympics will help grow the game around the world, especially in countries where it receives little attention. After all, we saw the impact the Olympics had on basketball. I'm not buying it for golf. Basketball requires a net and a ball. Golf is much more expensive, especially if you're looking to build from the grassroots level. I have doubts the money will be there, thus minimizing the impact of Olympic golf.

3. False promise, II. Thus far, Tiger Woods said he will compete in 2016. But it likely will be one-and-done for Woods, who will be 44 in 2020. Beyond Woods, there's no guarantee the other stars will become Olympic regulars. If 2020 Games are awarded to South Africa, several big name players will say thanks but no thanks to making such a long trek in the middle of the summer. If it becomes mostly a second-tier event, what's the point?

2. Diluted field. Speaking of not having the big names, the qualifications definitely will keep a number of them out of the field. As of this writing, the format guarantees only the top 15 players ranked in the world get in regardless of nationality. From there, the remaining 45 players will get in based on rankings, *but* each country can have only two players from this pool. As a result, you'll have several stars just outside the top 15 from the United States, England, and Australia not get in, whereas unknown players from Taiwan, Philippines, Finland, Russia ranked in the 300–500 range get spots. Does that make for a compelling field? Hardly.

1. Four majors. The reason why we care about sports like track and swimming once every four years is that a gold medal is the ultimate prize for these participants. We see how much it means to win or lose, and we get caught up in their stories. That won't be the case in golf. There isn't a golfer in the world who would trade a victory in a major for a gold medal in the Olympics. The majors are and always will be the defining and most desired tournaments in golf. Leave the gold for other sports.

★ ★ ★ ★

"The point is that it doesn't matter if you look like a beast before or after you hit it, as long as you look like a beauty at the moment of impact."

—Seve Ballesteros

THE WIT AND WISDOM OF LEE TREVINO

Lee Trevino surely was born with his eyes tightly shut but his mouth wide open. Over the years, the Texas native with six majors to his credit has been a quote machine on a wide variety of subjects, occasionally even golf, as the following list surely confirms.

15. One of the nice things about the Senior Tour is that we can take a cart and a cooler. If your game is not going well, you can always have a picnic.

14. When it comes to the game of life, I figure I've played the whole course.

13. You can make a lot of money in this game. Just ask my ex-wives. Both of them are so rich that neither of their husbands work.

12. I'm going to win so much money this year, my caddy will make the top 20 money-winner's list.

11. The older I get, the better I used to be.

10. His nerve, his memory, and I can't remember the third thing.

9. Putts get real difficult the day they hand out the money.

8. There's nothing I'm scared of except my wife.

7. My divorce came to me as a complete surprise. That's what happens when you haven't been home in 18 years.

6. How can they beat me? I've been struck by lightning twice, had two back operations, and been divorced twice.

5. My wife doesn't care what I do when I'm away as long as I don't have a good time.

4. No one who ever had lessons would have a swing like me.

3. You can talk to a fade, but a hook won't listen.

2. Pressure is when you play for $5 a hole and only have $2 in your pocket.

1. If you're caught on a golf course during a storm and are afraid of lightning, hold up a 1-iron. Not even God can hit a 1-iron.

★ ★ ★ ★

"Golf is an open exhibition of overweening ambition, courage deflated by stupidity, skill soured by a whiff of arrogance."

—Alistair Cooke

UPS AND MOSTLY SPLASHDOWNS ON 17 ►ES

The most exciting 132 yards in golf? That's easy: the par-3 17th at TPC Saw-grass. Every year, an estimated 150,000 balls land in the water surrounding Pete Dye's famous island green. Several of them were dunked by the world's best players during the Players Championship. The hole has created memorable moments. Most of them weren't good.

9. A 66. Somebody must have had a sadistic bent when they had Angelo Spagnolo play the hole in 1985. Spagnolo, a 31-year-old grocery store manager, won a contest for America's worst avid golfer. His reward was getting to play TPC Sawgrass. At 17, he knocked 27 balls in the water from the tee and drop area. Finally, officials told him to putt around the hazard and through the narrow path that leads to the green. It has since been named "Angelo's Alley." Spagnolo wound up with a 66 on the 17 and posted 257 for his round. Hey, he broke 300!

8. 12 for Bob Tway. Tway had his nightmare on 17 during the third round of the 2005 Players. With the wind blowing at 25 to 30 miles per hour, Tway needed five attempts before finally keeping his ball on the green. He wound up with a 12, the all-time worst for The Players.

7. Couples's par. Fred Couples had the most memorable par on 17. In 1999 he hit his tee shot in the water. Couples then pulled out another ball, took a swing and promptly put it in the hole. Give him a 3. With the crowd going wild, Couples seemed a bit embarrassed as he walked off the tee. Perhaps he still was upset about missing the tee shot.

6. Goydos run ends. Paul Goydos was everyone's favorite underdog in 2008. Sporting a Long Beach State cap, Goydos came out of nowhere to get in a playoff with Sergio Garcia. However, his dream died on the first playoff hole when he knocked his tee shot into the water on 17. Garcia went on to win the tournament.

5. Bad dive for Sluman. In 1987 Jeff Sluman was on the verge of winning a playoff over Sandy Lyle. He had a 5-footer for birdie. However, as he was lining up the putt, an idiot dived in the water. The fans started booing as the idiot was whisked away. Unfortunately, the delay broke Sluman's concentration. He missed the putt and then lost the tournament on the next playoff hole.

4. 9-iron nukes O'Hair. Sean O'Hair trailed by two shots when he arrived at 17 in 2007. He stood on the tee trying to decide between a 9-iron or wedge. He went with the 9. Wrong decision. His shot flew over the green. Then he messed up from the drop area, eventually leading to a 7. In one hole, he fell from second to 11th. Ol' 17 had claimed another victim.

3. Hang on. The world first learned of Tiger Woods's special powers at 17. During the 1994 U.S. Amateur final, he arrived at 17 all square in his match with Trip Kuehne. Woods's tee shot bounced on the right fringe and seemed destined for the water. The ball, though, held as if it miraculously found a strip of Velcro. Then for miracle No. 2, Woods made the improbable putt to take the lead and eventually win the match.

2. Mattiace heartbreak. Like O'Hair, Len Mattiace saw his dreams crushed on 17. He arrived at the hole trailing by a shot to Justin Leonard in 1998. All afternoon, NBC chronicled the story of the unlikely contender and his mother, who was fighting cancer. It all begged for a happy ending. However, 17 has no heart. Mattiace hit his first shot in the water. Then after finding the bunker, he promptly skulled his next shot across the green and into the pond again. It all added up to an 8, securing Mattiace a spot in 17 infamy.

1. Better than most. There are two positive entries on this list, and of course, both of them belong to Tiger Woods. During the third round in 2001, Woods faced a 60-foot putt from the back of the green. Gary Koch and Johnny Miller were talking about how Woods would be lucky to just get it close. Woods had other thoughts. As the putt rolled toward the hole, Koch let out his memorable description, "Better than most." Then when it dropped in, he yelled it again, "Better than most!" Woods pointed to caddy Steve Williams and the crowd exploded. A putt for the ages.

★ ★ ★ ★

"The first time I played the Masters, I was so nervous I drank a bottle of rum before I teed off. I shot the happiest 83 of my life."

—Chi Chi Rodriguez

BEST RYDER CUPS

Technically, the Ryder Cup began in 1927 with the United States facing golfers from Great Britain (and later Ireland, too). However, the Ryder Cup as we all now know it started in 1979 when the matches were expanded to include players from all of Europe. Previously, the Ryder Cup was a mostly obscure, one-sided exhibition that saw the United States go 14-1-1 after World War II. Enter Seve Ballesteros from Spain in 1979, and suddenly the Ryder Cup became a fierce, intense, and, at times, bitter rumble. The semi-annual event now is a highlight on the golf calendar every other year. Here's a list of the best U.S.-Europe Ryder Cups.

10. 2010 at Celtic Manor. Apparently, nobody told organizers that Wales gets a lot of rain in October. The wettest Ryder Cup in recent memory forced the event to spill over into Monday. But it turned out to be worth the wait. The United States rallied valiantly from a 3-point deficit in singles. Ultimately, it came down to the final match on the course. Facing supreme pressure, Graeme McDowell came through huge for Europe with a 2 and 1 victory over Hunter Mahan, giving captain Colin Montgomerie a 14½–13½ victory.

9. 1983 at PGA National. Initially, the expanded European team didn't change the course of the Ryder Cup. The United States easily trounced Europe in 1979 and 1981. Then things heated up considerably in 1983. The matches were even at 8–8 going into Sunday singles. During his match against Fuzzy Zoeller, Ballesteros hit a legendary 3-wood from a bunker on 18 and got up and down for par to secure a halve. Trailing by three to José Maria Canizares, Lanny Wadkins rallied for a key halve, which gave the United States a tight 14½–13½ victory. Europe may have lost, but it definitely proved it was "game on" for the Ryder Cup.

8. 1987 at Muirfield Village. Jack Nicklaus was the captain with the matches being held on the course he designed. He had reason to feel confident of a U.S. victory. Instead, he watched the Europeans bully the Americans. Europe built a 10½–5½ lead after two days and then held on for a 15–13 victory. Ben Crenshaw displayed the U.S. frustration. After snapping his putter during his singles match, "Gentle Ben" had to finish using a 1-iron and the edge of his sand wedge on the greens.

7. 1993 at the Belfry. This battle was tight from the beginning, with several matches being decided on the final hole. Europe held a 1-point lead going into singles, but the United States rallied for a 15–13 victory. Raymond Floyd, 51 at the time, was one of the heroes, sinking three birdie putts on the back nine to post a 2-up victory over José Maria Olazabal.

6. 2008 at Valhalla. Europe dominated the previous two Ryder Cups, winning by back-to-back scores of 18½–9½ and making the competition look more like Europe versus the United Emirates. U.S. captain Paul Azinger was out to change things in 2008. Using a pod system in which he matched players with similar personalities, Azinger found the right combinations. Despite playing without Tiger Woods, the United States got some pride back with a resounding 16½–11½ victory.

5. 1995 at Oak Hill. The United States was poised to win a third straight Cup, leading by two points going into singles. Europe, though, got unexpected singles victories from Philip Walton (1-up over Jay Haas) and Howard Clark (1-up over Peter Jacobsen). Europe's Ryder Cup fixtures also came through and they walked away with a 14½–13½ victory.

4. 1989 at the Belfry. At the gala the night before the matches, U.S. captain Raymond Floyd introduced his team as "the twelve greatest players in the world." That didn't go over well, considering Europe won the previous two Ryder Cups. The Spanish pairing of Seve Ballesteros and José Maria Olazabal had something to prove to Floyd. They recorded 3½ points in team competition. The United States rallied in singles to produce a 14–14 tie. However, because Europe was the defending champ, the Ryder Cup stayed on its side of the pond.

3. 1985 at the Belfry. Europe arrived and it wasn't even close. Manuel Piñero had four points and Ballesteros picked up 3½ in Europe's 16½–11½ victory. When Sam Torrance made a birdie putt on 18 to win his match over Andy North, the Europeans had their first title in 28 years. Torrance was so overcome with emotion, tears streamed down his face. Tells you how much it meant for Europe.

2. 1999 at Brookline. The United States looked doomed after two days. Europe held a 10–6 lead going into singles. However, U.S. captain Ben Crenshaw refused to lose faith. During his Saturday news conference, Crenshaw said, "I'm a big believer in fate. I have a good feeling about this. That's all I'm going to tell you." Crenshaw was right. Stacking the lineup with his best players at the top, the United States got off to a quick start to pull back even with Europe. The drama built, climaxing on 17 when Justin Leonard hit a putt for the ages; his 45-footer for birdie secured the winning point and a 14½–13½ U.S. victory.

U.S. Ryder Cup team member Justin Leonard celebrates.

1. 1991 at Kiawah. "The War by the Shore" proved to be the measuring stick for all other Ryder Cups. With the United States seeking to win its first Cup since 1983, the matches were an epic battle, producing one dramatic moment after another. Fittingly, it came down to the last match and then the last putt. Bernhard Langer needed to convert a 6-footer for par on 18 to win his match against Hale Irwin and keep the Cup in Europe's hands. As the putt skittered past the hole, a photographer captured the famous image of Langer grimacing in defeat. The United States had a 14½–13½ victory and the Cup.

BEST RYDER CUP PLAYERS

The best golfers don't necessarily make for the best Ryder Cup players. For instance, you won't find Tiger Woods on this list. The world's best golfer has been decidedly underwhelming in Ryder Cup play. Sergio Garcia, meanwhile, has played like Tiger Woods at times in team competition. Go figure. Again, we'll be examining the best players in Ryder Cups after 1979, when the matches were expanded to include all of Europe. Sorry, Jimmy Demaret (who went 6-0 in Ryder Cup play from 1947–51).

14. Hal Sutton. Picking up 3½ points in five matches, Sutton was the star of the U.S. team's thrilling victory against Europe in 1999 at Brookline. He opened singles with a 4 and 2 victory over Darren Clarke, sparking the Americans' comeback. Captain Ben Crenshaw called him "the backbone of the team."

13. Ian Woosnam. "Woozie" always played big in Ryder Cups. His strength was in fourballs, where he posted a 10-3-1 mark. He went on to be the winning captain for Europe in the 2006 Ryder. The celebration provided the memorable image of champagne going up Woosnam's nose. Memorable, but not exactly a pretty picture.

12. Corey Pavin. He was a bulldog for the United States, sporting an 8-5 mark in three Ryder Cups. Pavin shined in the 1995 Ryder Cup, going 4-1 in five matches, even if it wasn't enough to keep Europe from winning the Cup that year.

11. Payne Stewart. He only went 8-9-2 in five Ryder Cups, but that's not the full measure of his impact on the U.S. team. Stewart was a fierce competitor and team leader who inspired other players. He also showed tremendous sportsmanship when he conceded a long final putt to Colin Montgomerie during singles in 1999 to halve their match. The United States already had clinched the Cup, and the fans were giving Monty a hard time. Montgomerie never will forget the gesture.

10. Paul Azinger. Like Stewart, Azinger was another U.S. player who "got it" when it came to the Ryder Cup. Even though he was only 5-7-3 in four Ryder Cups, he was a driving force in bringing the Americans together. He had some epic rumbles with Seve Ballesteros, gaining the ire of the Spaniard. He dunked a bunker shot for birdie on 18 to halve a singles match against Sweden's Niclas Fasth in 2002. Using the lessons he learned as a player, he went on to be the winning captain for the United States in 2008.

9. Bernhard Langer. His Ryder Cup legacy always will be tied to the putt he missed at Kiawah to give the Cup back to America in 1991. However, the German made more than his share of putts, compiling a 21-15-6 record in 10 Ryder Cups. He was the winning captain for Europe in 2004.

8. Larry Nelson. He was a go-to player for the United States, compiling a 9-3-1 record in three Ryder Cups. He won all five of his matches in his Ryder Cup debut in 1979. Considering he also won two PGA Championships, Nelson deserved a shot at being U.S. captain. It was a major slight that it never happened for him.

7. Tom Kite. He was a fixture on seven U.S. teams, compiling a 15-9-4 mark. However, he was the losing captain for the United States in 1997.

6. José Maria Olazabal. He and Ballesteros formed the most successful team connection in Ryder Cup history. "The Spanish Armada" went 11-2-2. With a short game that could rival Ballesteros's, Olazabal rose to the occasion in the Ryder Cup.

5. Sergio Garcia. Garcia has one of the shakiest putters in pro golf, which is the main reason why he has struggled to achieve true greatness. But put him in a Ryder Cup, and Garcia putts like Jack Nicklaus. Perhaps playing in the team format makes him more at ease. He knows if he misses, there will be somebody to pick him up.

4. Lanny Wadkins. He was a stud, compiling a 20-11-3 record in eight Ryder Cups. His 21½ points ranks third overall for U.S. players behind Billy Casper (23½) and Arnold Palmer (23). And Wadkins played against much tougher competition, facing the Europeans during the 1980s. Wadkins, though, did have one major Cup disappointment: He was the losing captain in 1995.

3. Nick Faldo. He played in his first Ryder Cup at the age of 20 in 1977 and his last in 1997 at the age of 40. His arrival, coupled with that of Ballesteros in 1979, signaled that things would be different going forward for Europe. He compiled 25 points in 11 Ryder Cups, the most for any player on either side.

2. Colin Montgomerie. The same scenario as Garcia. Put him in a major and watch Montgomerie wilt under pressure. But Monty reigns supreme in the Ryder Cup. He was 20-9-8 in eight Cups, compiling 23½ points. He once said, "If I tell you

I can remember every shot I hit in a Ryder Cup, it will go some ways in explaining how much this biennial competition means to me." Indeed, since he never won a major, the Ryder Cup will be his defining competition as a player. Then he secured his legacy, winning the Cup for Europe as a captain in 2010.

1. Seve Ballesteros. Quite simply, he made the Ryder Cup what it is today. Beginning with his entry in 1979, the same year the matches were expanded to include all European players, he transformed the competition with his shot making and gamesmanship. He inspired the Europeans and got under the skins of the Americans. Paul Azinger once accused Ballesteros of "always developing a cough at the Ryder Cup." He had a 20-12-5 record in eight Ryder Cups. In 1997 he was the winning captain for Europe with the matches being played in his home country of Spain. It was the crowning moment for the best of the best in the Ryder Cup.

★ ★ ★ ★

"One thing about golf is you don't know why you play bad and why you play good."

—George Archer

MY TOP TEN IN GOLF FICTION ►BY JOHN GARRITY

A fixture on the *Sports Illustrated* masthead since 1989, author and journalist John Garrity remains one of the most literate and prolific sportswriters
of his generation, a master of his craft as well as a single-digit handicapper
himself. We asked him to pick his all-time favorite works of golf fiction, and
we also recommend adding some of John's own books to your required
absolutely-must-read list, including two of his most recent works of non-
fiction, "Tiger 2.0" and "Ancestral Links: A Golf Obsession Spanning
Generations."

10. *Goldfinger* by Ian Fleming. Although not universally recognized as a golf
novel, Fleming's spy thriller gives us the best fairway duel in literature—suave James
Bond vs. conniving Goldfinger—as well as (in the film only) the most intimidating
caddy, Oddjob. Hats off to 007!

9. *A Nasty Bit of Rough* by David Feherty. Hailed as "The *Naked Gun* of
golf literature" by *Publishers Weekly*, this madcap farce by the former tour player from
Northern Ireland has absolutely no redeeming value—unless mocking the Brits is
your cup of tea. It happens to be mine.

8. *Train* by Pete Dexter. Looking for something a little darker for your golf
book collection? Dexter's crime novel, set in the San Diego of 1953, serves up bigotry,
classism, murder . . . and a black caddy who could outplay Bagger Vance without
mystical assistance. Golf noir at its best.

7. *Missing Links* by Rick Reilly. The gags practically overflow the pages, but
Reilly's novel about a shopworn Boston muni and its hard-gambling habitués is, in the
end, a misty-eyed tribute to publinx golf. Hail "Ponky"!

6. *Fast Greens* by Turk Pipkin. Daring to trespass on Dan Jenkins's Texas
landscape of rich white guys and golf hustlers, Pipkin delivers a novel that is pica-
resque but sincere—leaving the impression that the former stand-up comic borrowed
more from life itself than from Jenkins own self.

5. *Fore!* by Charles E. Van Loan. This long-out-of-print collection of original short stories, by the man Grantland Rice called "sport's greatest fiction writer,"

helped usher in the so-called Golden Age of Sports. Van Loan is far less arch than Wodehouse, but his portrayal of country club rivalries and golfing camaraderie is more than a confirming echo.

4. *Out of the Bunker and Into the Trees* by Rex Lardner, Jr. Subtitled "The Secret of High-Tension Golf," this faux golf-instructional-cum-memoir by the former chief writer for comedian Ernie Kovaks is golf's *Spinal Tap*. It is the funniest of all golf books, and it is my favorite of all golf books.

3. *Dead Solid Perfect* by Dan Jenkins. There is an actual PGA Tour, dominated by disciplined range rats and chapel-attending family men, and there is Jenkins's PGA Tour, populated by chain-smoking, bet-pressing, half-in-the-bag tail chasers and their cat-scratching women. Before the Tiger Woods flameout, who would have guessed that Jenkins's version is nearer the truth?

2. *Golf in the Kingdom* by Michael Murphy. Half of it is New Age mumbo-jumbo and the other half is dead-end narrative about a truth-seeking American and a Scottish golf pro, but Murphy's golf soliloquies are downright Shakespearean, unmatched for their lyricism and profundity. No other golf writing, outside of a few instructionals, has actually transformed its readers or spawned so many acolytes.

1. *The Golf Omnibus* by P. G. Wodehouse. Take it from the Oldest Member, Wodehouse will never be surpassed as a chronicler of golf and its attendant absurdities. His many novels and collected stories made the entire world safe for golf—even as the British Empire retreated—and gave the English language a sparkle it would not otherwise possess. ("The least thing upset him on the links. He missed short putts because of the uproar of the butterflies in the adjoining meadows.") Even Jeeves would concede that Wodehouse was top drawer.

★ ★ ★ ★

"Playing golf is like eating. It's something that has to come naturally."

—Sam Snead

Of the trillions of shots hit in golf history, only a precious few stand the test of time. They were so spectacular, improbable, and utterly clutch that they are forever seared in our memories. We can see them today as clearly as when we first saw them years ago.

The age of television tends to tilt this list more toward the modern era. We have clearer memories of what we actually saw. So apologies to any shot from the distant past that probably merited a mention. Having said that, a couple of them even made this list, including No. 1.

Here's our shot at the game's greatest shots.

11. Young Tom Morris, 1869 British Open. Young Tom recorded the first hole-in-one in any tournament. Only 18 at the time, he posted an ace on the 166-yard par 3 at Prestwick. Imagine how big that shot must have been at the time? The British Open debuted in 1860 and nobody had ever posted a 1 on their scorecard. The shot helped him win the tournament; his father was second.

10. Sergio Garcia, 1999 PGA Championship. Nobody will ever forget Garcia's shot at the 16th hole at Medinah. He knocked his drive up against the base of one of the thousands of trees at Medinah. Locked in a tight battle against Tiger Woods, Garcia, from 189 yards, decided to go for broke, risking life and limb. Closing his eyes, he lashed at the ball and then did a memorable Peter Pan dance down the fairway as he watched it land on the green. Even though Woods won the tournament, Garcia stole the show with that shot.

9. Constantino Rocca, 1995 British Open. Rocca needed to can a 65-foot putt off the 18th green at St. Andrews to force a playoff with John Daly. No way, right? When the putt rolled in, Rocca collapsed in a heap while Daly looked stunned, thinking he already had won the tournament. This putt probably would rank higher if Rocca actually walked home with the Claret Jug. However, Daly eventually won the playoff.

8. Bob Tway, 1986 PGA Championship. Tway put up a furious back-9 rally to tie Greg Norman going into the final hole at Inverness. However, he put his second shot into the bunker. With Norman on the green, Tway splashed the sand, landing the ball a foot onto the putting surface. It then rolled in for an improbable birdie. Norman then missed his putt, giving Tway the title.

7. Birdie Kim, 2005 U.S. Women's Open. Just like Tway, Kim also found a miracle in a bunker. The relatively unknown South Korean was tied with Morgan Pressel on the 18th hole at Cherry Hills. Trying to save par from the bunker, Kim lived up to her nickname by holing the shot for the winning birdie.

6. Tiger Woods, 2005 Masters. Battling Chris DiMarco down the stretch on Sunday, Woods went over the green with his tee shot on the par-3 16th. He faced a difficult chip to just get it close to save par. Sensing the moment, Woods landed his shot perfectly on the green. Then the entire golf world watched breathlessly as the ball rolled slowly toward the hole, stopping for a split-second on the rim. When it finally dropped, CBS's Verne Lundquist shouted, "OH, WOW!" Nobody will ever forget it.

5. Phil Mickelson, 2010 Masters. We have to include this shot because it still is so fresh in our minds. Stuck on the pine straw and surrounded by trees, most people expected Mickelson to play it safe with his second shot at the par-5 13th. Mickelson, though, isn't most people. Finding a narrow opening, he took a wicked slash with a 6-iron and then watched as the ball barely cleared Rae's Creek, landing safely on the green. Vintage Phil.

4. Jack Nicklaus, 1972 U.S. Open. You know the old saying, "Not even God could hit a 1-iron." Well, that didn't apply to Nicklaus. Nicklaus arrived at the par-3 17th at Pebble Beach holding a 1-shot lead over Bruce Crampton. Hitting into a stiff wind on the 206-yard par 3, Nicklaus's 1-iron shot hit the pin, leaving him a tap-in for birdie. He went on to win the tournament, and he had perhaps the defining shot of his career.

3. Tom Watson, 1982 U.S. Open. Watson waged another epic duel with Nicklaus in his bid for his first U.S. Open. Tied for the lead at the par-3 17th at Pebble Beach, Watson hit 2-iron in the deep, nasty rough surrounding the green. It looked like a bogey for sure. Watson, though, told his caddy, Bruce Edwards, "I'm not going to get it close. I'm going to make it." Sure enough, Watson and Edwards did a memorable dance after the ball went into the hole for unlikely victory. Watson had his U.S. Open title.

2. Larry Mize, 1987 Masters. Mize authored the most dramatic ending ever to a major tournament. Locked in a playoff with Greg Norman, he was off the green on the 11th hole. Facing a fast green flanked by water, all sorts of disaster loomed for Mize. You expect people named Hogan, Woods, or Nicklaus to pull off a miracle.

This time it was the unassuming Mize. He sent his chip skittering onto the green and into the hole. The Augusta, Georgia, native had his Green Jacket.

Larry Mize leaps for joy after winning the 1987 Masters.

1. Gene Sarazen, 1935 Masters. It is the most written about shot that virtually nobody saw. Battling Craig Wood down the stretch at only the second Masters, Sarazen grabbed a 4-wood from 245 yards for his second shot into the par-5 15th. He said, "I took my stance with my 4-wood and rode into the shot with every ounce of strength and timing I could muster. The split second I hit the ball I knew it would carry the pond. It tore for the flag on a very low trajectory, no more than 30 feet in the air."

Watching from the 17th hole, Byron Nelson had a perfect view of the shot. He saw the ball land in the hole. "It was pretty exciting," he said.

The double eagle helped land Sarazen in a 36-hole playoff against Wood the following day, which he won. Sarazen's thrilling moment gave immediate credibility to the new tournament. The shot few people saw became known as "The Shot heard around the world."

THE BEST NICKNAMES

Any follower of the game hardly needs a full name to identify their favorite players, particularly at the highest levels of the sport. It's just Jack or Arnie, Tiger or Annika, but those four have other monikers as well, and colorful nicknames have always been a tradition on both the PGA and LPGA Tours.

The King—Arnold Palmer

Urkel—Eldrick Woods

Golden Bear—Jack Nicklaus

El Niño—Sergio Garcia

Wild Thing—John Daly

Halimony—Hal Sutton

The Black Knight—Gary Player

The Haig—Walter Hagen

Dr. Dirt—Brad Bryant

Tank—K. J. Choi

Peanut—Mi Hyun Kim

Babe—Mildred Didrikson Zaharias

The Big Easy—Ernie Els

The Big Wiesy—Michelle Wie

Fluff—Mike Cowan

Lefty—Phil Mickelson

Popeye—Craig Parry

Spaceman—Jesper Parnevik

Alfie—Helen Alfreddson

Chi Chi—Juan Rodriguez

Miss 59—Annika Sorenstam

Veej—Vijay Singh

The Shark—Greg Norman

The Dark Shark—Ian Baker-Finch

The Walrus—Craig Stadler

Big Momma—JoAnne Carner

The Wee Ice Mon—Ben Hogan

Slammin' Sammy—Sam Snead

The Squire—Gene Sarazen

Spiderman—Camilo Villegas

Paddy—Padraig Harrington

Aquaman—Woody Austin

Elk—Steve Elkington

Beemer—Rich Beem

Pink Panther—Paula Creamer

DL 3—Davis Love III

Boom Boom—Fred Couples

Lumpy—Tim Herron

Bads—Aaron Baddely

Boss of the Moss—
Loren Roberts

Gentle Ben—Ben Crenshaw

Zinger—Paul Azinger

The Mechanic—
Miguel Angel Jimenez

Ollie—José Maria Olazabal

Champagne Tony—Tony Lema

Merry Mex—Lee Trevino

The Silver Scot—
Tommy Armour

Terrible Tommy—Tom Bolt

Lighthorse—Harry Cooper

Mrs. Doubtfire—
Colin Montgomerie

Sarge—Orville Moody

Lord Byron—Byron Nelson

Porky—Ed Oliver

Jumbo—Masahi Ozaki

Jules—Juli Inkster

PAR FOR A PRESIDENT

According to *Golf Digest*, 15 of the last 18 U.S. presidents were golfers, and a few of them were actually fairly decent players, despite the grinding demands of their day jobs.

Vice President Dan Quayle, the captain of his college golf team, was a heartbeat away from the presidency under George H. W. Bush and was a scratch or low single-digit player before back problems eventually sent his scores soaring. Vice President Joe Biden tried several times to run for president and also would have been one of the best First Golfers if he'd made it to the White House, considering he once carried an 8.2 handicap index. Speaker of the House John Boehner has been known to shoot in the low to mid-80s, and the Republican Congressman from Ohio has the deep tan to prove he definitely knows his way around golf venues coast to coast.

The following commanders-in-chief could also hold their own on any tee or green in the land. You'll also notice that Richard Nixon is not among our top ten, even if he did like to play. His swing was an ugly, Charles Barkley–esque lunge at the ball, and if the man was capable of covering up Watergate, do you think he might have moved his ball in the rough a time or two?

10. George W. Bush. A decent athlete, he preferred running and mountain biking during most of his eight years in office, though in the early years of his administration he played the occasional round of golf. He infuriated the golfing community during his second term when he said he was giving up the game because he didn't feel it was appropriate to play while the country was fighting wars in Iran and Afghanistan. Meanwhile, some of his troops were actually working on their swings practicing on Iraqi sand, and some wounded warriors even used golf to rehab their bodies and their minds when they came home.

9. Warren G. Harding. He was one of four presidents to become an early member of Congressional Country Club in Bethesda, Maryland, along with William Howard Taft, Woodrow Wilson, and Calvin Coolidge. Harding loved to play poker, occasionally slipped out of the Oval Office for a burlesque fix, and was said to play golf at least twice a week while in office. He practiced by hitting balls on the south lawn of the White House, with a favorite Airedale dog, Laddie Boy, trained to fetch them. Make that Caddy Boy.

8. Ronald Reagan. The Gipper played a little golf in his Hollywood days, but by the time he got to 1600 Pennsylvania Avenue in 1980, horseback riding and clearing brush at his California ranch were his main physical diversions. Still, he did manage to get in a few rounds in the 1980s and was decent enough to shoot in the low 90s. He also got a laugh the day he said that "my golfing friend Bob Hope once asked me what my handicap was. So I told him—Congress." Some things never change.

7. Franklin Delano Roosevelt. Until he was struck by polio at the age of 39, the Happy Warrior was said to be happiest on a golf course. He learned the game at a young age, played on a 6-hole course at the family estate in New York, and often shot in the low 80s. His love of the sport became a boon to golfers nationwide during the Great Depression because his New Deal policies to get Americans back to work included the construction or renovation of more than 600 municipal courses around the country, including Bethpage Black on Long Island, a two-time U.S. Open venue.

6. Gerald Ford. Arguably the most decorated athlete ever to attain the presidency, the former All-American center at the University of Michigan was an avid golfer for most of his life. He played in a number of pro-am events after leaving the White House, and there weren't ever enough Secret Service men on the grounds to protect all those bruised spectators from his well-documented errant shots. Still, despite Ford's follies off the tee, he more than occasionally broke 90 and hated his reputation as Hacker-in-Chief.

5. Barack Obama. Although basketball has always been his sport of choice, the former Hawaiian high school point guard took up the sport in his mid-30s and has become a devoted golfer in recent years, often slipping out on his weekends in Washington to play at Andrews Air Force Base, a 15-minute drive from the White House. He hits it left-handed and has said his personal bucket list includes playing as many of the world's great golf courses as he can, though not necessarily while he's the president. That's sort of comforting, actually.

4. Bill Clinton. He started playing golf at age 12 at an Arkansas country club where his uncle was a member. As governor of that state, he said he often teed off at 6:30 a.m. to get in a few rounds a week, and while he was president, averaged about five rounds a month when the weather was good. Clinton loved to gamble for small stakes and was known to take more than the occasional mulligan—otherwise known as Billigans. After all, would anyone ever dare to tell a president he was cheating . . . in golf, anyway?

3. George H. W. Bush. Poppy was a starter on the Yale baseball team and a decorated pilot during World War II, so all that outstanding hand-eye coordination also made him a decent golfer who once carried an 11-handicap. Before, during, and after his presidency, the man never liked to dawdle on the golf course. He was legendary for playing speed golf, whizzing his cart around 18 holes in less than two hours, the better to take care of really important matters of state.

2. John F. Kennedy. Many have said he was probably the best golfer of all the presidents, at least when he was healthy enough to play, carrying a 10-handicap and often posting scores in the high 70s. But JFK suffered from serious back problems for most of his adult life, so he usually was able to manage only nine holes before stiffening up and calling it day. He was also something of a closet golfer as president, not wanting to let on that he played a lot, the better to avoid comparisons to his predecessor, Dwight Eisenhower, who he and his aides often referred to as "Duffer-in-Chief."

1. Dwight Eisenhower. Ike liked golf—a lot. He had his own practice putting green installed at the White House and played over 800 rounds of golf during his eight years in office, many of them at his beloved Augusta National Golf Club, where the Eisenhower Cabin on the grounds is still very much in use. Journalist Don Van Natta, Jr., author of *First Off the Tee*, a history of golfing presidents, wrote that "Ike made the game accessible to the people and he made the game cool." He also managed to break 80 at least a dozen times. With all that practice, no surprise there.

President Barack Obama has never had any qualms about throwing the sticks in the trunk, saddling up his Secret Service detail, and ditching 1600 Pennsylvania Avenue for the tranquility of a mind-cleansing round of golf. In the Washington, D.C. area, he's got plenty of choices, ranging in degree of difficulty from several former U.S. Open venues to one of the busiest public courses in America, most within a 30-minute motorcade drive, a couple more less than an hour away.

Here's a list of places he's likely to sample over his tenure, and one politically incorrect, inside-the-beltway private club he'd be better off avoiding.

10. Be my guest. That's right, we'd be remiss in not inviting the president to Shapiro's home course, Loudoun Golf and Country Club in Purcellville, Virginia, the longest drive he'll have to make on our top ten list, about 50 miles door to first tee. It's worth it for a delightful day in the countryside, not to mention a challenging 6,500-yard test at a totally unpretentious club built in 1927 that doesn't even require a tee time. Not to worry, Mr. President, guest fee on me.

9. River view. East Potomac is the shortest drive of all from the White House, maybe ten minutes to a popular public course, one of only three in the District of Columbia. Averaging over 100,000 rounds a year, the 6,600-yard course hugs the Potomac River, and there are lovely views of Reagan Airport on the Virginia shore, not to mention all those pesky jets flying overhead at the top of your backswing. This may be the place where the president, who reportedly shoots in the low 90s, might get down to the low 80s, especially if he brings Bill Clinton along, guaranteeing mulligans on virtually any poor shot or lousy putt.

8. Female friendly. Bethesda Country Club, an Arthur Hills design, is a relatively tight, tree-lined 6,700-yard course opened in 1947. The LPGA Championship was contested at the course from 1990 to 1993, and three of the four winners—Beth Daniel (1990), Betsy King (1992), and Patty Sheehan (1993)—are Hall of Famers. The '91 champion was Meg Mallon, who also won the U.S. Women's Open the same year. Sadly, the tournament left town in 1994 when Mazda pulled its sponsorship, but it's still a world-class course that, early in its illustrious history, encouraged single women to join, no husband necessary.

7. No Tin Cup. The Robert Trent Jones Golf Club in Lake Manassas, Virginia, actually hosted four Presidents Cup competitions before PGA Tour officials moved it in 2009 to San Francisco's Harding Park, a public course named for former president Warren G. Harding. RTJ is a relatively new venue, but it offers one of the country's more demanding layouts as well as an extremely diverse membership that includes former Urban League executive director Vernon Jordan and former Supreme Court Justice Sandra Day O'Connor.

6. Military golf. We're not talking about hitting balls left, right, left, right, but rather the Army Navy Country Club in Arlington, where a number of past presidents have played over the years. The club, with many current and retired military men and women holding memberships, boasts three challenging 9-hole courses.

5. Pardon the interruption. Tony Kornheiser of ESPN and *Washington Post* fame is a member of Columbia Country Club. This Chevy Chase institution, the oldest golf club in the area, originally started with twenty members in 1898. The current course was built in 1911 and was said to be President Woodrow Wilson's favorite place to play. It also hosted the 1921 U.S. Open, won by Englishman Jim Barnes, with President Harding presenting the championship trophy.

4. That's a mouthful. It's recently been renamed to the TPC Potomac at Avenel Farms, perhaps to hide the fact that in its previous form, the old TPC at Avenel was considered a big-time dog track by the PGA Tour pros who played there during the old Kemper Open. That tournament is now long gone, and the course and clubhouse have both been recently renovated into what many players now say is a world-class facility, definitely fit for a president. The Constellation Energy Open, a major on the Champions Tour, was contested here in 2010.

3. Let's fly away. If the president so desires, a helicopter can land on his south lawn and transport the commander-in-chief across the Potomac to the Maryland side, the better to play one of three championship courses at Andrews Air Force Base, also the home of Air Force One, the presidential airplane. Only current and retired military and anyone working for the federal government can play the course, which obviously qualifies POTUS for membership.

2. Black history. Langston Golf Club in Northeast Washington was opened in 1939 at a time when the District's other segregated public courses did not allow African Americans to play. Heavyweight champion Joe Louis was a regular at Langston any time he came to the nation's capital, and the course once was operated by Lee Elder, the first African American to play in the Masters. If he goes, the president might want to get some inspiration from a master athletic motivator who also plays the course several times a week. That would be Herman Boone, the former head coach at T. C. Williams High School in nearby Alexandria, Virginia, played by Denzel Washington in the blockbuster movie *Remember the Titans*.

1. The very best. That would be Congressional Country Club, the site of three U.S. Opens and a PGA Championship. Opened in 1924 with two 18-hole courses on the property, the club's membership includes Congressmen, high-powered lobbyists, and other movers and shakers in the nation's capital. The championship Blue Course, originally designed by Devereux Emmet, has been renovated for majors both by Robert Trent Jones, Sr. (1957) and his son, Rees Jones (1989 and 2006), and it stretches over 7,200 yards, playing to a par of 70 for the pros and 72 for the members. If the president needs a seasoned caddy, Mike "Fluff" Cowan, a super-looper for Tiger Woods (formerly) and Jim Furyk (currently), might help out. After all, he's a Congressional member himself and plays to a single-digit handicap.

A word to the wise. President Obama may very well be tempted to sneak over to the exclusive Burning Tree Club in Bethesda, where President Dwight Eisenhower once had a locker and a regular game. But the club, which includes Bryant Gumbel, Jim Nantz, and Ken Venturi as members, could be politically toxic, seeing as how Burning Tree has never allowed a female to join the all-boys-all-the-time club. John F. Kennedy played a round of golf at Burning Tree the day of the Bay of Pigs invasion, but presidents of the twenty-first century would be wise to stay away, at least until they've been elected to a second term.

★ ★ ★ ★

"Stick your butt out, Mr. President."

—Sam Snead to President Eisenhower

AROUND THE WORLD

▶ BY DAVE KINDRED

In 1994 longtime, award-winning sports columnists Dave Kindred and Tom Callahan set off on a dream assignment, funded by a book advance from their publisher, Doubleday. They traveled the world (though not by hot-air balloon) in search of the most unique golfing venues on the planet. Kindred listed his four favorite holes from that trip and the most unusual golf shot of his life from quite the historic teeing ground.

(The book is *Around the World in 18 Holes* by Tom Callahan and Dave Kindred, Doubleday Publishing, 1994.)

5. The 17th at Akureyri Golf Club, Akureyri, Iceland. A par 5 of 518 yards, mostly uphill between black lava-rock fields. At 3:17 a.m.—this was June near the Arctic Circle with 24 hours of daylight—I hit a driver off the tee. Then I hit the driver off the fairway. Because the wind was coming into us, I hit a third driver toward the green—whereupon I made a new Rule of Life: Never play uphill into a wind that five minutes ago crossed the North Pole.

4. The 13th at the Lost City Golf Course, Sun City, Bophuthatswana. A par 3 of 178 yards, the tee shot struck from a cliff side high above a green made in the shape of the African continent. In a massive stone pit cut about where the Atlantic Ocean would touch Nigeria, there lurked maybe 40 crocodiles up to 14 feet long, yawning, sunning, and swimming near unnecessary signs suggesting BEWARE OF CROCODILES. My tee shot came to rest near one croc. I left it there.

3. The 3rd at Royal Nepal Golf Club, Kathmandu, Nepal. A par 4 of 456 yards on a fairway of ankle-deep grass (no powered mowers there) to oiled-sand greens. The 9-hole layout became "Royal" in 1965 when His Majesty King Mahendra Bir Bickram Saha Dev signed a proclamation by the glow of a Zippo lighter rushed into duty when the lights went out, a daily occurrence at the Everest Hotel. We made bogeys at the 3rd after waiting for three little men to pass carrying a corpse bundled in a bright orange shroud on its way to cremation alongside a river that would carry the ashes to the sacred Ganges.

2. The 10th at Le Golf du Château de la Salle, Macon, France. A par 4 of 430 yards on a course designed in the shape of a woman named Nicole, once the architect Robert Berthet's mistress. Every curve, every contour, every titillating mound on the course—no doglegs, "many womanlegs," Berthet said—was shaped according to photographs for which Nicole posed nude. The green at the 10th was Nicole's foot tucked up over an ankle, guarded by five sand traps arranged as toes.

1. The not really a hole at the Great Wall of China. It was impossible. It was unthinkable. It would have been unbecoming of any golfer to walk on the Great Wall without hitting a shot from its surface. So I dialed my adjustable club to an 8-iron setting, teed up a Titleist on the peak of my baseball cap—and here's what my coauthor, Tom Callahan wrote, "It flew majestically. Not the ball, the bill of his cap. Just the bill." The ball, we never saw. So Callahan teed up on the remains of my cap "and took my own slash at history. Somewhere in the undergrowth of Mutianyu, two dimpled orbs are waiting to drive the anthropologists nuts."

★ ★ ★ ★

"One of the advantages bowling has over golf is that you seldom lose a bowling ball."

—Don Carter

BATS AND BALLS

Long before the Diablo drivers, the Machspeed irons, the Pro V1 golf balls, the basic tools of the game had much kinder, gentler monikers, now mostly forgotten by so many players with little sense of history. Modern space-age clubs are mostly selected from the bag by number, and golf balls are branded with the corporate names of their respective manufacturers, a far cry from the days when many of the early implements had far more exotic names.

Doesn't the sound of a brassie or a niblick stir the golfer's soul so much more than the metronomic mention of a 2-wood or 9-iron? Wouldn't it be more fun to watch the flight of a feathery ball, or hear the sound of a gutta-percha plop on to the green? There was a time when true craftsmen made clubs and balls by hand, not assembly line, and so we offer a brief primer on clubs and balls of old.

CLUBS

Cleek: driving iron

Mid-mashie: 3-iron

Mashie: 5-iron

Spade-mashie: 6-iron

Mashie-niblick: 7-iron

Niblick: 9-iron

Jigger: wedge

Spoon: 3-wood

Brassie: 2-wood

EARLY BALLS

Feathery: Wet goose feathers, enough to fill a top hat, then stuffed in a leather pouch, circa early 1800s.

Gutta percha: Made with a sap-like substance molded at 212 degrees Fahrenheit that held its shape when cooled, circa mid- to late 1800s.

The bramble: An offshoot of the Gutta Percha, with a surface like a berry, the better to control the flight of the ball in the air, circa late 1800s.

The haskell: The first rubber-cored ball surrounded by rubber thread and covered with a balata cover, made from the gum of a bully tree, circa early twentieth century.

JOHN DALY BY THE NUMBERS

John Daly, a.k.a. "Wild Thing," has long been the bad boy of the PGA Tour, even if he remains immensely popular with many fans. Just how bad he's been was graphically revealed in Daly's 456-page PGA Tour confidential personnel file that became part of the public court record when Daly sued the *Florida Times Union* in Jacksonville for libel in 2005.

The case ultimately was dismissed in 2009, with Daly also ordered to pay court costs and attorney fees. But far more damaging were the revelations in his file concerning Daly's long history of misbehaving between 1991, his first year on the PGA Tour, through 2008. The numbers tell it all.

5. Number of Daly's PGA Tour victories.

2. Number of his major championships.

21. Number of times he was cited by the tour for "failing to give best efforts."

11. Number of times he was cited by the tour for "conduct unbecoming a professional."

5. Number of suspensions handed out by the tour.

6. Number of times he was placed on probation by the tour.

7. Number of times he was ordered by the tour to seek counseling or enter an alcohol rehabilitation program.

$100,000. The total amount he was fined by the tour from 1991 through 2008.

$30,000. The largest fine of his career, for launching golf balls over the heads of spectators sitting in bleachers behind the practice area during the 1993 Fred Meyer Challenge in Portland, Oregon.

$20,000. A fine for hitting into the group in front of him during the final round of the 1994 World Series of Golf in Akron, Ohio. After the round, Daly screamed obscenities at the mother of Joe Roth, the player who had complained about Daly's on-course behavior, and Daly got into a fight with Roth's father. He also was suspended for the rest of that season.

$10,000. A fine for passing out in a Winston-Salem, North Carolina, bar in 2008 after being publicly intoxicated, refusing medical treatment, and spending a night in jail.

$5,000. A fine for trashing his hotel room at the Sawgrass Marriott Hotel in Ponte Vedra Beach, Florida, during the 1997 Players Championship. He also was ordered to pay an additional $1,500 to cover damages to the room.

110. The number of pounds Daly lost following lapband surgery on his stomach in 2009.

4. Number of ex-wives, which prompted this famous line in one of his songs, "All my exes wear Rolexes."

$9.35 million. Career earnings on the PGA Tour through 2010.

Millions. The amount of money Daly has blown through gambling, bad investments, and so forth.

★ ★ ★ ★

"Grip it and rip it."

—John Daly

NOTABLE ATHLETE-GOLFERS

▶ES

Notice we didn't title this category Best Athlete-Golfers. There are scores of athletes who could light it up on the links. We wanted this list to show athletes from other sports that also made an impact in golf, either through good or bad play. Basically, this is a glorified way to get Charles Barkley into this list.

Having said that, here are our notable, but not necessarily the best, athlete-golfers.

11. Ralph Terry. Pressure wasn't going to faze the former Yankees pitcher. Two years after giving up Bill Mazerowski's World Series–winning homer in 1960, he was on the mound to record the final out in the seventh game of the 1962 Series. Terry then tried golf after retiring. He played in 96 Senior Tour events, recording one top-ten finish. He was one of two former athletes to be fully exempt on that circuit.

10. Mark McGwire. Let's assume McGwire didn't take steroids to help him on the course. He actually has a strong game. I saw it on display when McGwire played in the Western Amateur, a top amateur event. Besides the crazy length, he had a strong short game and could putt. He didn't make the cut, but he didn't embarrass himself either.

9. Charles Barkley. We have to include Sir Charles for all the exposure he has brought to golf. His swing is so bad, it gets spoofed from CNN, ESPN, to *Saturday Night Live*. He also makes us feel better. If one of the greatest basketball players of all time, a man with exceptional hand-eye coordination, struggles with golf, then perhaps we shouldn't get so down on ourselves. As Charles would say, "Golf is harrrrd."

8. Michael Jordan. Jordan isn't Barkley when it comes to golf, but he isn't like his buddy Tiger either. There are plenty of guys at your club who could beat Jordan. Nevertheless, he has also been a high-profile ambassador for golf. If Michael plays, then it must be cool. He also brings his fierce competitive nature to the course. Once I was standing with him on the first tee. He hit his opening drive way right. Because it was an informal game, somebody suggested he should take another one. He declined, saying, "Then I won't be able to break the course record."

7. Babe Ruth. There's a YouTube clip of Ruth swinging the golf club. He hardly was the Babe Ruth of golf. He had a major sway in this backswing and then had a nice reverse pivot. Still, he had enough skills to shoot in the 70s. But like Jordan, it wasn't about the kind of golf he played; it was the fact that Ruth played golf, and that brought more attention to the game.

6. Dan Quinn. The former hockey player, who once scored 40 goals for Pittsburgh, made a name for himself on the Celebrity Players Tour, winning several tournaments. Quinn then found himself inside the ropes on the PGA Tour, but not as a player. He does some work as a part-time caddy for Ernie Els. That says something about how Els feels about Quinn's handle on golf.

5. Rick Rhoden. The former pitcher was the Babe Ruth/Tiger Woods/Michael Jordan of the Celebrity Tour. He dominated, winning numerous events. He also played in several Champions Tour events, once finishing as high as fifth.

4. Ken Harrelson. Even though he led the American League in RBIs in 1968, he quit baseball in 1971 at the age of 29. He decided to pursue a career in golf. "Hawk" got further than most. He qualified for the 1973 British Open, missing the cut by a stroke. But that was about it, as Harrelson went on to become a popular announcer with the White Sox. Of his attempt to master golf, he once said, "If I can hit a curveball, why can't I hit a ball that is standing still on a course?"

3. John Brodie. The former great quarterback of the San Francisco 49ers also was an outstanding golfer. He qualified for two U.S. Opens and then won $735,000 on the Senior Tour. The highlight came when Brodie won a tournament in 1991, beating Chi Chi Rodriguez and George Archer in a playoff.

2. Joe Louis. The legendary heavyweight champion became a fine golfer. He even once made the cut in a PGA Tour event. But his impact on the game goes much further. Tournaments wanted to capitalize on his fame and offered him spots in the field. This came during a time when the Tour had its infamous Caucasian-only clause. His indignation over the rule and subsequent protests helped open the door for African Americans like Charlie Sifford, Ted Rhodes, and Bill Spillner.

1. Babe Didrikson Zaharias. When it comes to athletes who gained fame in other sports and then excelled in golf, nobody rivals this "Babe." The 1932 Olympic champion in track took up golf in the 1940s. All she did was become a founding member of the LPGA Tour and win 41 tournaments and 10 majors. Her excellence in golf was one of the big reasons why Zaharias was named the greatest woman athlete of the first half of the twentieth century.

ENTERTAINING GOLFERS

The golf bug has struck many of the biggest stars in the various arts. In the process, their passion for the sport enabled them to be some of biggest ambassadors for the game. Their exploits on the course also have proved to be entertaining, although usually not in a way they preferred. There is no shortage of people we could have put on the list. Here are a few.

13. Johnny Carson. He didn't play golf. Tennis was his game. However, he ended every monologue by simulating a golf swing. As a result, a generation of Americans went to bed every night with a vision of golf in their heads.

12. Larry David. David's obsession with golf has been a constant theme on *Curb Your Enthusiasm*. A classic episode featured David killing the swan belonging to the owner of the club and trying to cover it up to save his rear end. Also, David weighed in with his own commentary on slow play. When a player in front of him grinds play to a halt, David berates him to the point that he drops dead. It's dangerous to play golf with Larry.

11. Clint Eastwood. The legendary actor lends considerable star power as the host of the annual Pro-Am at Pebble Beach. Eastwood also is a part-owner of the course. He once said, "We just felt that an American resort like Pebble Beach should be owned by Americans." Amen.

10. Jack Nicholson. Nicholson took up the game at 52 and now adores it as much as his beloved Lakers. I'll never forget seeing Nicholson at the Masters being whisked around Augusta National in a cart. From the look on his face, you knew Jack was loving every minute of it.

9. Katherine Hepburn. The legendary actress was quite a golfer. She displayed her swing in the classic golf movie, *Pat and Mike*, costarring Spencer Tracy. Tracy was her longtime love, but she had another notable relationship with Howard Hughes. It began on the golf course. While playing at Bel-Air in Beverly Hills, Hepburn watched as Hughes landed his plane on the course. He took out his clubs and asked if he could join them.

8. John Updike. He couldn't sing and dance, but he did have a way with words. One of the country's best writers, Updike was a passionate golfer who preferred to carry his own bag. He penned memorable pieces getting to the essence of the game. Updike wrote, "Golf appeals to the idiot in us and the child. Just how childlike golf players become is proven by their frequent inability to count past five."

7. Justin Timberlake. The singer is emerging as this generation's most notable golfer from the entertainment side. A strong player with a single-digit handicap, Timberlake showed his commitment to the game by attaching his name to the PGA Tour event in Las Vegas.

6. Jackie Gleason. "The Great One" loved to play and hosted his own PGA Tour event in Florida. But his lasting contribution to the game might have been a classic *Honeymooners* episode in which he tries to learn how to play golf. Ralph spoofs the game, wearing a ridiculous outfit. Then he watches as Norton (a.k.a. Art Carney) utters the immortal line, "Heelllooo ball." Makes me laugh every time.

5. Charles M. Schulz. Schulz was one of my biggest heroes thanks in no small part because he loved golf. A low-handicap player at his peak, Schulz made golf the subject of many *Peanuts* cartoons. He often had Snoopy in the role of "World Famous Pro." Schulz once said, "The things I like best are drawing cartoons and hitting golf balls."

4. Alice Cooper. You wouldn't think the conservative game of golf would be the favorite pastime for the outrageous rock star. But he turned to the game while trying to overcome drug and alcohol abuse. He became a single-digit handicap player who can't get enough. He even became an endorser for Callaway. You could say he traded one addiction for another.

3. Bill Murray. A former caddy on Chicago's North Shore, Murray created golf's most memorable character in movies: Greenskeeper Carl Spackler in *Caddyshack*. He also has stolen the show many times at the Pro-Am at Pebble Beach. All of his antics have obscured the fact that Murray actually is a decent golfer. As Spackler would say, "Cinderella story. Outta nowhere. A former greenskeeper, now, about to become the Masters champion. It looks like a mirac . . . It's in the hole! It's in the hole! It's in the hole!"

2. Bing Crosby. The famous singer spent as much time as he could on the golf course. He was an excellent player, good enough to enter the U.S. and British Amateurs. He then helped popularize the game by creating the celebrity "Clambake" at Pebble Beach in 1958. The last thing in his life he did was play golf. While coming off a course in Spain, he suffered a heart attack and died at the age of 73. His final words were "That was a great game of golf, fellas." Not a bad way to go out.

1. Bob Hope. The man entertained troops carrying a golf club. Need we say more? Golf never was far from Hope, whether he was in Hollywood or Vietnam. He used golf to unite presidents, getting Gerald Ford, George H. W. Bush, and Bill Clinton, who was in office at the time, to play with him at his tournament in Palm Springs. He actually was a low handicapper, but he had more fun joking about his game. His famous line about golf was "If you watch a game, it's fun. If you play it, it's recreation. If you work at it, it's golf."

Hope's contributions earned him a spot in the World Golf Hall of Fame. His plaque reads, "Not a golf champion but a great champion of golf."

Bob Hope (R) jokes around with The King.

INSPIRING PLAYERS

►BY AI MIYAZATO

For a long time, Miyazato was known as the best woman's player to come out of Japan. Then in 2010 she simply became known as the best player in the world. A breakout year on the LPGA Tour saw her vault to the No. 1 ranking. Miyazato had plenty of help to get to the top. Here are some of the people who inspired her, in her own words.

6. Juli Inkster. Words can't describe how much respect I have for Juli. To still be playing on tour and contending at her age is just amazing. Not only is she a great person off the course, but she is a great mother as well. As a woman and golfer, Juli is someone that I'd like to emulate.

5. Karrie Webb. I called her my "Teacher Webb" up until high school. I loved the way she competed and still have so much respect for her. She is a great friend on tour and I enjoy being around her.

4. Annika Sorenstam. I was fortunate to play with Annika before she retired. I am still amazed at how she played and approached the game. I share something in common with her in Vision54, and I hope that one day I'll play the game as well as she did.

3. Lynn Marriott and Pia Nilsson (Vision54). I met Lynn and Pia soon after I became a professional in Japan, and a few years later, I asked them to coach me. Since then, I've learned so much about myself and the game. I would not have achieved what I've achieved so far if I hadn't met them. They always amaze me with their way of thinking and lead me on the correct path.

2. Kiyoshi and Yusaku Miyazato. I began playing golf because my two older brothers were playing golf. They are professional golfers on the Japan Tour and they are the nicest brothers! Maybe I wouldn't have picked up the clubs if they didn't play golf and take me to the course.

1. Masaru Miyazato. He is my father and instructor. He learned the game on his own and made me and my two brothers into professional golfers. He is the instructor that knows my swing the best and still is a key person that guides me through the season.

AUSSIE RULES

►BY IAN BAKER-FINCH

Known as "The Dark Shark" when he started winning golf tournaments around the world in the 1980s and early '90s, Ian Baker-Finch is a tall, dark, and handsome player who seemed to be the formidable heir apparent to his fellow Australian, Greg Norman. Baker-Finch won the '91 British Open at Royal Birkdale with rounds of 64 and 66 on the weekend, then went into a mysterious slump in the mid-'90s before giving up competitive golf in favor of television commentary. Now a valuable member of the CBS Sports golf coverage team, we asked "Finchy" to pick the ten greatest Australian golfers. He graciously recused himself from consideration, though that British Open win as well as 17 professional victories on four different continents certainly would have made him a contender.

10. Norman Von Nida. A prominent player in the 1940s and '50s, he had four top-ten finishes in the British Open between 1946 and 1952. He had 30 professional victories, mostly on the Australian and European circuits, 19 of them between 1947 and 1949 in a career that was interrupted by World War II in the prime of his golfing life.

9. Steve Elkington. "Elk" has had a long and distinguished career that includes ten wins on the PGA Tour and the 1995 PGA Championship, his only major title, when he beat Colin Montgomerie in a playoff. Winner of the '95 Vardon Trophy for lowest scoring average on the PGA Tour, he also won the prestigious Players Championship in 1991 and '97 and was a four-time Presidents Cup participant.

8. Geoff Ogilvy. With two improbable pars, including a chip-in at 17, on the final holes of the 2006 U.S. Open at Winged Foot, Ogilvy became the first Aussie to win a major since Elkington's triumph in '95 and only the second ever to win an Open title. He's also won three World Golf Championship events, including two Match Play titles, and he got as high as No. 3 in the world rankings in 2008.

7. Graham Marsh. He was a regular winner on the European, Australasian, and Japanese tours in the 1970s and '80s and has 69 professional victories to his credit. His only win on the PGA Tour came at the 1977 Heritage, but he won six times on the senior Champions Tour, including two majors—the 1997 U.S. Senior Open and the 1999 Tradition.

6. Bruce Crampton. He had 14 wins on the PGA Tour between 1961 and 1975 and was runner-up in four major championships, each time finishing second to Jack Nicklaus in one Masters, one U.S. Open, and two PGA Championships. As a senior player, he won 20 Champions Tour events and led the money list in 1986.

5. Kel Nagle. He's the all-time winner on the Australasian Tour with a record 61 career titles. More important, at the age of 39 he won the 1960 British Open, beating rising star Arnold Palmer by a shot at St. Andrews. Two years later he finished second by six shots to Palmer at Royal Troon, and he also was runner-up in the 1965 U.S. Open, losing a playoff against Gary Player at Bellerive in St. Louis.

4. David Graham. He became the first Aussie ever to win a U.S. Open when he prevailed by three shots over George Burns and Bill Rogers at Merion in the Philadelphia suburbs, overcoming a 3-shot deficit after 54 holes. Two years earlier he won the PGA Championship despite a double bogey at the 72nd hole that forced a playoff against Ben Crenshaw. Graham holed two long putts in sudden death to keep the match going, and then he finally won with a birdie on the third extra hole. He had 38 professional wins on six different continents.

3. Karrie Webb. The all-time greatest Australian female golfer, "Webbie" became the youngest winner of the Women's British Open at age 21, a portent of greater things to come. She's won 50 times worldwide as a professional, including 36 victories on the LPGA Tour through 2010, with seven major championships. She easily qualified for the LPGA Hall of Fame at age 30, the youngest player at the time ever to earn that honor. She has at least one victory in every major championship in women's golf and remains one of her sport's most popular players.

2. Greg Norman. The Shark once spent 331 consecutive weeks as the No. 1 player in the world in the 1980s and '90s and has 88 career victories—20 on the PGA Tour, including two British Open titles, his only major championships. Norman was so close so often in majors, suffering a number of heartbreaking losses when opponents made miracle shots to cost him the title. He was runner-up in majors eight times and will forever be remembered for blowing a 6-shot 54-hole lead in the '96 Masters when he shot 78 in the final round and lost to Nick Faldo (67) by five. Still, Norman's swashbuckling style and dominance of the game made him an inspirational figure to several generations of Australian players, many of them now often contending for titles on the PGA Tour.

1. Peter Thomson. He will always be remembered for his five British Open championships, and he remains the only man ever to win the tournament three consecutive years in the twentieth century. The feat was accomplished between 1954 and 1956 in an era when most of the top American players did not bother to enter, unwilling to invest the time and money to travel abroad. That changed in the early 1960s, and Thomson's victory at Royal Birkdale in 1965 against a field that included Arnold Palmer, Jack Nicklaus, and Tony Lema was his greatest triumph. Over a storied career that included 81 professional victories, Thomson won the national championship of ten different countries, had a highly successful senior tour career, and also made a name for himself as a course designer and prolific golf writer for the *Melbourne Age* newspaper.

★ ★ ★ ★

"A hole in one is amazing when you think of the different universes this white mass of molecules has to pass through on its way to the hole."

—Mac O'Grady

Each year, the Masters is the most anticipated tournament in golf. We live to see the emerald green fairways. It rarely disappoints, adding new chapters to the history of the game. Some Masters, though, rank a cut above, delivering to golf iconic moments that will last forever. Here are the best of the best.

12. 2004: Finally. The long wait for Phil Mickelson ended on the 18th green on Sunday. Mounting a rally down the stretch, Mickelson faced a 15-footer for birdie and the victory over Ernie Els. When the putt dropped to seal his first major, Mickelson leaped into the air. It didn't matter that his vertical jump was only a couple inches. With the monkey finally off his back, nobody flew higher than Mickelson on this day.

11. 1954: Heavyweight fight. From 1951 to 1954 Sam Snead and Ben Hogan switched off winning the Green Jacket. Hogan won in 1951 and 1953 and Snead took the honors in 1952 and 1954. It concluded with an epic battle in 1954. An amateur, Billy Patton, actually led the tournament during the fourth round, but a 7 on 13 doomed his hopes. Snead and Hogan eventually tied, forcing an 18-hole playoff. Snead then shot a 70 to win by a stroke. It was Snead's third and final Masters victory.

10. 2001: Slamming. Tiger Woods came to the 2001 Masters on the heels of winning the last three majors in 2000. If he won, he would be the first player to hold all four major titles at the same time. Of course, Woods delivered. After opening with a 70, Woods put on a clinic, shooting 66-68-68 to win by two shots over David Duval. Woods had his "Tiger Slam."

9. 1956: Venturi heartbreak. Jackie Burke, Jr. won the 1956 Masters, but this tournament will be remembered for the second-place finisher, Ken Venturi. An amateur, Venturi held the lead going into the final round. However, the pressure got to him, as he stumbled home with an 80. That allowed Burke to make up an 8-shot deficit and beat Venturi by a stroke. Venturi never would win a Green Jacket.

8. 1987: Nice chip. Seve Ballesteros and Greg Norman were two of the biggest stars of the day in 1987. On the final day Ballesteros was making a run for his third Masters; Norman was going for his first. Yet they were both trumped by an unlikely contender, Larry Mize. The Augusta native made a 6-footer for birdie on 18 to get into the three-way playoff with Ballesteros and Norman. After Ballesteros went out in the first playoff hole, it came down to Norman and Mize. Mize stunned Norman and the golf world, chipping in from 140 feet for birdie on 11 to provide the most dramatic ending ever for the Masters.

7. 1996: Norman collapses. Once again, it was the loser everyone remembered. In 1996 it looked to finally be Greg Norman's year as he entered the final round with a 6-shot lead. Norman, though, wilted under the pressure, shooting a 78. The pain of watching Norman stumble was heartbreaking to watch. Forgotten in all the carnage was winner Nick Faldo, who rose to the occasion to shoot a 67 to win by five shots over Norman. It was Faldo's third Masters title.

6. 1942: Former caddies duel. In 1942 Byron Nelson and Ben Hogan, who grew up together in Texas, went neck-and-neck at Augusta National. Tied after 72 holes, Nelson shot a 69 in the playoff to beat Hogan by one shot. Nelson went 5-under over the final 13 holes to record his second Masters title. Hogan would have to wait another nine years before winning his first Green Jacket in 1951.

5. 1975: Nicklaus wins slugfest. The 1975 Masters proved to be one of the most thrilling ever. Johnny Miller shot a 66 in the final round to get into the hunt. Tom Weiskopf, on the strength of a 66 during the third round, also made a bid for the title. But ultimately, it was Jack Nicklaus who got the job done, winning by a shot. Again, it was Nicklaus coming through in the clutch, as his 40-foot birdie putt on 16 helped give him his fifth Masters title.

4. 1935: Sarazan's double eagle. In only the second year of the tournament in 1935, Gene Sarazan put the Masters on the map with his "shot heard around the world." His famous double eagle on the par-5 15th tied Craig Wood for the lead in the final round and forced a 36-hole playoff, which Sarazan won. For the record, Sarazan used a 4-wood from 235 yards to make history on 15.

3. 1960: The King rules. The 1960 Masters elevated Arnold Palmer to superstar status. Playing with his typical go-for-broke style, Palmer rallied with birdies on the final two holes to beat Ken Venturi by a shot. The comeback victory thrilled the nation, making Palmer the game's biggest star.

2. 1997: One for the ages. In 1997 Tiger Woods redefined the game. Only 21, Woods put on an incredible performance, shooting a record 18-under to win by a record 12 strokes. The sight of a man of color winning at Augusta National forever changed how the game would be perceived. As Jim Nantz said when Woods's final putt fell on 18, "One for the ages." Indeed, it was.

1. 1986: The Bears roars again. The 1986 Masters always will be remembered as Nicklaus's defining moment. And it was. But the tournament also had superb star power with Tom Kite, Seve Ballesteros, and Greg Norman making their bids to win the title. One by one, the top players wilted down the stretch, perhaps collapsing under the weight of the Augusta roars being generated by Nicklaus. Eventually, Norman's bogey on 18 opened the door, giving everyone the champion they most wanted to see on this unforgettable day.

STUFF YOU PROBABLY NEVER KNEW
ABOUT THE MASTERS

It's the most watched golf tournament on television year after year, with an international press corps on the grounds as well. Despite all that media exposure, there's still plenty of room for more information on some of the more obscure tournament factoids. So allow us to fill in a few blanks.

10. Green Jacket. It wasn't always awarded to the champion, but the tradition began when Sam Snead won the tournament in 1949.

9. Aces Wild. They've held the par 3 tournament on Augusta National's short course since 1960, two years after it was built. The 9-hole course measures 1,060 yards, and through 2010, 70 holes-in-one have been recorded in the Wednesday event, including a record five in 2002. No player who's ever won the par 3 tournament has gone on to win the Masters.

8. Olden Bear. Jack Nicklaus holds the record for completing a 72-hole tournament after the age of 50. Nicklaus did it nine times, one more than Sam Snead. His last appearance was in 2000, when he tied for 54th at the age of 60.

7. Magnolia Lane. Players always say it's a goose-bump moment when they steer their cars through the front gate and head up Magnolia Lane toward the clubhouse. For the record, there are 61 magnolia trees dating back to the late 1850s lining both sides of the lane. Magnolia Lane is 330 yards long and was first paved in 1947.

6. Stormy weather. They've had rain for 42 of the first 73 tournaments, but only eight days of play have ever been postponed. The last Monday finish because of postponed rounds occurred in 1983.

5. The chairman. There have only been six chairmen of Augusta National Golf Club since 1934, and the current Lord of the Masters, William Porter Payne, took over in 2007. Billy Payne was a three-year starter for the University of Georgia football team and was named to the all-SEC team his senior season in 1968.

4. Knee knockers. Only four players in tournament history have won the Masters on the final putt of the final round—Arnold Palmer in 1960, Sandy Lyle in 1988, Mark O'Meara in 1998, and Phil Mickelson in 2004.

3. Going low. Among players who have completed 100 or more rounds in the Masters, Jack Nicklaus has the lowest scoring average on the par-72 course—71.98 strokes over 163 rounds. Tom Watson is second at 72.36 over 118 rounds.

2. Eagle eye. Only two players have ever had back-to-back eagles on consecutive holes—Dan Pohl in 1982 at No. 13 and 14 and Dustin Johnson in 2009, also at 13 and 14.

1. Double eagle. Golf fans around the world know that Gene Sarazen made a double eagle at the 15th hole on his way to a victory in the 1935 Masters. But how many also are aware that only about 30 spectators actually witnessed the shot or that it allowed Sarazen to get into a 36-hole playoff against Craig Wood, and then win it by five shots.

Clubhouse at the Augusta National Golf Course.

Everyone knows the Green Jacket is the most coveted piece of clothing in golf. However, it isn't the only prize handed out by the good folks at Augusta National. The tournament doles out all sorts of goodies, giving the players a good chance that they will walk away with something from their trip to the Masters.

8. Crystal vase. Starting in 1954, the Masters began to give players additional awards for play during the tournament. The Crystal Vase is awarded to the player with that day's lowest score. Brandel Chamblee won only one tournament during his career and never came close to seriously challenging in the Masters. But in 1999 he had a share of the first-round lead. You can be sure the Crystal Vase he received for the feat sits prominently in his trophy case.

7. Pair of crystal goblets. The Masters dishes out the fancy goblets each time a player records an eagle. Longtime Masters participants Arnold Palmer and Jack Nicklaus must have a warehouse full of these goblets. I can remember after a so-so round, Nicklaus, searching for a bright spot, once said, "I got an eagle, so those goblets will make [wife Barbara] happy."

6. Large crystal bowl, part 1. This is a nice way to commemorate a lifetime memory at Augusta. A crystal bowl is awarded to the player who records a hole-in-one. Through 2010 the most popular place to score an ace was on the par-3 16th, with 13. The toughest was No. 4; in 1992 Jeff Sluman became the first and only player to post a 1 on the hole. With the tee now pushed back to 240 yards, Sluman's feat could stand for a long time.

5. Silver cup. With Bobby Jones as its founder, the Masters always has put a premium on honoring amateurs. In 1952 it awarded the first Silver Cup to the low amateur, and in 1954 it gave a silver medal to the amateur runner-up. In order to receive the award, the amateur must make the 36-hole cut. Interestingly, Tiger Woods never claimed the prize in 1995 and 1996 when he played as amateur. He missed the cut both times.

4. Silver salver. Beginning in 1951, the runner-up in the Masters was awarded the Silver Medal. Then in 1978 it gave the second-place finisher something more substantial: a Silver Salver. Greg Norman has three of these Silver Salvers. Given his heartbreaks at Augusta, I doubt they are prominently displayed at his house.

3. Large crystal bowl, part 2. Double eagles are rarer than hole-in-ones in golf. During the first round of the 1967 Masters, Bruce Devlin made a double eagle on the par-5 8th hole. It was the first double eagle at Augusta since Gene Sarazan's legendary shot in 1935. Masters Chairman Clifford Roberts announced that Devlin would be awarded a large crystal bowl for his shot. However, Roberts decreed that Sarazan would have to get one first.

2. Champion trophy. Yes, in addition to the Green Jacket, the Masters winner also receives a trophy. And it's a nice one. First presented in 1961, the original trophy was made in England and consists of more than 900 separate pieces of silver. A model of the famed clubhouse rests on a pedestal, and bands of silver provide space to engrave the names of the winner and runner-up. The original trophy remains at the club. In 1993 a sterling replica was presented to the champion along with the Gold Medal.

1. Money, money. When Horton Smith won the first Masters in 1934, he pocketed all of $1,500. Now the winner receives more than $1 million and earns millions more through endorsement opportunities that come with owning a green jacket. Yet money seems secondary here. I'm betting that every player would trade the money for the honor and prestige of being the Masters champion.

★ ★ ★ ★

"Golf is not, on the whole, a game for realists. By its exactitudes of measurements it invites the attention of perfectionists."

—Heywood Hale Broun

AUGUSTA NATIONAL: THE BAD AND THE UGLY

►LS

The Lords of The Masters would have us all believe they run the world's finest golf tournament—also known in syrupy southern lingo as the "toon-a-ment." That contention is definitely up for debate, especially because they keep lengthening the course, now nearly 7,500 yards, and turned the once-thrilling birdies-in-bunches back nine on Sunday into a U.S. Open–like survival contest.

And though there still is plenty to love about the first major championship of the season, there is lots to dislike as well. At the risk of jeopardizing our annual press credentials, the following represents the dark side of the exclusive club and its famous April event.

10. Hold the cheese. The club's signature green cellophane–wrapped pimento cheese sandwiches sold for a proper pittance in concession stands all around ought to come with a free sample of Pepto-Bismol. Plaster that yellowish goop between a few bricks and you could build a pretty cheesy new clubhouse wing.

9. Bibs are for babies. Not for the poor caddies forced to don those white one-piece, long-pants coveralls that make an already tough march around the hilly property a sweat-soaked nightmare for the lowly loopers. It's one dehumanizing tradition the toon-a-ment could easily get along without.

8. Oh, the hypocrisy. Augusta National counts among its members a number of former past presidents of the U.S. Golf Association, the governing body of the sport that is charged, among other noble goals, with making the game accessible to one and all. Wouldn't it be far more appropriate for all of them not to pay dues to a club that has never allowed female members?

7. Outside the ropes. The Masters is the only event on the PGA Tour schedule that does not allow credentialed media to cover the sport from inside the gallery ropes, a major handicap for enterprising golf writers trying to give readers more than what they just watched on television. It's tough to judge how long that putt was when you're at the back end of a ten-deep crowd around the green.

6. Hypocrisy continued. Augusta National is listed as a main sponsor of the First Tee, a nationwide initiative designed to attract youngsters, especially inner-city kids, to the game. Last time we checked, the boys and girls enrolled in the city of Augusta's First Tee program have never been invited to play the Augusta National course or even use its world-class practice facility, though they do get a few free tickets to the Masters. How generous.

5. Fan patronizing. A golf fan is a golf fan everywhere, that is, except Augusta National, where they are pretentiously referred to as patrons. And poor Jack Whitaker, the longtime CBS Sports broadcaster and essayist who, in 1966, described a gaggle of spectators as a "mob" on the air. The next year, and for many more after that, he was asked to stay home.

4. A little reverence. Surely that must be in the User's Guide for all CBS broadcasters assigned to the Masters telecasts. Hushed tones are mandatory, and hold the one-liners, thank you very much Gary McCord. On the air, he once described Augusta National's warp-speed greens as being as slick as bikini wax. The next year, he was Whitaker-ed off the broadcast team forever more.

3. User unfriendly. As much as the Lords of the Masters say they care about their precious patrons, they don't do much about the outrageous ticket scalping going on outside their gates or on the Internet. During the practice rounds, although attendance figures are never divulged, crowds of 60,000 or more swarm around the course, making for a mob scene behind the ropes, a clogged elbow-to-elbow merchandise area, and long lines at the beer counters leading to even longer lines (and uncomfortable waits) to use the restrooms. Oh yes, during regulation play, there are no walking standard-bearers conveniently showing spectators the scores of every player in the group, a standard feature of every other event on the schedule.

2. For shame. It took until 1975 for the first African American player, Lee Elder, to "qualify" for the Masters, even if Charles Sifford should have been invited years earlier when he won the 1967 Greater Hartford Open. Not until the PGA Tour mandated that all clubs hosting an official event not discriminate on the basis of race, religion, or gender did Augusta National admit its first African American member in 1990. The club won't disclose anything about the make-up of its membership, but you could probably count the number of African American and Jewish members on two hands. Maybe one.

1. Where the girls aren't. The club has no female members, though women are at least allowed to play the golf course as guests. You want more hypocrisy? How about the PGA Tour recognizing all Masters statistics and prize money in its official stats, including the money list and world rankings, despite its much-ballyhooed antidiscrimination policies. The Tour reasons that because Augusta National runs this major event, not the Princes of Ponte Vedra, and all of their players would kill to participate, they have no power to force the issue. Oh, please.

★ ★ ★ ★

"When I putt, my emotions collide like tectonic plates. It's left my memory circuits full of scars that won't heal."

—Mac O'Grady

THE CASE FOR WOMEN JOINING AUGUSTA NATIONAL

►LS

Augusta National is not the only all-male golf club in America, but it is the only single-gender club in the country that puts on a very public golf tournament, one of the four major championships, every year. So how come 51 percent of the American public—the 51 percent who happen to be female—is not eligible for membership? Len Shapiro offers the Lords of the Masters a few reasons why they really should change the policy.

10. Corporate hypocrites. Countless Augusta National members are CEOs of public companies that specifically reject discrimination on the basis of race, religion, or gender in their hiring, firing, and promoting practices. So how do these guys in good conscience join a club that does allow women to play as guests but very specifically discriminates on the basis of gender when it comes to being a full-fledged member? And shouldn't they be leading the charge to change the exclusionary policy?

9. Now children. You're a member of Augusta National. Your daughter loves golf and is rising through the junior ranks with every passing week. How do you explain to your darling child, the pig-tailed daddy's girl with the swell swing and the deft putting touch, that when she grows up, there's not a chance in hell she'll be allowed to join her father's golf club, boasting one of the finest courses on the planet, just because she's a woman?

8. Public trust. The Masters uses the public airwaves to transmit its television signal around the world. Public funds are used to handle traffic, to keep thousands of out-of-town visitors safe and secure all around town and even to handle the trash from all those lime-green cellophane sandwich wrappers and plastic cups. Shouldn't all of the public—the people who pay the taxes that fund those public services—be eligible to join?

7. Fashion statement. Wouldn't Nancy Lopez, Annika Sorenstam, Judy Rankin, Condoleezza Rice, Sandra Day O'Connor, among many, many others, look smashing in a green jacket?

6. Start a movement. Maybe if Augusta National opened its doors to women, CBS, the television network that has aired the tournament forever, might actually add a female to its golf announcing team, properly altering a tradition unlike any other.

5. More hypocrites. Several current officers and other high-ranking officials as well as countless past presidents of the U.S. Golf Association are members of the club. Last time we looked, the USGA is golf's governing body of the sport in the United States, charged with growing the game nationwide, and not just among boys and men. The presence of all those USGA people, past and present, on the Augusta National roster represents a classic conflict of interest, and unless the club starts to admit women, they should not be members.

4. Party on. Just exactly who do all those green-jacketed guys dance with when they have a fancy function at the club? Better yet, when it's boys' night out at Augusta National, what are all those wives and girlfriends up to? Could it be don't ask, don't tell, both ways?

3. A matter of taste. Admit a woman. Put her on the tournament concessions committee. Perhaps then, and only then, the dreaded pimento cheese sandwich that would have caused Julia Child to choke at first bite, might be forever removed from public consumption.

2. Big bid-ness. I'm a boy banker trying to convince you to deposit your considerable assets in my institution. I'm a girl banker trying to do the same. Boy banker takes client out for a round of golf, drinks, and dinner at Augusta National. Girl banker takes same client to her friendly little country club for Sunday brunch. Who do you think closes the deal?

1. Do the right thing. Gentlemen, it's time.

MOST EXCLUSIVE
AMERICAN GOLF CLUBS

▶ LS

Money has its privileges, and one of them includes the ability to become a member at virtually any private golf club on the planet. Then again, big bucks are hardly the only requirement for membership in our list of exclusive American golf clubs. Sometimes it's about playing ability. Occasionally, and sadly, it has to do with race, religion, and/or gender. Often, it's all about the social register or family ties. Old money is king; gauche nouveau rich need not apply. And if you have to inquire about the price tag for initiation and dues, you probably don't belong.

10. Winged Foot, Mamaroneck, New York. With two classic A. W. Tillinghast courses, "The Foot" is considered by many to be the finest pure golf club in the New York area, with a membership that includes titans of Wall Street, glitterati from the worlds of sports and entertainment, and a huge number of highly skilled players, one of the more important criteria for membership.

9. Burning Tree, Bethesda, Maryland. The men-only club in the Washington suburbs has been a popular retreat for members of Congress, high-powered lobbyists, and presidents, though it's become far more politically correct for occupants of the White House to stay away in recent years, for all the obvious reasons. Women are not allowed to play, but they do let the ladies on the property at Christmas, the better to purchase gifts for the man of the house, and no doubt the manor as well.

8. The Country Club, Brookline, Massachusetts. The oldest country club in the nation was founded in 1882 by a small group of Boston bluebloods far more interested in horseback riding than golf. The first course was created in 1893, and two years later the first U.S. Open was contested on the premises of a club that was one of the five charter members of the U.S. Golf Association. The membership is a Who's Who of Boston society, and some say it's almost as difficult to gain membership now as it was in the beginning.

7. Chicago Golf Club, Wheaton, Illinois. Also one of the first five USGA member clubs, it's the site of the country's first 18-hole course and also hosted the first

U.S. Open not contested in the East in 1897. There are just over 100 members with what one publication described as "a steeplechase worth of hurdles to clear in order to get in." The club did admit its first female member in 2001.

6. National Golf Links of America, Southampton, New York. When the seaside club on the tip of Long Island opened in 1911, it had 67 members from around the country, including a Vanderbilt, hence "The National." It often has been described as the snootiest club in America. The great-grandson of famed course designer Charles Blair Macdonald, the man who built the venue, once told me he was not allowed to play the course unless a current member invited him.

5. Fishers Island Club, Fishers Island, New York. This island course not far from the Connecticut shore is only accessible by ferry, making this bastion of high society just as difficult to get to as it is to join. The good news is that in peak summer season, the first tee is usually wide open, with nary a spiked-shoe soul in sight anywhere on the course.

4. Cypress Point Club, Pebble Beach, California. Bob Hope, who belonged to the club himself for more than 40 years, once joked that "one year they had a membership drive at Cypress. They drove out 40 members." The club, with a magnificently scenic seaside course designed by Alister MacKenzie, took itself out of the rotation for the old Bing Crosby annual PGA Tour event in 1991 when it chose not to abide with tour rules that required clubs not to discriminate on the basis of race, religion, and gender. At the end of the year, they add up the operating costs and divide it equally among the members.

3. Seminole, Juno Beach, Florida. All you have to know about this breathtaking all-male club hard by the Atlantic is that it once turned down Jack Nicklaus for membership. This was Ben Hogan's favorite golf course in the world, a venue where he spent 30 days every year preparing himself for the upcoming PGA Tour season. The yawning locker room, with mounted animal trophies hung on walls all around, must be seen to be believed.

2. Augusta National, Augusta, Georgia. Bill Gates is a member now, but he was kept out for many years simply because he had said very publicly he wanted to be part of this very exclusive fraternity. Membership in the all-male bastion of Southern gentlemen and corporate titans is by invitation only, and the club actually encourages its dues-paying minions not to use the facilities all that often, the better to protect its world-famous golf course from all those divots and ball marks on the greens. Members wear green jackets, but only on the grounds, the most famous piece of clothing in golf.

1. Pine Valley, Pine Valley, New Jersey. Considered by many the best and most demanding golf course in America, the club was founded in 1913 by a group of well-to-do Philadelphians. There are now 1,300 members from every corner of the globe, many of whom stay on the property in swank cottages when they come in to play. It also has an all-male membership, by invitation only from the club's board of directors, with scads of scratch or single-digit players on the roster. Women are allowed to play the course on Sundays, and like any other guests, must be accompanied by a member. And if you ever are invited, try the world-class mock turtle soup after a day on a world-class course.

★ ★ ★ ★

"Actually, the only time I ever took out a 1-iron was to kill a tarantula. And it took a seven to do that."

—Jim Murray

THE TEN BEST COURSES YOU CAN PLAY

The great thing about golf is that many of its best courses are open to the public. Now, you might have to pay premium rates, especially if the track is affiliated with a resort. But the bottom line is that you can play them. Here are the best of best. (A confession: I'll admit to being partial to some of the courses I've played.)

10. Cog Hill No. 4. Okay, so this might be a hometown pick. However, don't underestimate "Dubsdread." The longtime home of the Western Open and BMW Championship, the course features a vintage parkland layout. Originally designed by Dick Wilson, No. 4 recently was updated by Rees Jones. The course is one of four at Cog Hill, making it perhaps the best public facility in the country. The public golfers are king there. Don't be surprised if owner Frank Jemsek greets you at the first tee. It's that kind of place.

9. Plantation Course at Kapalua. As you'll see by this list, I have a thing for courses on the water. The scenery is simply breathtaking at Kapalua. You'll likely see whales in the distance if you go during the right part of the year. Perched high on the hills in Maui, the course's extreme elevation changes often make it seem like a roller-coaster ride. Truly memorable.

8. Chambers Bay. I haven't seen this new course in Seattle, but the fact that it already landed the 2015 U.S. Open is a strong indication that this is a special place. The pictures look amazing. Golf.com called Chambers Bay "Bethpage Black-by-the-Sea." Stunning views against the backdrop of Puget Sound and sprawling dunes make for an unforgettable experience. After 2015 everyone will know about Chambers Bay.

7. Torrey Pines South. This course, located north of San Diego, always looks great on TV during the annual Farmer's Insurance Open, with camera shots of paragliders floating over the Pacific Ocean. Torrey also proved its chops as the site of Tiger Woods's memorable 2008 U.S. Open victory. However, the best part about Torrey is that it is a true muni. You won't have to pay resort prices to play it, provided you can snag a tee time.

6. Pinehurst No. 2. This course is considered Donald Ross's masterpiece. It is all about the greens at Pinehurst. The contours, slopes, and other tricks turn probable pars into double bogeys or worse. To get yourself prepared, practice on a hilly driveway. Then give it up and pay homage to Mr. Ross. You wouldn't want to play this kind of course every day. But you'll always have the memories from playing it just once.

5. TPC at Sawgrass. The home of the Players Championship, this course provides plenty of thrills during the tournament. There is also plenty of excitement for recreational players. The 17th gets the fanfare, but the Pete Dye course features many other interesting holes. It all builds to the grand finale when you get your shot at Pete Dye's famed par 3 with an island green at 17. For the record, I posted a par in the only time I played the hole. So yes, this course rates high on my list.

4. Whistling Straits. Living in mostly flat and uninteresting Illinois, it is hard for me to believe something like Whistling Straits exists just two hours from my front door. Designed by Pete Dye with lots of money from Herb Kohler, the course boasts stunning views, with several holes looking down on Lake Michigan. The links' design, complete with dunes and fescue grasses, is a vintage Dye thrill ride. Whistling Straits actually has sheep grazing on the course. Close your eyes and you'll think you're in Scotland, not an hour outside of Milwaukee.

3. Bethpage Black. This Long Island public course has become a superstar thanks to hosting U.S. Opens in 2002 and 2009. You'll have to camp out overnight to get a tee time, but Black regulars such as our coauthor (it was Len's home course) will tell you it is worth losing some sleep to play. The rolling hills provide an interesting landscape, and the A. W. Tillinghast design, with an update from Rees Jones, is a classic. However, check your ego at the door because you'll be hard-pressed to find a harder course. Also, Bethpage is more than about the Black. There are four other courses in the facility, including the highly regarded Red layout.

2. Pacific Dunes. The immense dunes and views of the Pacific Ocean make this course something to behold. Designed by Tom Doak, this was the second course at the Bandon Dunes resort in Oregon. The links' layout produces all sorts of unexpected twists and turns. It is a memorable experience from beginning to end. Though all of the Bandon Dunes courses are treasures, this one is just a cut above.

1. Pebble Beach. Views, history, views, history, views, history. It's hard to describe the thrill of playing what is essentially "America's Course." You can go to 17 and check out where Tom Watson holed his legendary chip to win the 1982 U.S. Open. You won't find a more dramatic finishing hole than its famous par 5 on the ocean. The stretch from holes 5 through 10 is staggering. I've always told my wife it would be worth the price just to be able to walk the course. Just the same, you'll probably want to take your clubs.

How many fathers will tell you the most enjoyable rounds of golf they ever played included one or more of their own children tagging along, from toddler to teenager to adult. Some of the game's best-known fathers also proudly watched their sons gain lofty stature in the game as well, both on and off the course.

10. Claude and Butch Harmon. As the longtime head golf professional at Winged Foot in the New York suburbs and Seminole in South Florida, Claude Harmon also won the 1948 Masters. All four of his sons, Butch, Dick, Craig, and Bill, became teaching pros, with Butch gaining the most notoriety as Tiger Woods's teacher from 1993 until they parted ways in 2004. Butch Harmon also now works with Phil Mickelson and has had a number of other big-name stars as clients, including Greg Norman, Davis Love III, Fred Couples, Adam Scott, Justin Leonard, Stewart Cink, and Natalie Gulbis.

9. Fred and Jeff Klauk. Fred Klauk was the longtime course superintendent at the TPC at Sawgrass until his retirement in 2008. His son Jeff learned the game growing up at the Ponte Vedra, Florida, course and joined the PGA Tour full time for the 2009 season after becoming one of only five players ever to earn more than $1 million in purses playing on the Nationwide Tour, where he won twice. As a PGA Tour rookie in 2009, he finished 71st on the money list and easily retained his playing card.

8. Jack and Gary Nicklaus. The son, Gary, had the toughest act of all to follow when he decided to try professional golf, a sport once dominated by his father, Jack, the winner of a record 18 major championships. Gary joined the PGA Tour in 2000 and came agonizingly close to winning the rain-shortened BellSouth Classic in Atlanta that year, only to lose a sudden-death playoff to Phil Mickelson. Gary lost his tour card after the 2002 season, joined his father's course design business, and regained his status as an amateur. At the age of 40, he tried and failed to qualify for the Tour again in 2009, but his day job was still waiting.

7. Jay and Bill Haas. Jay Haas learned the game from his uncle Bob Goalby, the 1968 Masters champion, and won nine times on the PGA Tour, with many more victories on the senior circuit in recent years. Jay's son Bill was an outstanding collegiate player at Wake Forest, where his father won the 1976 NCAA championship on a team that also included two-time U.S. Open winner Curtis Strange. Bill was a three-time All American at Wake and joined the PGA Tour as a rookie in 2006. He broke through for his first Tour victory at the 2010 Bob Hope Classic a week after his father and Uncle Bob gave him a tip on repositioning his feet on his swing.

6. Craig and Kevin Stadler. If it walks like a walrus, talks like a walrus, and looks like a walrus, it must be PGA Tour pro Kevin Stadler, the son of The Walrus, Craig Stadler. Both men constantly battle the bulge, both shamble down the fairway, and both hitch their pants exactly the same way in their respective pre-shot routines. Craig won 16 times on the PGA Tour, including the 1982 Masters and now plays the Champions Tour. Kevin made the PGA Tour in 2007, a year after his biggest victory as a professional—the Johnnie Walker Classic on the European Tour.

5. Robert Trent Jones, Sr., Robert Trent Jones, Jr., and Rees Jones. It once was said that the sun never sets on a Robert Trent Jones, Sr. golf course, and the same also could be said for the work of his two sons. RTJ, Sr., the renowned architect, designed courses around the world until his death in 2000 at the age of 94. Both his sons, Robert, Jr. and Rees, joined him in the family business before each went off on his own. Robert, Jr. has designed more than 270 courses in 40 countries, and his younger brother has over 100 courses to his credit. Rees is best known as "The Open Doctor" for overseeing the renovation of classic U.S. Open venues like Congressional, Torrey Pines, and Oakland Hills.

4. Bob and David Duval. There have been eight winning father-son combinations in the history of the PGA Tour, but only one of them won tournaments on the same day. In 1999 David Duval, once the No. 1 ranked player in the world, captured the Players Championship on the regular Tour, the same day his father Bob won the Emerald Coast Classic on the Champions Tour. Bob, who spent most of his career as a club pro, taught David the game and watched him soar to the upper echelons of the sport, winning the British Open in 2001, the last of his 13 tour victories before going into a prolonged swoon. His game began coming around again in 2009 when he was in late contention for the U.S. Open title at Bethpage Black.

3. Davis Love, Jr. and Davis Love III. The father was considered one of the country's finest golf instructors and also was in contention for the 1964 Masters title. He taught his son how to play and watched him blossom into a highly skilled amateur and college golfer who made it to the PGA Tour in 1986. Two years later he was killed in a tragic plane crash, and in 1997 Davis Love III paid tribute to his father with his book *Every Shot I Take*, honoring his father's lessons on golf and life. Davis Love

III has won 20 times on the PGA Tour, including the 1997 PGA Championship, his only major title.

2. Earl and Tiger Woods. Earl was a former Green Beret officer who learned to play the game early in his Army career at a public course in Brooklyn, New York. He put a club in his youngest son's hands not long after young Tiger came out of the womb and shepherded the lad's career from cradle to the eventual No. 1 ranking in the world. Tiger always said his father was his best friend, even if, as he was growing up, his old man coughed on his backswing and rattled his car keys before he was about to make a key putt. It was perfect training for his son, who went on to become the youngest Masters champion when he won in 1997 at the age of 21, the first of his 14 major titles. Earl died in 2004 after being diagnosed six years earlier with prostate cancer.

1. Old and Young Tom Morris. By far the most successful father-son juggernaut in golf history, Old Tom lived in St. Andrews Scotland, the home of golf, where he became a renowned greenskeeper, club and ball maker, instructor, and course designer. He could play the game as well, winning his first of four British Open titles in 1861. Young Tom first beat his father at the age of 13, and they would often partner as a virtually unbeatable team in alternate shot and best-ball competitions. Young Tom won four straight British Open titles starting in 1868, succeeding his father, the 1867 winner, as champion. Young Tom almost certainly would have won more, but he died at the age of 24. Some say the cause of death was a broken heart, four months after his wife and their baby died in childbirth.

MY TEN FAVORITE GO-TO GOLFERS

►BY JOHN FEINSTEIN

Prolific author and sports journalist John Feinstein has done a number of golf-themed books, including the runaway best-seller *A Good Walk Spoiled*, which focuses on 17 players as they make their way through a season on the PGA Tour. His latest golf effort now available in bookstores is *Moment of Glory: The Year Underdogs Ruled Golf*. We asked Feinstein for his personal list of the most cooperative, media-friendly players in the game. Tiger Woods, surprise, surprise, didn't make the cut in this competition.

10. Joe Ogilivie. He's so smart, he's almost as smart as he thinks he is. The difference between Joe and some players is that you can joke with him about how smart he thinks he is—and he's really smart. He has a lot of ideas—some off the wall—but they're really interesting to hear. He's also one of those guys who knows everything that's going on, so he's a go-to guy when you want to know what's happening on tour. And his educational background (Duke, of course, also my own alma mater) is impeccable.

9. Kevin Sutherland. Paul Goydos's running-mate and pal, the best thing about him might be that he always has the latest Goydos story to tell. He and brother David both love to talk basketball. The difference is that David will ask my opinion and then say, "Here's why you're wrong." Kevin will ask my opinion and then say, "I like that—it proves that David's wrong." He's also a "never says no" guy. Doesn't matter how he played, he always has time to talk. (Just like Tiger, right?)

8. Steve Stricker. First time I ever interviewed him I asked about his parents. "They're typical Midwesterners," he said. "Very quiet and polite, sort of the anti–New Yorkers." I said, "Yeah, coming from New York I know exactly what you mean." He went white and said, "Oh God, I'm so sorry, I didn't mean to insult you . . . " I told him I wasn't at all insulted because it was a very good way to describe someone. The next day I was walking with his group. There was a wait on a par 3 and he walked over to me and said, "Geez, I couldn't sleep last night because I felt so bad about what I said." I told him, speaking as a New Yorker, to shut the hell up because he didn't say anything wrong. To this day when I see him, he says, "Oh boy, here comes the rude New Yorker."

7. John Cook. Just the nicest professional golfer you'll ever meet. The only player he ever mistreats is John Cook. He gets so angry at himself on the golf course that his nickname is "Mr. Happy," which he willingly jokes about. Once, when he shot 78 to miss a cut and we were supposed to talk, I said, "John we can do this another day." He said, "Absolutely not, I made a commitment." I said, "Look, I understand you want to get out of here, I'm not on deadline." He thanked me profusely. That was 15 years ago. About twice a year he still thanks me for letting him off the hook that day.

6. David Duval. That's right, I think he's great. He doesn't suffer fools, but he has a knack for storytelling and is completely honest when he gets to know you—far more important than you knowing him. Once, he was talking about his reputation as an "intellectual" on tour. "Reading Ayn Rand doesn't make you an intellectual," he said. "Of course, out here reading anything other than *USA Today* apparently makes you an intellectual."

5. Jay Haas. He offered one of the great lines ever when the Golf Writers Association of America gave him the Jim Murray Good Guy award several years ago: "I guess you could call this the 'Curtis (Strange) blew us off so let's go talk to Jay,' award." He once told me a story about his only fine on tour. In the midst of shooting 77 on a Saturday at Milwaukee, a fan yelled at him, "Hey, Haas, you suck!" after he chunked a chip. Fed up and overheated, Haas turned to him and said, "Fuck you." The next day, rules official Wade Cagle called him in because the fan had filed a complaint. Cagle said, "Jay, I'm sure you said 'thank you,' to the guy, right?" Jay shook his head and said, "Nope, he's got it exactly right. How much do I owe you?"

4. Billy Andrade. One of the few athletes I've ever met who always asks about your children—by name—when you see him. He'll always return a call and will always find time for you. For better or worse, he is also the first person who pointed Tiger Woods out to me: on the driving range at Riviera in '94. "That's Tiger Woods," he said. "He's supposed to be the next big thing out here." This was about five minutes before the then 18-year-old Tiger walked past about a dozen kids asking for autographs without even looking at them. Billy stopped and signed every one, of course.

3. Davis Love III. I think this might surprise some people because Davis tends to come off as pretty dry. Get him one-on-one, though, and he has a lot of honest thoughts and never ducks a question. Here's another story from *A Good Walk Spoiled*: During our first session, after we spent about two hours talking, I said, "How are you set on time?" He said, "Well, you're writing a book, so I just cleared the whole afternoon." I thought I'd died and gone to heaven.

2. Nick Price. I'm not sure there's a nicer man on the planet. The first time I met him was in 1993 when I was researching *A Good Walk Spoiled*. He was ranked number one in the world. He asked me to give him a call when he knew his '94 schedule to set up a time to talk for the book. I figured he'd given me his agent's number. I called and Nick answered. (This was before cell phones.) It was his home number. He was changing a diaper. He is what my mom used to call a mensch.

1. Paul Goydos. Sure, I'm biased, but I'm not the only person who feels this way. What makes Paul unique is that he's always accessible and always has something to say worth listening to: funny, smart, and makes you think. He's even convinced me I was wrong a couple of times, which is virtually impossible.

★ ★ ★ ★

"A golf ball is like a clock. Always hit it at 6 o'clock and make it go toward 12 o'clock. But make sure you're in the same time zone."

—Chi Chi Rodriguez

DAN JENKINS HIS OWN SELF

▶ BY DAN JENKINS

To mark the occasion when Dan Jenkins was honored by the Golf Writers Association of America in 2005 with the William D. Richardson award, given annually to "an individual who has consistently made an outstanding contribution to golf," his editors at *Golf Digest* published a short book entitled *The Dogged Victims of Dan Jenkins*, which included some of his brilliant magazine work. He's been with the *Digest* since 1984, following a previously distinguished career in newspapers, with *Sports Illustrated*, and as the author of a wide variety of sports classics, from *Semi-Tough* to *Dead Solid Perfect*.

In the book's afterword, his daughter Sally Jenkins, an award-winning sports columnist for the *Washington Post* and an equally prolific author, perfectly summarized her father's unique style:

> Look again at the writing of Dan Jenkins and ask yourself if it could have been as effortless to write as it is to read. Peruse the easy rhythms and the jauntiness of the phrasing, and yet the unfailing truthfulness and the nail-on-the-head precision in each description. Consider the fact that, despite the ease with which the sentences pass, he almost never employs a shopworn, over-used word, but rather finds the unexpected one, which also happens to be utterly right.

Judge for yourself from Jenkins's writings in *Golf Digest* about some of the greatest names in golf.

On Arnold Palmer's last U.S. Open: On Friday, Arnold Palmer conducted the most memorable non-press conference after playing in his final Open. He uttered 20 difficult words in about five minutes but was so overcome with emotion he was forced to excuse himself. There weren't many dry eyes in the audience either, and suddenly, for one of the few times in their cynical lives, the press inhabitants spontaneously gave this most cooperative athlete they would ever know a standing ovation. Somewhere in that unique moment was a lesson for today's stars.

On Sergio Garcia's first British Open: The day before the championship began, the young Spaniard was in the interview room pleading with the press to refer to him simply as "Sergio," like Cher or Elvis, you could only guess. "Call me Sergio," he said. Then he shot 89-83, walked away tearfully in the arms of his mommy, and became "call me a cab."

On Seve Ballesteros: Seve's the most glamorous golfer who ever forgot to be born with blonde hair.

On Phil Mickelson winning the 2004 Masters: It was my 54th Masters in a row, and I must confess that in all those years I have never seen anything as thrilling, exciting, or dramatic as Phil Mickelson's victory. Now that Phil has done it, who's the best American player who has never won a major? I look around the dismal landscape and see only one answer. Michelle Wie.

On Gary Player: If Gary ever played a golf course that wasn't the finest he'd ever seen, I must not have been there.

On Greg Norman losing the 1986 Masters: What do you do if you're Greg Norman in the 18th fairway of the Masters on Sunday and you're trying to get Jack Nicklaus into a playoff? You hit a half-shank, push-fade, semi-slice 4-iron that guarantees the proper result for the history books. Oh well, Greg Norman always has looked like the guy you sent out to kill James Bond, not Jack Nicklaus.

On Jack Nicklaus winning the 1986 Masters: If you want to put golf back on the front pages again and you don't have a Bobby Jones or a Francis Ouimet handy, here's what you do: You send an aging Jack Nicklaus out in the last round of the Masters and let him kill more foreigners than a general named Eisenhower. On that final afternoon of the Masters tournament, Nicklaus's deeds were so unexpectedly heroic, dramatic, and historic, the taking of his sixth Green Jacket would certainly rank as the biggest golf story since Jones's Grand Slam of 1930. That Sunday night, writers from all corners of the globe were last seen sitting limply at their machines, muttering, "it's too big for me."

On Fred Couples winning the 1992 Masters: It took Fred Couples 12 years to win a major. Possibly that's because it takes that long to find a ball that will stop short of the water going straight downhill. No ball hitting the bank short of the 12th green ever stopped short of the water before. Not on Sunday. Not in all the Masters tournaments that had ever been played.

On John Daly winning the 1995 British Open: So now John Daly has a British Open to go with his PGA, which makes him an even larger drawing card for golf—I say the largest today—and maybe it's dawned on everybody that if Arnold Palmer once took the game to the people, John Daly has now taken it to the people in the RV parks.

On Jean Van de Velde losing the 1999 British Open: You can't throw away a major championship the way Jean Van de Velde did. Just can't happen. When a double bogey wins a major, you don't turn yourself into a martyr with a triple. But that's what Jean of Argh did on Carnoustie's 487-yard par 4. How bad was it? There was a rumor in the press tent that Van de Velde is French for Greg Norman.

On the death of Ben Hogan in 1997: If this is a remembrance, let me make clear right away that the Ben Hogan I knew was nothing like the image he inadvertently presented to the public: cold, steely-eyed, unapproachable, seemingly rude, utterly private. It's true he didn't suffer fools easily, had no patience for small talk, was highly opinionated on certain subjects, remained overly protective of his name, and had little regard for people who didn't work hard at their jobs, whatever their jobs might be. Frankly, I found those traits admirable. But let me tell you what else he was: rather shy, incredibly modest, fantastically gracious in victory and defeat, engagingly courteous, and chivalrous around women, a person who had acquired exquisite taste, a guy who enjoyed trading jibes with good friends, a guy with a well-concealed sense of humor.

On Tiger Woods: I covered Tiger winning his 14 professional majors, but I can't say I know him. I knew the smile he put on for TV. I knew the orchestrated remarks he granted us in his press-room interviews. I knew the air he punched when another outrageous putt went in the cup. That's it. I once made an effort to get to know the old silicone collector. Tried to arrange dinners with him for a little Q&A, on or off the record, his choice. But the closest I ever got was this word from his agent: "We have nothing to gain." Now it's too late. I'm busy.

★ ★ ★ ★

"I know I am getting better at golf because I'm hitting fewer spectators."

—Gerald Ford

HOGAN'S GREATEST TRIUMPHS ►BY DAN JENKINS

Dan Jenkins, author, journalist, raconteur, and just about the most dead-solid perfect golf writer of all time grew up in Ft. Worth, Texas, and had the good fortune to caddy for, play with, and write about another Ft. Worth guy: the great Ben Hogan. A newspaperman back in those days, Jenkins covered Hogan for many years and was there to witness all of his greatest days on the golf course. He chose the five best.

5. 1953 Masters. He shattered the existing Masters 72-hole record by five shots with a 14-under total of 274, the first of his three major wins that year. No one had ever won three professional majors in a single season until Hogan did it in '53.

4. 1967 Masters. All he did was shoot a 30 on the back nine at Augusta National for a third round 66. That week he tied for 10th place—at the age of 55—and Jack Nicklaus missed the cut after winning the tournament in 1965 and '66.

3. 1959 Colonial. Tied Fred Hawkins after 72 holes and then whipped him in the playoff for his fifth Colonial title and his last of 64 career victories, including nine major championships.

2. 1953 U.S. Open. In the year of his then-unprecedented Triple Crown, he fought off and then buried Sam Snead by six shots to win his last U.S. Open at Oakmont, the same year a 24-year-old amateur from nearby Latrobe played in his first Open. Arnold Palmer missed the cut.

1. 1951 U.S. Open. He came in with a 67 in the final round at Oakland Hills outside Detroit, the greatest last round in history on the world's toughest golf course.

GRIP IT AND SIP IT

A number of professional golfers have a passion for the game—and the grape, evidenced by so many of them getting involved in the wine business, either lending their names to a private label vintage or actually investing in vineyards to produce their own reds and whites or anything in between. The following players definitely can all handle a corkscrew as deftly as they can a lob wedge.

11. John Daly. Yes, even downscale JD is associated with this upscale pursuit, and although you might joke that he's more likely to be a connoisseur of Ripple and Cold Duck, his John Daly Wines label was introduced in 2008 and has produced a Chardonnay, a Cabernet Sauvignon, and even what he calls a "Perfect Round" Bordeaux blend.

10. Duffy Waldorf. He's been collecting wines for years and reportedly has 2,000 bottles in his personal cellar back home in Southern California. He's involved with several California vineyards that use his name on a wide variety of wines.

9. Mike Weir. The Canadian started the Mike Weir Estate Winery in 2005 to showcase wines from the Niagara region of Canada and upstate New York. Proceeds from the sale of Weir wines goes directly to the Mike Weir Foundation to support children with medical or other needs, including his first vintage in 2007, a Cabernet Merlot.

8. Annika Sorenstam. The Swedish star loves to cook and occasionally have a sip on the side as she toils in the kitchen. The Annika label is produced by Wente Vineyards in California's Livermore Valley. Her first effort was the Annika Vineyards Syrah, launched in 2009.

7. Luke Donald. The Englishman and product of Northwestern University has the Luke Donald Collection in partnership with the Terlato Wine Group of Napa Valley, California, that began with a claret-style wine blend in 2008.

6. Nick Faldo. The six-time major champion's label is produced by Katnook Vineyards in Coonamara, Australia, a vineyard known for its fruity red wines, particularly a Faldo Shiraz and a signature Cabernet Sauvignon.

5. Arnold Palmer. The King's non-alcoholic beverage of choice is a blend of ice tea and lemonade that bears his name in restaurants, bars, and supermarkets around the country. In 2003 he also partnered with the Luna Vineyards of Napa Valley, owned by longtime friend Mike Moone, to produce an Arnold Palmer label of premium wines marketed to high-end eateries.

4. Gary Player. One of the fittest golfers on the planet always avoids the fries and chocolate cake, but the antioxidants in fine wine suit his healthy lifestyle to a tee. His Black Knight Wine is produced by Quoin Rock Winery in South Africa, launched with a 1959 Muirfield vintage that is part of the Gary Player Major Championship Series, which will introduce 18 different vintages over the next decade.

3. Greg Norman. The Shark's vast business empire includes the Greg Norman Estates label, which produces reds, whites, and sparkling wines from vineyards he owns in Australia and California. Sour grapes? Ask Chris Evert, his latest ex-wife.

2. Ernie Els. The three-time major champion has been in the wine business for quite a while, partnering with his friend Jean Engelbrecht in a South African vineyard that bears both their names. The first vintage came out in 2000, and there are five different varieties of Bordeaux wines under the label. A Big Easy on the palate, for sure.

1. David Frost. No professional golfer knows more about making wine than the South African native, who grew up and worked on his family's vineyard when he wasn't off working on his golf game. Frost bought his own 300-acre vineyard in South Africa in 1994, and his David Frost Wine Estate released its first vintage in 1997. Frosty also produces Cabernet Sauvignon, Merlot, and Shiraz as well as what he calls "Par Excellence," a traditional red blend.

★ ★ ★ ★

"When I die, bury me on the golf course so my husband will visit."

—Author Unknown

Aaaah, the 19th hole, the ideal spot to wet your whistle, commiserate over the card, and replay that heroic 140-yard shot from the sand that finished stiff to the pin. A cold brewski or two in the grille room or snack bar has always been our favorite way to wind down from a draining round of golf, but the sport also has a wide variety of golf-themed adult libations to ease the pain of that dreaded snowman or toast that 30-foot putt for that elusive eagle you finally bagged after all these years. A small tasting:

10. Whiskey Mac. The libation of choice at the Littlestone Golf Club in Rye, England, just combine ginger wine and your favorite whisky, and the pain of that triple bogey at 18 eases considerably with every sweet little sip.

9. Western Comfort. Available at the bar at Celtic Manor in Wales, home of the 2010 Ryder Cup, it's a mix of bourbon, Grand Marnier, and ginger ale on ice.

8. Fresh Cut Fairway. White rum, peach schnapps, apple schnapps, and orange juice offers lots of vitamin C to counteract the alcohol.

7. Famous Grouse. The single-malt Scotch is so popular in the British Isles that the company sets up its own booth/bar at the British Open every year, not far from the Moet champagne tent that also attracts three- and four-deep crowds.

6. Valhalla Ryder Cup Martini. Served at the Louisville golf club of the same name that hosted the 2008 Cup, it's a blend of bourbon, amaretto, and pineapple juice—and hold the vodka and vermouth.

5. Happy Gilmore. In honor of the whacky Adam Sandler character in the golf movie of the same name, mix Kahlua, Frangelico, crème de cocoa, and a sprinkle of cinnamon.

4. The Slammer. They'll know what you're talking about at Sam Snead's old stomping grounds at the Greenbrier Resort in West Virginia. Two types of bourbon, Bols Amaretto, and sloe gin.

3. Arman de Brignac Champagne. In 2009 the exclusive French company put out a limited edition of its Brut Gold in a green bottle to honor the Masters, and 2009 champion Angel Cabrera was delighted to taste the bubbly shortly after they fitted him for a green jacket.

2. Devil's Spruce. Named for the famous fourth hole at the Fairmont Banff Springs Hotel, known as the Devil's Cauldron, it's a mixture of Belvedere citrus, lime juice, mint, and juniper.

1. Arnold Palmer. The King of all golf drinks, a simple mixture of half-lemonade and half-unsweetened iced tea that's always been Palmer's favorite postround pick-me-up. Now available ready-made at your local supermarket under the Arizona brand, add the liquor of your choice, hitch up your pants, and have a ball.

★ ★ ★ ★

"The golf swing is like a suitcase into which we are trying to pack one too many things."

—John Updike

LOSING IT

The history of professional golf is littered with gifted players who soared to the highest levels of the game, only to crash and bottom out to the lower depths of the world rankings and the money list. It might have been a swing change gone amuck, an ill-conceived switch of equipment, or illness/injury. Some fortunate players eventually managed to pull out of the nose dive, but some have been flailing and failing for years, trying to get back to those past heady heights.

10. Notah Begay. Tiger Woods's old Stanford teammate won four times in his first two seasons on the PGA Tour starting in 1999, but he hasn't been among the top 200 on the tour's money list since 2004. He got up as high as No. 19 in the world rankings in 2000, but a chronically bad back has been the primary reason for Begay's on-course woes.

9. Len Mattiace. In 2003 he fired a final round 65 in the Masters before losing a playoff to Mike Weir during a season when he climbed to No. 24 in the world rankings. But Mattiace injured both knees in a serious skiing accident in December 2003 and hasn't been the same since. He lost his tour card after the 2005 season and has been playing most of his golf in recent years on the Nationwide Tour.

8. Todd Hamilton. After spending the early portion of his career on the Japanese Tour, Hamilton finally earned his PGA Tour card in 2004 at the age of 38. He went on to win the Honda Classic and the British Open that season, and he then earned over $3 million in purse money and was named Rookie of the Year. It's been mostly downhill ever since, due to what he once described as a "mental problem" in trying to recreate that magical season. Hamilton lost his PGA Tour card after the 2009 season and now plays mainly on the European Tour, where the British win earned a 10-year exemption.

7. Chris DiMarco. With over $20 million in earnings, DiMarco was ranked as high as No. 6 in the world in 2005, with three runner-up finishes in major championships. But a rib injury after a 2006 skiing accident followed by shoulder and wrist problems sent him into a prolonged slump that included finishing 146th on the money list in 2008 and 135th in 2009. DiMarco did show some flashes of his old form in 2010, playing mostly pain-free for the first time in a while. He also said his confidence was coming back as well. "A mind can be a terrible thing," he said, "and mine was in a terrible place."

6. Corey Pavin. Once known as the gritty little Bruin from UCLA, Pavin won 14 events, including the 1995 U.S. Open, between 1984 and 1996 and also was a highly successful Ryder Cup player. Then came the tailspin, some say induced by a change in equipment, bad swing habits, and a loss of confidence. Pavin went 242 straight events without a victory until he prevailed in Milwaukee in 2006, ending a 10-year drought. He's back in form again, now playing the senior Champions Tour.

5. Michael Campbell. When he won the 2005 U.S. Open at Pinehurst No. 2, he became the first New Zealander to capture a major championship since Bob Charles in the 1963 British Open. But Campbell, who now plays the European Tour primarily, has been in steady decline ever since. A shoulder injury has plagued him over the last few years, and he may have hit rock bottom when he shot 83 in the opening round of the 2009 Masters. Campbell says of his own roller-coaster playing history, success has often bred failure. When he wins, "I take it too easy, get into a comfort zone, and stop practicing and working out."

4. John Daly. So much talent, so long off the tee, such a wonderful touch around the greens, and yet this two-time major champion has been getting in his own way for years, dealing with a wide variety of addictive demons, a string of failed marriages, and a long history of bad behavior on and off the golf course. Though he's still a gallery favorite wherever he goes, "Wild Thing" is now forced to play on sponsor's exemptions and hasn't finished higher than 188th on the PGA Tour money list in the last five seasons.

3. Chip Beck. Between 1988 and 1989 he spent 40 straight weeks in the top ten of the world rankings, and then he shot a Holy Grail 59 in the 1991 Las Vegas Invitational, at the time only the second man in PGA Tour history to go that low. But things got truly on the down low for this likeable fellow after finishing second in the 1993 Masters. He began tinkering with his swing, a fatal mistake that once led to a run of 46 straight missed cuts in one stretch of the 1997 and 1998 seasons, and he eventually left the game and started selling insurance in Chicago. He has since found new swing thoughts and has returned to competitive golf on the Champions Tour.

2. David Duval. Until his stirring second place finish at the 2009 U.S. Open at Bethpage Black, Duval, once the No. 1 ranked player in the world in 1999, had not finished in the top ten of a tournament since 2002, a streak of 116 events. His downward spiral began not long after he won the 2001 British Open, his first and only major championship. Duval dropped to 80th on the money list in 2002 and hasn't cracked the top 125 ever since. He had a series of injury problems with his back, wrist, and shoulder, suffered issues with vertigo, and then seemed to lose some interest in the game, preferring to focus more on his family life. He's been playing more frequently over the last few years, with modest success, but that British Open triumph remains his last victory.

1. Ian Baker-Finch. Once known as "The Dark Shark" and considered the likely successor to Australian countryman Greg Norman as one of the top players in the world, Baker-Finch won the 1991 British Open with finishing rounds of 64 and 66 earning, a 10-year exemption on the PGA Tour. But he never won on tour again. His form started to desert him, and by the mid-1990s, after a series of swing changes failed to produce better results, his confidence was shattered. He reached his professional nadir at the 1995 British Open when, playing with Arnold Palmer at St. Andrews, he hooked a tee shot out of bounds across two fairways, and then in the '97 British Open, shot 92 in the first round and decided to retire from competitive golf. He's been a successful television analyst ever since and also began regaining enough semblance of a swing to consider occasional forays onto the Champions Tour.

★ ★ ★ ★

"Golf is the cruelest game, because eventually it will drag you out in front of the whole school, take your lunch money and slap you around."

—Writer Rick Reilly

MY TEN COMMANDMENTS OF LIFE

► BY GARY PLAYER

People often say that the game of golf is a mirror of life.

Having played this great game professionally all over the world through the course of six decades, I've found this to be true. A round of golf, like life, is a journey between whose start and finish an almost unimaginable variety of triumphs and tragedies unfold.

Like golf, business is also a wonderful metaphor for life. Adversity often presents unexpected opportunities; imagination, creativity, and patience are the keys to problem solving; and hard work truly pays off.

In fact, success in golf and success in business have a great deal in common. I've tried to encapsulate some of the lessons I've learned into what I call *10 Maxims for Life and Business*, with an emphasis on the link between golfing and business excellence.

1. Change is the price of survival.

2. Everything in business is negotiable except quality.

3. A promise made is a debt incurred.

4. For all we take in life we must pay.

5. Persistence and common sense are more important than intelligence.

6. The fox fears not the man who boasts by night but the man who rises early in the morning.

7. Accept the advice of the man who loves you, though you like it not at present.

8. Trust instinct to the end, though you cannot render any reason.

9. The heights of great men reached and kept were not attained by sudden flight but that while their companions slept were toiling upward in the night.

10. There is no substitute for personal contact.

★ ★ ★ ★

"The reason the pro tells you to keep your head down is so you can't see him laughing."

—Phyllis Diller

THE PERFECT GOLFER

Some golfers are known for their prodigious drives, others for their delicate touch around the greens. Many others are known for their mental tenacity or their ability to think their way around a golf course. But what if you take the absolute best qualities of the world's best players, male and female, and packaged them all together into one player we'll call Golfenstein. If we were Mad Scientists, here's who we might invite over to our lab.

The killer instinct of
Tiger Woods

The guts of
Paul Azinger

The imagination of
Phil Mickelson

The charisma of
Greg Norman

The course management of
Jack Nicklaus

The swagger of
Arnold Palmer

The short game of
José Maria Olazabal

The cool of
Ernie Els

The ball striking of
Sergio Garcia

The ego of
Gary Player

The work ethic of
Annika Sorenstam

The scrambling ability of
Seve Ballesteros

The putting touch of
Ben Crenshaw

The will of
Tom Watson

The power of
John Daly

The sweet personality of
Lorena Ochoa

The flexibility of
Camilo Villegas

The looks of
Adam Scott/Natalie Gulbis

The driving accuracy of
Fred Funk

The humbleness of
Kenny Perry

The placid demeanor of
Fred Couples

The fire in the belly of
Justin Leonard

The genes of
Davis Love III

The cockiness of
Anthony Kim

The eyes of
Padraig Harrington

The sense of humor of
Paul Goydos

★ ★ ★ ★

**"It took me seventeen years to get 3,000 hits.
I did it in one afternoon on the golf course."**

—Hank Aaron, 1971

THE DIFFERENCES BETWEEN
THE PROS AND US

Every weekend we watch the pros and marvel at how they make the game look so easy. Then we go out and play and quickly are reminded (usually with the opening tee shot) that golf is a difficult game, squared. What's the difference between the pros and the rest of the world? Noted instructor and CBS analyst Peter Kostis says, "I like to say to it's 180 degrees of separation. The average player is 180 degrees different than the tour pro."

7. The grip. Most recreational players are doomed from the moment they place their hands on the club. Asked what flaw consistently stands out among his pro-am partners, Tiger Woods didn't hesitate. "It's the grip," Woods said. "Most amateurs have never been taught the foundation of a good grip. A lot of flaws are attributed to the grip because you have to make a lot of different compensations along the way in the golf swing to square up the club face.

"I think the best thing amateurs can do is focus on the simplest thing, which is the grip and your setup. It's amazing how much better you can play from a correct and solid foundation."

Listen to Tiger and get a grip.

6. Weapons. You probably bought your clubs off the rack at your local store. Golf, however, isn't a one-size-fits-all game, and the chances that those clubs meet your exact specifications are small. The pros, meanwhile, spend hours, days, months testing their equipment. Every calibration is measured by experts with advanced degrees in physics. At the end of the process, the pros have equipment that allows them to maximize their performance. As for you? . . . Hopefully, you have a nice set of head covers.

5. Trapped. Nowhere is the gap wider than in the bunkers. The pros look as if they are throwing darts to the pins from the sand. It's almost an automatic up-and-down. For us, it usually is an automatic down-and-down. We simply are clueless with the sand under our feet and often resort to tossing the ball out. "It's an easy shot most of the time if you know how to play it," said Luke Donald. "You can create a lot of spin on the ball. That makes it easy to control."

Easy for him. Impossible for us.

4. Work ethic. Obviously, the pros have to work harder on their games. It is their livelihood. But the differences go deeper than quantity of practice. There also is the issue of quality. The vast majority of amateur players are wasting their time at the driving range. "The average player never practices anything he doesn't do well," said Butch Harmon. "If he doesn't hit fairway woods, well, you'll never see him practice with those clubs. With the tour player, whatever he doesn't do well, that's what he'll spend all his time working on." Harmon noted that the amateur's poor practice habits are good for his business. "It keeps me busy," he laughed.

3. Choking. It is the one thing we have in common with the pros: We both choke. However, our stakes are considerably lower than, let's say, winning a tournament with thousands of dollars on the line. Nevertheless, a choke still is a choke, whether it occurs at the Masters or your local muni on Sunday. "It's the most interesting thing in golf," said NBC's Johnny Miller. "When you have a $2 Nassau with six presses going, and you've got a 3-footer in front of the clubhouse with everyone watching, it's all about whether you can make the putt. That's why golf is such a great game. You get to see if the guy has it in him to hit the shot that needs to be hit."

2. Mentally fried. Most amateurs simply go brain dead when they get on the course. They dwell too much about swing thoughts, a fatal error, and they usually are clueless about strategy. The pros, meanwhile, leave their swing thoughts on the driving range and focus on the task at hand. "The pro knows what he can do," Harmon said. "He doesn't try to do things he can't do. The average player, meanwhile, thinks he can hit a ridiculous amount of yardage. He thinks because he once hit a 6-iron 170 yards, that's the club he should use. That's unrealistic. You have to be realistic to play golf."

1. Athleticism. At the end of the day, it still comes down to strength, flexibility, and superior hand-eye coordination. The pros have it, and we don't. "Supposedly, one of the appealing things about golf is that you don't have to be an athlete to play the game," Kostis said. "Well, that might be true if you want to be a 20-handicapper. But if you want to be good, you have to be athletic."

THE GREAT BOB JONES

▶ BY ERRIE BALL

Errie Ball played in the first Masters in 1934, then known as the Augusta National Invitational. He received a personal invitation from the tournament's founder, Bobby Jones.

Jones had considerable impact on Ball's life. Here Ball shares his memories of the great golfer—and why the headline for this list refers to Jones as Bob, not Bobby.

7. First meeting. I first saw Bob Jones when I was 15 years old. I saw him play in the 1926 Open Championship. I played in that Open, too. I was the youngest player to compete in a major for more than 80 years. Now that's a pretty good record. I didn't fare too well, but it was just exciting to be around all those great players. And to see Jones. That was something. The fans loved him. It was like he was one of their own.

6. Coming to America. My uncle Frank Ball was the golf pro at East Lake Country Club in Atlanta. That was Bob's club. A few years later, my father—he was a golf pro, too—he took me over to meet Bob. Frank wanted me to come over to the United States, but I wasn't sure I wanted to. I talked to Bob. He said, "Errie, I think you'll do well over there."

Well, I wasn't about to go against the advice of Bob Jones. If he tells you to do something, you do it. So I decided to do it. In 1936 I met my wife Maxie on a ship coming back to the United States from England. If it wasn't for Bob, I never would have met her. He changed my life.

5. Invitation to the Masters. I went over there and I had some success early on. I won the Southeast PGA. Back in those days, that was a pretty good tournament. It showed Jones that I was a pretty good player. I think it had a lot to do with Bob asking me to play in the first Masters.

I was thrilled to death. We all were. We knew if Bob put his name on it, it would be top notch.

4. Playing with Jones. I played quite a few times with him in exhibitions. Sure, I got nervous. I'm sure they get nervous when they play with Tiger. Bob was wonderful to me. He tried to give me some advice. You always listened when he told you something.

173

3. Jones, the golfer. The thing I remember the most was his beautiful swing. His swing was the best. The swing is different today. It's short, more compact. Bobby had this long, flowing swing. He crossed the line at the top of his swing. They never would teach that today. Back then that's the way they swung.

But he never came over the top. At the start of his downswing, his clubhead was further away from the ball than at the completion of his back swing. He had such wonderful tempo. He could play any type of shot. He had everything.

2. Jones, the person. He was so smart, brilliant. He got his law degree in nothing flat. To me, he was one of the nicest people I ever met.

1. Just Bob. The first thing you have know about Bob Jones was that he didn't like to be called Bobby. He got that from the Scots. They called him Bobby. But he always wanted to be called Bob.

Bobby Jones and his wife, Mary, during a ticker tape parade in New York City.

THE BEST

►BY ERRIE BALL

Nobody has seen more golf history than Errie Ball. He played in the 1926 British Open at the age of 15. More than 80 years later, he was still active, hitting balls and giving lessons. Here is Ball's breakdown of the best players he has seen in golf.

Best driver: Sam Snead. Sam was long and straight. He had one of the best swings.

Best iron player: Tommy Armour. Solid. He just hit everything so purely. He could put the ball wherever he wanted.

Best putter: Bobby Locke. He could putt the eyes out. I played in a Western Open with him. Once he took a long time over a short putt. When he walked off the green (after making the putt), a man said to him, "Mr. Locke, you took a long time over that putt." Locke said, "Yeah, you know I missed one once."

Best showman: Walter Hagen. I played behind him once at Pinehurst. On one hole, he missed a green to the right. He had some trees blocking him. He starts walking around forever, studying the shot. Meanwhile, I'm standing in the middle of the fairway. I thought he'd never get through. Finally, he hits his shot, and gets up and down for 4.

Damned if I didn't put my shot in the same spot. But when I walked up, I saw the opening was as big as a house. He was just showing off for the crowd. . . . But I didn't get my par.

Best competitor: Ben Hogan. Nobody knew more about the game. He had it down to a science. When he went out on the golf course, he was determined to win. He wasn't going to lose.

Best player: Tiger Woods. He is the best I've ever seen. He has everything. If Bob Jones had the same equipment, I don't know who would win. They would have a real go at it.

BEST BALL STRIKERS

You hear it all the time during golf telecasts: some golden-throated analyst raving about a player being a great ball striker. But what exactly does that mean? Plain and simple, it refers to a golfer's ability to take a full swing and put the clubface on the ball in the perfect place upon impact, time after time, with enough skill to make a shot go left or right or whatever it takes to get the job done. Basically, it's consistently hitting a golf ball where you want it to go. We know we're leaving many worthy candidates out here, but here's one man's list of ten of the best ball strikers.

10. Sergio Garcia. The temperamental Spaniard has all the right shots off the tee and from the fairway. Now, if he could only make a few key putts, he might earn a few more big victories.

9. Raymond Floyd. His swing was a tad herky-jerky, but the man known as "Tempo Raymondo" almost always hit it flush over his brilliant career, including some nice work on the Champions Tour.

8. Nick Faldo. A technician of the highest quality, Faldo prided himself on his ball-striking abilities, particularly in crunch time.

7. Nick Price. He didn't really hit it that far. But in his prime (the early to mid-1990s), this Price was almost always right in the short grass off the tee and hitting greens in regulation with stunning consistency.

6. Tiger Woods. Some might wonder why arguably the greatest player of all time is not ranked higher. Well, when he's on, his ball striking can be stunning. When he's off, there's a tad too much left, right, left, right in the mix.

5. Lee Trevino. The man had just about every shot in the book and could make his low-flying ball do amazing things at just the right time, even from lousy lies.

4. Jack Nicklaus. Anyone ever see Nicklaus hit a really, really bad shot? Probably not, because he hardly ever did, and hoo-hah, not only was he long off the tee, he was deadly accurate with the long irons, also a key indicator of ball-striking prowess.

3. Byron Nelson. His swing has been the model for the U.S. Golf Association's robotic club and ball-testing machine—"Iron Byron," they call it—and Ken Venturi once said of Nelson that "nobody kept the ball on the club face longer through impact than Byron did."

2. Sam Snead. If you loved Slammin' Sammy's sweet swing, the results were even better for a self-taught Hall of Famer who was still hitting it down the middle well into his 80s, often scoring lower than his age.

1. Ben Hogan. A magician with all his clubs, but particularly a 1-iron, a club Trevino said you avoided carrying in a lightning storm because "not even God can hit a 1-iron." God and Hogan, that is, as evidenced by his famous 1-iron approach that produced a 72nd hole par at Merion in the 1950 U.S. Open to get him into a playoff that he won, just over a year after a car accident nearly ended his career and his life.

BEST SHORT GAMES

Short-game guru Dave Pelz once did an exhaustive three-year study on the importance of the short game and estimated that 60–65 percent of an 18-hole round involves shots inside 100 yards of the hole. The short game encompasses pitching, chipping, bunker play, and putting, and Pelz's study concluded that the biggest money winners were not usually the biggest belters of the ball but rather the short-shot magicians. Here's a list of ten of the all-time best, with many more contenders just a short pitch-and-a-putt behind.

10. John Daly. Don't laugh. Vijay Singh once said Long John had the finest short game he'd ever seen. What a shameful waste of talent squandered by his loopy lifestyle and nonexistent work ethic.

9. Seve Ballesteros. It was often said that the swashbuckling Spaniard could make par from the parking lot, and he once did in a British Open. The Spaniard's stellar short game made up for his many years of scattershot driving.

8. José Maria Olazabal. Ballesteros's protégé and countryman also was a wizard with a wedge in his hand, a creative shot maker and clutch putter, particularly around Augusta National, where he won two Masters on arguably the toughest short game course in golf.

7. Tom Watson. Remember that chip-in with a sand wedge from 18 feet at the 17th hole at Pebble Beach in the 1982 U.S. Open? He was so confident in his short game prowess, when Watson's caddy, the late Bruce Edwards, told him to hit it close, Watson responded, "Get it close? Hell, I'm going to make it."

6. Tiger Woods. Just think 2005 Masters, the chip shot that rolled up the bank and back down the bank and went into the hole for an improbable birdie, the swoosh-logoed ball hanging on the edge just long enough to make the perfect Nike commercial when gravity took its course.

5. Billy Casper. He liked to eat buffalo meat and other exotic protein when that wasn't so fashionable back in the 1960s, but it never affected his ability to find a way to get the ball in the hole in a hurry from anywhere within 50 yards of the flag.

4. Lee Trevino. He never hit it all that far, but with a wedge in his soft hands, he was a killer, playing for thousands or a $10 Nassau with an empty wallet at the local Texas muni—where you'd better knock it inside the leather or get yourself knocked out when you can't cover the wager.

3. Gary Player. Some believe The Black Knight may have been the greatest sand shot player in the history of the game. If you ask him, he'd probably agree, and it would be hard to argue with a man with nine major championships on a résumé that also includes 110 worldwide victories.

2. Walter Hagen. "The Haig" was so confident in his short game, he'd often psyche out match-play opponents by telling his caddy to pull the pin, even when faced with long chips or pitches from far off the dance floor. He made more than his share, too.

1. Phil Mickelson. When your old man installs a putting green and a sand trap in the backyard when you're a kid, you better hit it stiff from close-in more often than not. Mickelson was always a brilliant short game player (with the possible exception of too many missed three-foot putts), and then he got even better when he hooked up with Dave Pelz a few years ago to become as good as anyone in the history of the game inside 100 yards.

★ ★ ★ ★

"The world's No. 1 tennis player spends 90 percent winning, while the world's No. 1 golfer spends 90 percent of his time losing. Golfers are great losers."

—David Feherty

Not surprisingly, most of the best putters also are among the greatest players of all time. Tournaments are won and lost on the greens, and the player who can convert the 15-footer—or even the 5-footer—on a regular basis usually wins. For other top putters who weren't great all-around players, their time on the greens proved a great equalizer. It's pretty simple: You can't win if you can't put the ball in the hole. These ten made that often tricky and nerve-wracking process look simple.

10. George Low. He didn't win many tournaments, but he won a ton of money in putting contests. Low thought he was golf's greatest putter, and he received few arguments on that front. He was perhaps the first putting guru, advising Byron Nelson, Arnold Palmer, and Jack Nicklaus, among others. His book, *The Master of Putting*, is considered a classic.

9. Loren Roberts. His nickname, "Boss of the Moss," says it all. Roberts didn't have the overall game to match many of the champions, but his prowess with the putter enabled him to win eight PGA Tour events. During a long career on the PGA Tour that began in 1975, Roberts averaged only 28.3 putts per round. Tough to beat that.

8. Brad Faxon. Like Roberts, he had weaknesses elsewhere in his game. But his work with the putter made Faxon the envy of a lot of other players. One of the game's good guys, Faxon showed across eight PGA Tour wins, beginning with the 1991 Buick Open, that a solid putting stroke can carry you a long way.

7. Dave Stockton. The two-time PGA Championship winner (1970 and '76) was a terrific putter. He went on to share his insights as a top putting instructor. His pupils in recent years have included Phil Mickelson and Michelle Wie.

6. Ben Crenshaw. Tom Kite, who grew up with Crenshaw in Texas, once said, "I don't remember Ben ever missing a putt from the time he was 12 until he was 20." "Gentle Ben" also didn't miss many after that in his Hall of Fame career. His putting stroke was responsible for him winning two Masters, including in 1995 when he didn't post a single 3-putt on Augusta's treacherous greens.

5. Bobby Locke. He was the player who came up with the famous phrase, "You drive for show and putt for dough." The South African won a lot of dough on the greens during a career spanning from 1938–59. He used a 38-inch hickory-shafted putter that allowed him to move putts from left to right. A magician.

4. Billy Casper. Chi Chi Rodriguez had a terrific assessment of Casper's prowess with the putter: "(Casper) was the greatest putter I ever saw. . . . When golf balls used to leave the factory, they prayed they would get to be putted by Billy." Those balls that had their prayers answered went in the hole early and often during Casper's 51 PGA Tour victories.

3. Bobby Jones. His famous putter, known as "Calamity Jane," had a wood shaft with a simple offset and suffered few calamities on the greens. You don't win as much as Jones did without being a great putter.

2. Jack Nicklaus. Nicklaus was a study in concentration on the greens. He took his sweet time studying every nuance of a putt. Then Nicklaus would calmly make the putt, time and time again. If he isn't the game's all-time clutch putter, then who is? . . .

1. Tiger Woods. For my money, it is Woods. Perhaps I'm biased because I got to see him up close much more than I got to see Nicklaus. It just seems like Woods never misses. He has to be the greatest ever in making that 5- or 6-footer to save par. He always talks about how those mean more than making a birdie. As for clutch putts to win tournaments, where do you begin? You always knew Michael Jordan would make the big shot and that Woods will make the big putt.

★ ★ ★ ★

"I've never had a coach in my life. When I find one who can beat me, then I'll listen."

—Lee Trevino

WORLD GOLF HALL OF FAME

►BY JACK PETER

If you love the history of golf like us, then you must make a pilgrimage to the World Golf Hall of Fame. Located in St. Augustine, Florida, the Hall breathes the game. Walking through the exhibits is like taking a journey through the eras of Vardon, Jones, Hogan, Nicklaus, and so forth. We asked Jack Peter, the senior vice president and chief operating officer for the Hall, to compile a list of some of the unique items that are on display. Here are a few. Trust us, there is much, much more.

Annika Sorenstam's 59 scorecard. Annika Sorenstam was the first player in LPGA competition history to shoot a round of 59 when she did so at the 200 Standard Register Ping. The Hall displays the scorecard from her historical feat.

Charlie Sifford's PGA card. Sifford was the first African American to play full time on the PGA Tour and the first African American inducted in to the World Golf Hall of Fame. The Hall holds Sifford's first—and very meaningful—PGA card given to him on March 28, 1960.

Jack Nicklaus Andy Warhol painting. The original Warhol portrait of Nicklaus is one of 10 in Warhol's "Athlete Series" featuring elite athletes from the 1970s. Other athletes included boxer Muhammad Ali, figure skater Dorothy Hamill, and basketball player Kareem Abdul Jabbar.

Bob Hope's PGA of America money clip. The PGA of America recognized Hope's commitments and contributions to the game of golf by giving the amateur golfer a money clip in 1942. The memento was so special to Hope that he carried the clip every day throughout the remainder of his 100-year life.

Johnny Miller's 1973 U.S. Open medal, glove, and ball. Miller's medal, glove, and ball are representative of his final-round 63 at the 1973 U.S. Open—the first 63 shot in major championship history. It remains the lowest final-round score in U.S. Open history.

Lloyd Mangrum's locker. One of the many who stormed Normandy in World War II, Mangrum received numerous honors including a purple heart, which is on display. During that time, he also tore a $1 bill and gave half to a good friend in war, in hopes of once again reuniting someday. The friend was lost, but Mangrum kept his half.

Jack Nicklaus's fly fishing rod. Nicklaus has shared his passion of not only golf but also of another hobby, fly fishing. Currently, he is a national spokesperson on behalf of the Federation of Fly Fishers as well as Honorary Chairman of the FFF Presidents Club. See Nicklaus's fly fishing rod and reel, custom made for him in 1980.

Nick Price's locker key. Golfer Nick Price made his debut in the Open Championship at St. Andrews in 1978 when he was 21 years old. Price shot 74-73-74-72 to tie for 39th, but was uncertain if he'd ever return to the championship venue again. So before leaving, he took his locker key from The R&A Clubhouse as a souvenir. Of course, Price returned and was victorious in 1994, but kept his key . . . now on display at the Hall of Fame.

The great triumvirate. The historical footage from The R&A features extremely rare and restored moving images of Hall of Fame members Harry Vardon, James Braid, and J. H. Taylor, who combined to win 16 Open Championships between 1894 and 1914. The footage on display dates from between 1904 and 1909 and includes short biographical pieces on each player, allowing Hall of Fame visitors to study the champions' swings in detail.

"Voices of the Hall." The museum's audio tour features over two and a half hours of exclusive content from Hall of Fame members. Hear Arnold Palmer recounting stories with "Ike," Byron Nelson speaking about how he turned professional, Tommy Bolt talking about his temper, Ben Crenshaw talking about Harvey Penick and his emotional Masters win, and much more.

Karrie Webb's Hall of Fame moment. Karrie Webb officially qualified for the World Golf Hall of Fame at the 2005 LPGA Championship. Her golf bag and clubs she used to achieve that feat are displayed in her locker at the World Golf Hall of Fame.

Babe Zaharias's harmonica. The professional golfer, most well known as changing the game of golf for women, also was a harmonica player, much to the surprise of some golf fans. A star-billed harmonica performer in vaudeville in the 1930s, Babe's own personal harmonica is displayed at the Hall of Fame.

It is known simply as "The Open," except, of course, in the United States, where we've got a pretty good Open of our own. Still, the British Open, first contested in 1860 and the oldest of the major championships, has every right to consider itself the Open that matters most. The Brits even take it a few spiked steps further, proclaiming the winner to be "champion golfer of the year," no matter who prevails in the other majors that season. And they consider the Claret Jug that goes to the winner to be the most coveted trophy in the game. No argument here as we offer a dozen of the best Opens—British that is—of all time.

12. Norman conquest. Though he began the 1993 tournament at Royal St. Georges with a double bogey, Greg Norman never played any better in a major championship, becoming the first player in Open history with four rounds in the 60s. The Australian posted a final round 64, and his 72-hole total of 267 remains the lowest aggregate score in tournament history. Gene Sarazen, a special guest on the grounds that week, said afterward, "I just saw the most awesome display in my 70 years of golf."

11. Aussie, Aussie, Aussie. Long before there was Norman, Peter Thomson helped set the stage for a boom in Australian golf when he won five Open titles (one short of Harry Vardon's record six) between 1954 and his last championship at Royal Birkdale in 1965. By the mid-'60s, the best American players were entering the tournament in droves, and with Jack Nicklaus, Arnold Palmer, and South African great Gary Player in the field, Thomson still prevailed by two shots.

10. Irish eyes. Padraig Harrington had a 1-shot lead as he came to the 72nd hole at Carnoustie in 2007, but two balls splashed into the Barry Burn, leading to a double bogey six, and the Irishman was certain he'd lost. Wrong, Paddy. Sergio Garcia, needing to make par at the 18th to win his first major, instead couldn't get up and down from a bunker, missing a ten-foot putt for par that forced a 4-hole aggregate playoff. Harrington, who made up a 6-shot deficit in the final round to force the playoff, won it by a shot, ending an eight-year European drought in the Open.

9. Wild thing. John Daly had never seen St. Andrews before he played it in the 1995 Open, but the venerable venue obviously suited his long game. He was able to drive six of the par 4s and reach all of its par 5s in two shots. Daly, 66-to-1 in the betting parlors at the start of the week, had to survive Italian Costantino Rocca sinking a totally improbable 65-foot putt from the Valley of Sin at the 72nd hole to force a playoff. But the American ultimately prevailed when Rocca made a triple bogey out of the Road Hole bunker at 17 on a day Daly shot 1-under in the extra session for his second major title in four years.

8. The Wee Ice Mon. Ben Hogan had never felt the need to play in the Open, but after his near-fatal car wreck in 1949, he decided to take a flier and head to Carnoustie in 1953 after winning both the Masters and the U.S. Open. Despite those victories, Hogan had to play two qualifying rounds just like everyone else in the field. He also had to take warm baths every night to ease the pain in his legs, but his game got stronger as the week progressed. Though he opened with a 73, his scores improved every day, and with a final round 68, he prevailed by four shots over a gang of four tied for second, including young Peter Thomson, who would win the next three Opens.

7. Choke of the century. Frenchman Jean Van de Velde's collapse in the 1999 Open at a brutally set-up Carnoustie course will go down as one of the greatest folds in golf history. Details can be found on another list (see "Biggest Chokes"). It's almost too painful to repeat. And did we mention that Scotsman Paul Lawrie won in a forgettable playoff in pouring rain against Van de Velde and Justin Leonard?

6. Slammin' St. Andrews. Sam Snead had never played in a British Open until 1946, but contractual obligations with his sponsors compelled him to enter at St. Andrews. Coming into town by train, he thought the Old Course was actually an abandoned golf course and said of the landscape, "Down home we wouldn't plant cow beets on land like that." Still, after he had secured a 4-shot victory over Bobby Locke and Johnny Bulla, he sang a different tune. "Until you play it, St. Andrews looks like the kind of real estate you couldn't give away. Once I got on the golf course, I respected it more each time I played it."

5. Tiger slam. The 2000 Open was no contest. A month after winning the U.S. Open at Pebble Beach by 15 shots, Woods again decimated the field at St. Andrews, prevailing by eight in a week when he shot a course-record 19-under 267. The victory also allowed Woods to claim a career grand slam, a victory in each of the four majors, at the age of 24, two years earlier than Jack Nicklaus had achieved the same rare feat. "He's the best who ever played," said his friend, Mark Calcavecchia. "And he's 24."

4. The King arrives. That would be Arnold Palmer, who helped change the face of the Open when he played an Open for the first time in 1960. Though Palmer finished second by a shot to Kel Nagle that year at St. Andrews, his visit drew worldwide media coverage and also marked a turning point in convincing other top American players to try to qualify for the championship. Palmer won the next two Opens, both nationally televised back in the States, and atoned for his loss to Nagle in 1960 by winning over the Australian by six shots in 1962 at Royal Troon.

3. Duel in the sun. As they stood on the 16th tee at Turnberry that memorable Sunday in 1977, tied for the Open lead at 11-under, Tom Watson turned to final-round playing partner Jack Nicklaus and said, "This is what it's all about, isn't it?" Replied Nicklaus, "You bet it is." Watson had just holed a 60-foot putt from in front of the 15th green for birdie to catch Nicklaus. He then opened a 1-shot lead when he birdied 17 and Nicklaus missed a 3-footer, settling for par. At the last, Nicklaus gouged a miracle shot from ugly, deep rough to within 35 feet, then somehow made the birdie putt. But Watson, after a brilliant 7-iron stiff to the flag, sank his own 20-inch birdie putt to clinch the victory in arguably the greatest major championship duel ever.

2. Toom time. Watson nearly completed what would have been the most remarkable golf story of all in the 2009 Open at Turnberry. The 59-year-old, five-time Open champion came to the 72nd hole needing par to win the tournament and become the oldest-ever major winner. But his adrenaline-induced approach carried over the 18th green and was followed by a chip to ten feet and a badly missed par putt, forcing a playoff that was never even close. Stewart Cink won it by six shots and carried home the Claret Jug. But "Toom," as he is affectionately known all around Scotland, earned even more admiration and respect as a golfer for the ages. All ages.

1. Grand slam. Bob Jones made it well known in 1930 that his intention was to win all four major championships in the same year, a feat no one had accomplished before or has since. He began the quest by taking the British Amateur at St. Andrews, then two weeks later prevailed by two shots over MacDonald Smith and Leo Diegel in the Open at Hoylake in the Liverpool suburbs. Jones would go on to win the U.S. Open at Interlachen in Minnesota and the U.S. Amateur at Merion, completing what his good friend and sportswriter O. B. Keeler famously called, "The Impregnable Quadrilateral."

BEST TOURNAMENT TO COVER:
BRITISH OPEN

▶BY JOE LOGAN

If you asked golf writers to rate their favorite tournament to cover, nine and a half out of ten would say the British Open. Sure, the Masters is special, especially the first time you go, when you're on sensory overload, soaking up every sight, every sound, every moment. But nothing compares to the experience of being at a British Open. Not that covering the tournament is without its challenges.

Joe Logan was the longtime golf writer for the *Philadelphia Inquirer*. Now the host of his own golf Web site, myphillygolf.com, Joe lists his five best and worst things about covering golf's oldest championship.

5 BEST

5. The newspapers. Newspapers in the UK are much more lively and fun to read than their serious and often bland counterparts in the United States. There are a couple of earnest and subdued papers—namely, the *Times of London* and the *Guardian*—but most are tabloids that scream at you from the newsstand with headlines that cannot be ignored. In the UK, newspapers are more in the entertainment business than the news business.

4. The fans. You can spend an entire week at the British and never once hear anybody yell, "Get in the hole!" British Open golf fans tend to be very knowledgeable, very well behaved, and, above all, very, very proper. In the event of a good shot, they offer up a polite round of applause. If it's a fantastic shot, they ratchet up the enthusiasm a couple of clicks. Golf fans over there also make sure to bring along a sweater or pullover and an umbrella for the inevitable afternoon shower and chill, although if the sun comes out, they slather on sunscreen so thick they look like Casper the friendly ghost.

3. Change of scenery. If the golf courses are different, so is everything else, starting with the surroundings. British Opens tend to be played in small towns and villages far from the big cities. To get there, you generally must fly into a big city then drive through small, ancient villages that are as innocent and picturesque as something out of *Robin Hood*. Once you get off the thoroughfares, the roads are extremely narrow, having been built in the days before modern, wide-body cars. Because of the constant rain in the UK the fields and meadows you see from those roads are the richest hues of green and yellow that will stick in your mind forever. It's like going back in time, to a world you may never have known existed.

2. St. Andrews. Of all the British Open venues, none compares to the Old Course, and no host city compares to St. Andrews, the small, medieval city that is the original home of golf. Although it is home to the University of St. Andrews, the third-oldest university in the English-speaking world, St. Andrews is more like a small town, with only about 16,500 residents. There's a downtown commercial district several blocks away, but the heart and soul of St. Andrews is a short walk from the Old Course, where golf shops, souvenir shops, pubs, and hotels abound. If you walk off the back of the 18th green, turn right, and proceed about 100 yards up that narrow street, you come to a busy corner with a major tourist-attraction golf shop on one corner and a popular restaurant/pub on the other. During Open week, laughter and well-oiled golf fans spill out into the streets.

At the 2005 Open I shared a house with three other writers that abuts the 18th fairway. Whereas most of our colleagues rented dorm rooms at the university, we stumbled across this house on the Internet—a one-minute walk to the golf course.

1. The courses. The difference between golf over here and golf over there cannot be overstated. Whether you're lucky enough to play one of the exalted courses in the British Open rota or some no-name loop on the outskirts of town, it is a different kind of golf in every way. You will be called upon to hit golf shots we simply don't have to hit over here, say, the 100-yard bump-and-run over an insane series of mounds and the 80-yard putt from the fairway come to mind. Leave your 60-degree wedge at home because you won't hit it more than twice during a week of golf in the UK. They play a ground game, and you learn to adapt pretty quickly.

On many courses, another issue is the gorse, or heather, which is a benign-sounding name for shin-deep wiry grass that is impossible to play out of—assuming you can find your ball. Lay your bag down in that stuff and you can lose your bag—which is also why, if you aren't straight off the tee, you are wise to leave the driver in the bag in favor of a long iron or hybrid.

The weather cannot be ignored. During the course of a single round, it can go from sunny and calm to windy and raining sideways and then back again. Never a dull moment.

5 WORST

5. The flight over. Most flights to the UK leave in the early evening, fly all night (eight hours) and arrive about 8 a.m., just in time for rush hour in Europe.

If you can sleep on the plane, you're fine. If you cannot, and I cannot, you arrive stiff, cramped, and exhausted, just as a new day is dawning.

4. Driving. Driving on the left side is not something you do without training and practice.

In 1998, when I was headed to my first British Open. I was concerned about the 45-mile drive from the airport in Manchester, England, to Southport, home of Royal Birkdale. One of my golf writer buddies who I was sharing a house with told me not to worry. He was a veteran of several British Opens and of driving on the left. He'd rent a car for the week and I could ride shotgun. Sounded like a plan, until we were standing in the Hertz office at the Manchester airport and my buddy discovered he had managed to leave his driver's license back home in New Jersey. Hertz would rent him a car, but he was not allowed to drive. "No problem," he said, handing me the keys. Ten minutes later, I was behind the wheel, merging into morning rush-hour traffic on Manchester's equivalent of an L.A. expressway. By the end of the week, I was an old pro, weaving in and out of traffic, whizzing around narrow, country roads, negotiating round-abouts like a New York cabbie.

3. Smoking. The antismoking craze that swept across America years ago has yet to reach the shores of the UK. Restaurants, bars, media centers—they're all full of smoke.

2. The food. All the snarky clichés you hear about how lousy the food is in the UK—true, all true. So much of the cuisine is inexplicably bland and borderline inedible, which is surprising considering we're talking about such an ancient and cultured part of the world. Try starting the day with the "Full English" breakfast (eggs, fatty bacon, fried bread, and baked beans) or Bangers and Mash (fatty sausage and mashed potatoes) or Shepherd's Pie (minced lamb, veggies, and mashed potatoes). While in Scotland, be sure not to miss the haggis (don't even ask). The thing is that even when it is a food or dish you recognize and like back home, they have a way of preparing it in the most unappetizing way. Even the pizza joints and Chinese "take-away" places don't measure up. One of the favorite meals over there—sort of their answer to a burger and fries—is fish and chips, or fried fish and fries. Not a bad concept, except they have a way of making the fish and the chips so limp and greasy as to be revolting. One year, one of the guys I was sharing a house with left a half-eaten order of fish and chips in a paper bag on the dining room table. The next morning, the grease had leeched out of the bag and eaten through the varnish on the table.

The good news is that I always counted on the British Open to help me lose five pounds.

1. Prices. Depending on the exchange rate between the U.S. dollar and the British pound, figure on everything costing 50 to 100 percent more than back home. Hotels, restaurants, car rentals, soft drinks in a convenience store, a round of golf—everything is expensive. You can drive yourself nuts pinching pennies, or you can grin and bear it.

Still, minor annoyances aside, the British Open is the best tournament in golf.

★ ★ ★ ★

"Some of us worship in churches, some in synagogues, some on golf courses."

—Adlai Stevenson

GOLF CLICHÉS

You've heard the announcers use them on TV. You use them on the course. Clichés are part of golf's official language. Here are the best of the best, or worst of the worst.

18. "Better than most." We have Gary Koch to thank for this one. He uttered the famous line several times while describing Tiger Woods making a miracle putt on 17 at TPC Sawgrass. Now we do the same thing when he bags one from long distance.

17. "It's in the hole!" We have Carl Spackler, a.k.a. Bill Murray, to thank for this one.

16. "Touch of a blacksmith." The perfect description for that finesse chip that you just skulled 30 yards over the green.

15. "Worm burner." Oh, for the innocent worms that have perished when we sent out drives skittering along the grass. Pause now for a moment of silence.

14. "Don't worry, it's a par 5." This one often is heard after you hit that worm burner off the tee on a par 5. The phrase gives you the false hope that you still can make up for your bad shot.

13. "Good miss." This is a favorite. It means you hit a bad shot but still managed to get a good result. A stay of execution if you will.

12. "You're in jail." Not a good miss. With your ball stuck behind a tree or some other treacherous spot, you're well on your way to a scorecard-busting hole.

11. "Snowman." The dreaded snowman. The ugliest creature in golf, especially when you have to record an 8 on a par 3.

10. "Time to let the big dog eat." Yep, you're ready to unload with your driver. The trouble is that for most of us, the big dog usually goes hungry.

9. "Hit it on the screws." A blast from the past, referring to an era when drivers actually had screws. I didn't hit it on the screws back then, and I still don't now.

8. "Dance floor." Yes, you're on the green. My favorite version of this cliché came when I was playing with a novice golfer, who said, "I'm on the lawn."

7. "Short grass." Otherwise known as the fairway. Most of us still are looking for the short grass.

6. "Never up, never in." Makes only sense. There's a strong chance you won't make your putt if the ball doesn't reach the hole. Of course, there's also a strong chance you'll 3-putt if you knock your first putt 15 feet past the hole.

5. "Nice putt, Alice." Another term for a tentative, wimpy putt that comes up far short. Chauvinistic to be sure. I'm sure there's an Alice who made more than her share of putts.

4. "Still a little meat left on that bone." Another dog reference. You've just been told by your opponent that he's not conceding you that 3-footer for triple bogey.

3. "I hit a great putt." Those of us in the press room have heard this cliché many times from Tiger Woods in talking about a missed putt. Maybe that's what makes him so great. In his mind, he never thinks he hit a bad putt.

2. "How did that stay out?" Surely, there was some supernatural force that kept the ball out of the hole. There can't be any other explanation.

1. "Drive for show, putt for dough." The essence of golf. The 300-yard drive counts the same as the 4-putt. There are a million guys who can hit the ball a long way, but the guys who can make the 4-footers in the crunch time, a small fraternity, cash the checks.

★ ★ ★ ★

"Golf is a game in which you yell 'fore,' shoot six, and write down five."

—Paul Harvey

THE TOP TEN MISUSED TERMS IN GOLF

▶BY TRAVIS LESSER

A Rules of Golf Associate with the U.S. Golf Association, Travis Lesser answers thousands of telephone and e-mail questions every year about the Rules of Golf is acutely sensitive to mistakes made on the game's traditional terminology. Lesser, a former teaching professional and tournament director, knows all too well when golfers use terms incorrectly that are not defined in the rules. This list first appeared in several USGA publications.

10, 9, and 8. Through the green, Rough, Fairway. These terms are typically misused when referring to areas of the course. The misnomer with the first term is that most people tend to believe "through the green" means the area over the back of the green. However, if an area of the golf course is not a hazard (i.e., a bunker or a water hazard) and is not the teeing ground or the putting green of the hole you are playing, it is "through the green."

Next, the words "rough" and "fairway" appear only once in the Rules of Golf when used to define the term "closely mown area" with regard to a player being entitled to relief from a ball embedded in its own pitch-mark in Rule 25-2. Although all golfers at all skill levels use these terms, you will not be able to find these words as a reference point when attempting to look up a Rule pertaining to the Rules of Golf book. Both of these areas simply fall under one term: "through the green."

7. Waste area/Waste bunker. Many modern golf courses have areas people sometimes referred to as "waste areas" or "waste bunkers." These are generally areas that don't meet the definition of a water hazard, in that they are not an open water course (whether or not containing water), and they do not meet the definition of bunker as they are not a prepared area where soil has been removed and replaced with sand. Generally, these areas are unmaintained natural areas installed by modern-day course architects to add another test for golfers to negotiate and, alas, are simply "through the green." Conversely, some such areas do meet the definition of bunker but are erroneously termed by the committee in charge of a golf course as "waste bunkers" and played as "through the green," which is contrary to the Rules of Golf.

6. Trap. Because we've touched on bunkers, let's get another misnomer out of the way. Most people refer to these sand-filled areas as traps or sand traps. Now, the last time I checked, a "trap" is not something anyone or anything wants to be in (i.e., bear traps, rat traps, speed traps) and are difficult if not impossible to escape. A bunker, however, has a much more positive connotation to it and is the proper term as defined in the Rules of Golf. What's more, if you would attempt to look up the word "trap" in the Rules of Golf, your search will be fruitless because the word does not appear in the Rules.

5 and 4. Cup and Pin. The next two most misused terms that are not defined in the Rules of Golf (and, along with "trap," the most commonly used) are "cup" and "pin." It is a bit of a mystery as to how these two words came to replace the proper terms of "hole" and "flagstick," as it is just as easy to refer to it as a "flag" or a "stick." I for one instinctively cringe when I hear television announcers refer to the hole location as the day's "pin placement." After all, the purpose of the game as laid out in Rule 1-1 is to put the ball in the hole, not in the pin.

3. Tee box. Another term used incorrectly to describe an area of the course is "tee box." The area where play of a hole begins is a rectangular area, two club-lengths in depth, and the width of the tee-markers. The proper term for this area as found in the Rules of Golf is "teeing ground."

2. Rub of the green. Next, a favorite golf term is "rub of the green," which is perhaps the most commonly misused term in the Rules. A rub of the green occurs when a ball in motion is accidentally deflected or stopped by an outside agency. Most think of it simply as bad luck, but bear in mind that a rub of the green can also be a good thing. Sure, it's frustrating when you hit a perfectly good shot and the ball heads toward the flagstick, only to have it strike the flag and careen into the greenside bunker. But a rub of the green can also occur when you hit a ball destined for out of bounds or a bad place and it miraculously strikes a tree and comes to rest in a more desirable spot or, as some like to call it, a "member's bounce."

1. Foursome. Most people refer to their group of golf buddies as their "foursome." For anyone who watched the Ryder Cup or Presidents Cup, they learned that foursomes is a form of play in which partners play one ball alternately from the teeing grounds and alternately during play of each hole. I'm sure a vast majority of you aren't alternating shots with your partner (nor would you possibly want to), so using that word to describe your group of four is not proper.

FAVORITE MOMENTS

►BY JIM NANTZ

CBS's Jim Nantz has a standard line about when he intends to retire. He says it will be on April 8, 2035, the day he finishes broadcasting his 50th Masters. "The voice of golf" figures to pick up more memories along the way. The first 25 years of announcing golf provided Nantz with a host of unforgettable moments. Here are his favorites.

10. 1997 PGA Championship. Davis Love III captures the title at Winged Foot. As he lined up his final putt, a spectacular rainbow appeared. Director Steve Milton had cameraman Davey Finch shoot it so the cup became the "pot of gold" at the end of the rainbow.

9. 1995 Masters. An emotional Ben Crenshaw, nearing the end of his competitive days, wins his second Masters just days after his longtime teacher and mentor Harvey Penick is laid to rest. My first Masters in the 18th tower. It was just so emotional to see him channel the spirit of Harvey Penick.

8. 1991 PGA Championship. PGA Tour rookie, John Daly, the ninth alternate, not only made it into the tournament at the last minute, but he also stunned the golf world with mammoth drives that tamed the long and difficult Crooked Stick course, leading to an improbable victory.

7. 1996 Masters. Nick Faldo wins his third Masters as Greg Norman inexplicably squanders a 6-shot lead in the final round. It was heartbreaking to see Norman fall short in the tournament he desperately wanted to win the most.

6. 2009 PGA Championship. Y. E. Yang of South Korea outduels Tiger Woods in the final round at Hazeltine to become the first Asian-born golfer to win a men's major title. It was also the first time that Woods failed to win a major that he had led after 54 holes.

5. 2004 Masters. Phil Mickelson claims his first-ever major championship and Masters Green Jacket in a compelling back-nine shootout with Ernie Els. I love those stories in which the athlete silences all the questions. As Mickelson birdied the final hole, I summed up his frustration with the call: "Is it his time? Yes, at long last!"

4. 1997 Masters. Tiger Woods, 21 years and 104 days old, wins the Masters by 12 strokes over Tom Kite. It was the one Masters I broadcast that was devoid of drama, but it had its own kind of drama. It had so much significance that it transcended the sport. My call on 18: "A win for the ages."

3. 1986 Masters. Jack Nicklaus wins his historic sixth Green Jacket at the age of 46. When Nicklaus made his birdie on 16, I said, "The Bear has come out of hibernation." As much as I'd like to think that I had always been preparing myself for that moment, I must confess that I was so nervous, my teeth were chattering involuntarily. I was worried that my open microphone would pick up the noise emanating from my clicking molars. That night Ken Venturi told me, "You may be lucky enough to cover 50 Masters, but I promise you that you'll never see a greater one than the one you saw today."

2. 2010 Masters. Phil Mickelson's victory was the ultimate example of an athlete in an individual playing for someone other than himself. He wanted to win for his wife, Amy, who was suffering from breast cancer. Very emotional and memorable.

1. 1992 Masters. My college roommate at the University of Houston, Fred Couples, wins the Masters. I got to interview him for the Green Jacket ceremony, just as we rehearsed in our dorm room in 1979. I said, "It's a perfect fit. Fred Couples, Masters champion." I cannot imagine ever witnessing a moment that will touch me more deeply than this perfect fulfillment of a glorious dream that was shared by intimate friends for so many years.

★ ★ ★ ★

"Golf is the most fun you can have without taking your clothes off."

—Chi Chi Rodriguez

YO, TEACH

One of the best ways to improve your golf game, aside from practice, practice, and more practice, involves seeking out the best possible certified PGA of America instructor your budget will allow and take some lessons. Virtually all the pros, men and women, have their own swing gurus, and the following five are generally regarded among the best. None will take on just any old student off the street unless lots of zeroes are written on the check. We also did a little research and managed to uncover some pricey details that indicate they clearly don't teach cheap.

5. Jim McLean. A fine player who qualified for the U.S. Amateur four times and the U.S. Open twice, McLean's main operation, the Jim McLean Golf School, is located at the Doral golf resort in the Miami suburbs, with five other sites around the country. A three-day golf school taught by McLean instructors goes for $1,875. If you want McLean's individual attention, a package that includes a 90-minute lesson and 18 holes at Doral with McLean, it runs $5,000, lunch included. Among his past star pupils are Tom Kite, Ben Crenshaw, Cristie Kerr, Alexis Thompson, Dan Marino, Bill Murray, and Pat Riley. *Golf Digest* reported he gets $500 an hour for an individual lesson.

4. Dave Pelz. Generally acknowledged as the finest teacher of the short game and putting, Pelz has schools in seven locations around the country and another in Ireland. Ten of his pupils have won 18 major championships, including four-time major winner Phil Mickelson. A three-day Pelz golf school at the PGA National course in Palm Beach Gardens, Florida, runs $2,475, with Pelz's instructors handling the teaching. Pelz himself has a day rate of $30,000, usually targeted to corporations who want him to conduct clinics or offer instruction at a company golf outing.

3. David Leadbetter. The Englishman made his reputation as the man who helped Nick Faldo win six major championships, but his roster of students also includes players like Greg Norman, Nick Price, Ernie Els, Se Ri Pak, and Michelle Wie. Headquarters for the four-acre David Leadbetter Golf Academy are located in Orlando, Florida, with 27 other academies located in the United States and 12 other countries around the world. According to his Web site, a three-hour session with Leadbetter runs $3,500, and the so-called "David Leadbetter Experience" is a full day of one-on-one instruction with Leads himself as well as a fitness and flexibility analysis, a session with a sports psychologist, and a complementary custom-fitted Callaway driver, all for $10,000. They'll even spring for lunch.

2. Hank Haney. The native of Deerfield, Illinois, began teaching golf in 1976 and estimates he's given over 40,000 golf lessons ever since. For six years Haney was the swing instructor for Tiger Woods until they parted company in May 2010. Before that, he helped two-time major champion Mark O'Meara, who first recommended him to Woods. Haney has four golf schools, all located in Texas, with his main operation at Vista Ridge in the Dallas suburbs. A three-day golf school with one of Haney's "senior instructors" costs $2,279, but nowhere on the Haney Web site is there any mention of one-on-one with Haney himself. Still, wouldn't it be priceless to get a lesson from a man who actually taught Charles Barkley how to get his golf ball airborne. *Golf Digest* estimated his rate at $500 an hour.

Hank Haney (R) instructs Charles Barkley.

1. Butch Harmon. The son of 1948 Masters champion Claude Harmon, Butch played on the PGA Tour for several years until he turned to teaching in the early 1970s. He began working with Tiger Woods when the No. 1 player in the world was a teenager and stayed with him until they parted company not so amicably in 2004. Harmon's main charge these days is Phil Mickelson, and he also works with Adam Scott, Stewart Cink, and Natalie Gulbis among others, not to mention being the personal teacher for the King of Morocco. His base camp is at Rio Secco Golf Club in Las Vegas, and a three-day package with instruction that includes Harmon and his staff runs $5,900, including four nights at Caesars Palace. Harmon's Web site says he "does not offer personal lessons at this time." When he did, he was paid $600 an hour.

SWEETEST SWINGS

Who has the best-looking swing in the game? It's all in the eye of the beholder, of course, and very much open to debate. Here's our list, in several divisions.

CURRENT PGA TOUR

10. Rory McIlroy

9. Charles Howell III

8. Trevor Immelman

7. Steve Elkington

6. Tiger Woods

5. Ernie Els

4. Adam Scott

3. Luke Donald

2. Paul Casey

1. Geoff Ogilvy

CURRENT LPGA TOUR

10. Beth Bauer

9. Paula Creamer

8. Hee Young Park

7. Ai Miyazato

6. Suzann Pettersen

5. Grace Park

4. Se Ri Pak

3. Michelle Wie

2. Karrie Webb

1. Angela Park

ALL-TIME GREATS

10. Annika Sorenstam

9. Greg Norman

8. Johnny Miller

7. Jack Nicklaus

6. Tom Watson

5. Mickey Wright

4. Bobby Jones

3. Ben Hogan

2. Byron Nelson

1. Sam Snead

★ ★ ★ ★

"You are meant to play the ball as it lies, a fact that may help to touch on your own objective approach to life."

—Grantland Rice

SURPRISE MAJOR WINNERS

The majors usually are about Jones, Hogan, Nicklaus, Sorenstam, and Woods. But every once in a while, a no-name emerges from the pack and somehow manages to hang on to win. For several players, it is a one-and-done experience, as they never contend again. Regardless, they forever will be known as "a major winner."

There have been many surprise major winners. Here is our ranking of some of the most memorable.

14. Orville Moody. Known as the "Sarge," Moody had only one victory on the PGA Tour. But it was a big one. He won the 1969 U.S. Open, beating Deane Beman, Bob Rosburg, and Al Geiberger by a shot. Moody was an excellent ball striker, but he was held back by putting problems. However, for one week in 1969, he conquered the greens to become a U.S. Open champion.

13. Paul Lawrie. Nobody even mentioned his name during the 1999 British Open at Carnoustie. He was 10 shots back going into the final day, and the focus was completely on Jean Van de Velde. But when the Frenchman made his epic collapse on 18, Lawrie suddenly found himself in a three-way playoff; Justin Leonard rounded out the trio. Lawrie prevailed to win the Claret Jug. Of course, nobody remembers that tournament as the one in which Lawrie won. Nobody but Lawrie, that is.

12. Rich Beem. Even though Beem won the International a few weeks before, he hardly was a favorite going into the 2002 PGA Championship. He was better known for being the subject of a book by Alan Shipnuck depicting his wild rookie year. Beem, though, remained hot at Hazeltine and withstood a final round rush by Tiger Woods to win his major.

11. Louis Oosthuizen. Louis who? Nobody heard of the young South African before the 2010 British Open at St. Andrews. Then it took three days for people to learn how to pronounce his name. Oosthuizen wasn't just a surprise winner. He dominated, winning by seven shots. All hail Louis Oost-something.

10. Y. E. Yang. Hazeltine produced another surprise winner when the PGA returned in 2009. Again, Yang didn't come completely out of nowhere. He won the

Honda Classic earlier in the year. Still, nobody figured the South Korean had the game to do it in a major. Turns out he did, and like Beem, he beat Woods to become a major champion.

9. Shaun Micheel. The PGA produced a series of surprise major winners during the first decade of the twenty-first century. Micheel definitely was an unexpected champion at the 2003 PGA at Oak Hill. Ranked 169th in the world at the time, Micheel closed out Chad Campbell by hitting a spectacular approach to inches on 18 on Sunday, sealing the victory.

8. Birdie Kim. Led by Se Ri Pak, South Korea has produced a long line of top women golfers. Kim added her name to the honor roll with a stunning performance in the 2005 U.S. Women's Open. In only her second year on the LPGA Tour, she shocked Morgan Pressel and the golf world by holing out from the bunker for birdie on 18 to win the title by a stroke. As a result, Kim also landed on another list: "Greatest Shots of All Time."

7. Todd Hamilton. Hamilton found himself grinding on the Japan Tour during much his career. Tired of the commute, he rejoined the U.S. PGA Tour in 2003 and broke through by winning the 2004 Honda Classic. Still, it seemed highly unlikely he would challenge in, let alone win a major. But there he was at the 2004 British Open in a playoff with Ernie Els. Again, he was the big underdog, but using his hybrid off the green, Hamilton proved to have enough game to win his major.

6. Ben Curtis. Curtis was an unheralded PGA Tour rookie when he qualified for the 2003 British Open. Unheralded rookies don't win majors. Curtis, though, defied the staggering odds to play his way into contention. Then he benefited to win the title as Thomas Bjorn imploded down the stretch. He became the first player since Francis Ouimet in 1913 to win while appearing in his first major.

5. Andy North. North only won three times on the PGA Tour. However, two of them were at the U.S. Open, winning in 1978 and 1985. Both times, the titles were unexpected. North's career could be defined as a case of quality over quantity.

4. Hillary Lunke. Lunke has had one moment in her career—and it's a big one. In 2003 she won the U.S. Women's Open. She withstood a battle with Annika Sorenstam on Sunday and then defeated Kelly Robbins and Angela Stanford in an 18-hole playoff. It is her only top-ten finish in a major and her lone victory.

3. John Daly. He was the ninth alternate at the 1991 PGA Championship. It was an upset that he even got into the field. Daly made the most of his opportunity. Wrapping the club around his neck, the world got its first taste of Daly when he won the title at Crooked Stick. It wouldn't be the last.

2. Jack Fleck. Fleck's story is well known. He was the club pro from Iowa who shocked Ben Hogan in a playoff to win the 1955 U.S. Open. Most people assume it was his only moment of glory in golf. It wasn't. He won two PGA Tour events and finished third in the 1960 U.S. Open. So the Open victory wasn't just a one-shot deal for Fleck.

1. Francis Ouimet. He was golf's first true underdog winner in a major. The legendary story of the 20-year old amateur who won the 1913 U.S. Open made front-page news. It probably sparked America's love affair with the game. In 1913 only 300,000 Americans played golf. Ten years later the number was up to two million, thanks largely to Ouimet.

THE BIGGEST UPSETS

Unlike tennis, the gap between the best player and the No. 200 is minute. Usually the best player prevails, but the possibility always is there for a shocker. All it takes is for a player to hold it together for four rounds to make history. To qualify for this list, the underdog had to take down the top player in a major. Here is the list of the biggest upsets in golf.

7. Steve Jones over Tom Lehman and Davis Love III. A series of injuries derailed Jones's career in the 1990s. In fact, he hadn't qualified for the U.S. Open in five years when he entered the tournament as a sectional qualifier. Lehman and Love, meanwhile, were at the top of their games and were favorites to win at Oakland Hills. Both players, however, blew the opportunity. Lehman squandered a 3-shot lead during the final round, and Love missed a three-foot par putt on 18 that would have put him in a playoff. Jones's round of 69 was good enough for a 1-shot victory.

6. Kel Nagle over Arnold Palmer. Palmer was the toast of golf when he arrived at the 1960 British Open. He was looking to nab the third leg of the Grand Slam after winning the Masters and U.S. Open. Nagle, meanwhile, was a 39-year-old Australian who never had finished in a top ten in a major. Yet it was Nagle who proved to be a roadblock in Palmer's bid for history. His 1-shot victory saw him, not Palmer, walking off St. Andrews with the Claret Jug.

5. Larry Mize over Greg Norman and Seve Ballesteros. It was a case of what's-he-doing-in-this-picture when Mize found himself in a playoff against Greg Norman and Seve Ballesteros in the 1987 Masters. Norman and Ballesteros were the two top players in the game, whereas Mize had only one PGA Tour victory at the time. But it was Mize who wore the Green Jacket after stunning Norman with his famous chip-in at 11.

4. Hillary Lunke over Annika Sorenstam. Hillary who? Lunke came out of nowhere to play herself into contention at the 2003 U.S. Women's Open. Still, there was no way she was going to beat Sorenstam on the final day, right? Lunke did, as it was Sorenstam who folded, recording a bogey on the final hole on Sunday. Lunke actually had to defeat Angela Stanford and Kelly Robbins in a playoff the following day to win the title. But most people remember this victory for her ability to hold off Sorenstam.

3. Y. E. Yang over Tiger Woods. Woods looked like he was going to go wire-to-wire at the 2009 PGA Championship. He held a 2-shot lead going into the final round, and Woods never loses on Sunday. Padraig Harrington was expected to give him the biggest challenge, but he had a terrible day. Instead, it was Yang who stepped up. A relatively unknown South Korean, Yang didn't wilt playing with Woods; instead, it was Woods who stumbled, shooting a 75. Yang, who shot a 70, closed with a terrific shot to the green on 18, putting an exclamation mark on his stunning victory.

2. Francis Ouimet over Harry Vardon and Ted Ray. This upset was so big that Hollywood actually made a movie about it. Ouimet, a local caddy using a 10-year-old as his caddy surely would be no match for the accomplished Vardon and Ray in the 1913 U.S. Open. The 20-year-old hung tough to get into the three-way playoff. Then, amazingly, he won, becoming the first amateur to win the Open.

1. Jack Fleck over Ben Hogan. This one also should be worthy of Hollywood. Ben Hogan was seeking his fifth title at the 1955 U.S. Open. Fleck, meanwhile, was a club pro at a tiny 9-hole course in Iowa. Improbably, Fleck somehow advanced to an 18-hole playoff with Hogan by rolling in a birdie putt on the 72nd hole. The playoff was billed as a David-and-Goliath match, but actually Goliath (Hogan) was weary and aching for the playoff. He had nothing left, shooting a 72. Fleck, meanwhile, played superb, firing a 69 for the improbable and memorable victory for the ages.

When Johnny Miller first mentioned the word "choke" in the context of a golfer on an NBC telecast, there was an audible gasp in the golf world. How could Miller say such a thing? Miller countered that when a player 3-putts from five feet to lose a tournament, that's a choke. There's no other way to label it.

Golf has had more than its share of memorable chokes. In some cases, a fatal collapse in the clutch has gone on to define a player's case. If you say a player pulled a "Van de Velde," no further explanation is needed.

Here are the most infamous chokes in golf.

16. Retief Goosen and Jason Gore, 2005 U.S. Open. Goosen took a 3-shot lead over Gore into the final round at Pinehurst No. 2, but both men disintegrated on Sunday. Goosen shot 81, with 36 putts and nine lip-outs to tie for 11th, and Gore posted 84 to tie for 48th on a day when New Zealand's Michael Campbell came out of the pack and won the tournament, beating runner-up Tiger Woods by two shots.

15. Ken Venturi, 1956 Masters. Amateur sensation Ken Venturi had a 4-shot lead after 54 holes and was eight ahead of Jack Burke, Jr. when the final round began. On a day of high winds and brutal conditions that saw the field average 78.2 strokes, Venturi soared to an 8-over 80 and Burke posted 71, tying Sam Snead for the low round. Burke's 1-over 289 remains tied for the highest 72-hole score in Masters history, but his 8-shot comeback is a tournament record as well.

14. Tom Kite, 1989 U.S. Open. Everyone remembers Curtis Strange winning his second straight Open at Oak Hill in Rochester, but Kite will never forget opening a 3-shot lead after 57 holes and then missing an 18-inch putt to make triple bogey at No. 5 and blowing a 3-footer for a double bogey at the 13th. Kite shot 78 that day and said afterward, "my play stunk."

13. McDonald Smith, 1925 British Open. A native of Carnoustie, Mac Smith took a 5-shot lead into the final round at Prestwick, only to shoot 82 and finish fourth, three shots behind champion Jim Barnes. The great British golf writer, Bernard Darwin, described his meltdown as "a tragedy of frittering."

12. Patty Sheehan, 1990 U.S. Women's Open. Sheehan suffered a two-day meltdown at the 1990 U.S. Women's Open. She held a 12-shot lead during the third round. Game over, right? Nope. Sheehan played the final 33 holes in 9-over. Betsy King took advantage to win by a shot.

11. Sam Snead, 1939 U.S. Open. Sam Snead had one major gap on his résumé: He never won a U.S. Open. He could have taken care of that at the 1939 U.S. Open. He came to the par-5 18th hole needing a par to win. However, Snead didn't know that. He thought a birdie was required. As a result, he played aggressively, getting himself in all sorts of trouble. The end result was a triple bogey 8. No U.S. Open on this day—or ever—for Snead.

10. Mark Calcavecchia, 1991 Ryder Cup. Rarely has the pressure of the moment ever debilitated a golfer more than what happened to Mark Calcavecchia at the 1991 Ryder Cup. During his singles match with Colin Montgomerie in the famous "War on the Shore," Calcavecchia was 4-up with four holes to play. All he needed was to halve a hole to give the Ryder Cup to the United States. Calcavecchia couldn't do it, though, as he lost the next four holes to halve the match. The lasting image is of Calcavecchia shanking his tee shot into the water in the par-3 17th. Afterward, he was in tears. Even though the United States wound up winning the Cup, it was a bittersweet day for Calc.

9. Colin Montgomerie, 2006 U.S. Open. No list of chokes would be complete without Colin Montgomerie. He just couldn't get it done in a major. His opportunity seemed to be at hand at the 2006 U.S. Open. He came to Winged Foot's 18th hole tied for the lead. After hitting a perfect tee shot, he chunked a 7-iron, leaving him in heavy rough surrounding the green. He eventually took a double-bogey 6 and wound up tied for second with Phil Mickelson, who would have his own choke on this day.

8. Arnold Palmer, 1961 Masters. Leading by a shot going into the 72nd hole, The King played like a pitiful pauper on No. 18, going from greenside bunker to greenside bunker on his way to a disastrous double bogey. Gary Player managed to get up and down from the sand at 18 and, despite his own final round of 74, became the tournament's first international champion, prevailing by a shot over Palmer and amateur Charles Coe.

7. Phil Mickelson, 2006 U.S. Open. Phil Mickelson's course management skills always have been the subject of debate, but never more so than at the 18th hole on Sunday at the 2006 U.S. Open. Sitting on a 1-shot lead, he pulled out his driver despite hitting only two fairways for the day. He promptly hit a major cut that bounced off a hospitality tent. Instead of playing it safe from there, Mickelson tried for a miracle shot, which hit a tree branch. He ultimately made a double bogey 6, leaving him one shot behind Geoff Ogilvy. Afterward he said, "I am such an idiot." Nobody disagreed with him on this day.

6. Ed Sneed, 1979 Masters. Ed Sneed was a journeyman player on the verge of a career moment at the 1979 Masters. He held a 3-shot lead with three holes to play on Sunday. Then it all fell apart as he proceeded to bogey the next three holes. Just to torment him, his putt on 18 came agonizingly close to falling. Instead, he wound up losing in a playoff to Fuzzy Zoeller.

5. Doug Sanders, 1970 British Open. Doug Sanders had a successful run in the 1960s, but he never won a major. Finally, his big moment was at hand during the 1970 British Open at St. Andrews. Leading Jack Nicklaus by one shot, he needed only a 2-putt from 30 feet on 18 to win the Claret Jug. His approach putt left him three feet from victory. Sanders, though, couldn't get it done, as his short putt skimmed over the right lip. Nicklaus wound up winning an 18-hole playoff the following day.

4. Scott Hoch, 1989 Masters. Scott Hoch faced his ultimate moment at the 1989 Masters. On the first hole of a playoff against Nick Faldo, Hoch needed a two-and-a-half-foot par putt to seal the victory. He studied the putt forever, and that probably doomed him. He hit a terrible putt, knocking it five feet past the hole. He would make the comebacker to extend the playoff, but he would lose on the next hole. Unfortunately, his name didn't help matters on this day. "Hoch as in choke" made for an easy headline.

3. Arnold Palmer, 1966 U.S. Open. The final nine holes of the 1966 U.S. Open should have been a coronation for Arnold Palmer, who had a 7-shot lead. Then it all unraveled. Billy Casper did his part, shooting a 32 on the back nine to put pressure on Palmer. Palmer wilted under the pressure, shooting a 40 on the back nine. With the 7-shot lead gone, Casper eventually beat Palmer in a playoff the following day.

2. Greg Norman, 1966 Masters. Greg Norman had many close calls and heartbreaks in majors. But if there is one day that defines his career, it would be the final round of the 1996 Masters. Sitting on a 6-shot lead, Norman looked as if he finally would win the tournament he coveted the most. Early on, though, you could tell Norman was in choke mode. It was agonizing to watch as Norman made one mistake after another. In the end, it wasn't even close. Norman shot a 78, losing to Nick Faldo by 5 shots. Norman never would get his Green Jacket.

1. Jean Van de Velde, 1999 British Open. What can you say? Jean Van de Velde came to the 18th hole at Carnoustie needing only a double bogey to win the 1999 British Open. The par-4 18th is a diabolically tough hole, but with two 5-irons and a wedge to the green and then an even 3-putt, Van de Velde could have still won the title. Instead, in a fatal decision, Van de Velde takes the driver off the tee and blocks it way right. His second shot hits the grandstand around the green and careens into the heavy rough. A dismal attempt to hack it out saw the ball land in the burn.

Van de Velde thought about hitting it out, even taking off his shoes and socks and wading into the water. At this point, the entire scene was playing out like a tragic comedy. He ultimately decided against playing from the water. However, the damage was done, as Van de Velde took an unthinkable triple bogey 7. He then would lose in a playoff to Paul Lawrie, thus sealing his fate forever. Van de Velde would be another term for choke.

THE TEN GREATEST
CHAMPIONS TOUR PLAYERS ▶BY VARTAN KUPELIAN

Vartan Kupelian, the longtime golf writer for the *Detroit News*, covered a number of senior Champions Tour events over the years. In the summer of 2010, on the 30th anniversary of the founding of the Champions Tour, he came up with a list of his all-time top-ten players on the 50-and-over circuit, once described as a professional golfer's mulligan on life.

10. Tom Watson. He's won 12 times, including five senior major titles. And at age 59, he posted the best finish ever by a senior in a major championship when he finished second to Stewart Cink at the 2009 British Open at Turnberry, losing in a playoff. He also made the cut at age 60 at the 2010 U.S. Open at Pebble Beach. And he's not done yet.

9. Jim Colbert. Winner of 20 events, he was Champions Tour Player of the Year in 1995 and 1996 as well as Rookie of the Year in 1991 and Comeback Player of the Year in 1998.

8. Don January. He won the first event ever, in 1980, and the money title three times. January won 22 times and claimed multiple events six straight years. He also won the Byron Nelson Award five times.

7. Miller Barber. No. 4 on the all-time win list (with 24 wins), he won at least once a year over nine straight years (1981–1989). Barber won the U.S. Senior Open three straight years starting in 1982 and led the money list twice, 1981–82.

6. Gil Morgan. An outstanding record in the Hale Irwin era, which is saying a lot. His 68.83 scoring average in 2000 is the third lowest ever (Irwin's 68.59 in '98 is best). In 2000 Morgan had 31 subpar rounds, the most ever. In 1997 he had 26 subpar rounds, the second most ever. He's No. 3 on the all-time win list, with 25.

5. Bob Charles. The left-hander from New Zealand has the most top-ten finishes in a career, 203, and led the money list in 1988 and 1989. He ranks fifth overall, with 23 Champions Tour victories.

4. Jack Nicklaus. His Champions Tour career wasn't as lengthy as some, but his triumphs were significant, including the Senior Players Championship in 1980 with a 261 score, 27 under par, and still the 72-hole scoring record. Eight of his ten victories on the Champions Tour were in majors over a seven-year span.

3. Chi Chi Rodriguez. Four straight victories (1987) is still the record, and he is No. 6 in total victories, with 22, with eight straight years (1986–1993) with at least one victory. He may also be the most colorful player in the tour's history.

2. Lee Trevino. No. 2 on the win list, with 29, he holds the record for the most top-ten finishes in a season, 26, in 1990. Four Champions Tour majors include the Senior PGA twice, the U.S. Senior Open, and the JELD-WEN Tradition. Like Rodriguez, he was a huge crowd pleaser as well.

1. Hale Irwin. He dominated for a decade-plus, or more than one-third the history of the Champions Tour. He has 45 victories, 16 more than his closest rival, and for 11 years he won multiple events. His list of accomplishments goes on and on, including 19 straight top-five finishes from 1997 to 1998. Incredible.

★ ★ ★ ★

"The income tax has made more liars out of the American people than golf has."

—Will Rogers

THE GREATEST PGA CHAMPIONSHIPS

The PGA Championship has always been considered the least glamorous of the four majors, but that doesn't mean it's not among the most coveted titles in the game. In recent years the PGA of America, which runs the event, also has made a significant push to contest the tournament at a classic golf course, definitely improving its stature among players and fans alike.

From 1916 to 1957 the PGA Championship was decided in a match-play format before switching to stroke play in 1958. The tournament also has had some rather obscure winners, many of them counting the PGA as their only major title.

11. May day. Tiger Woods found himself two shots behind on the front nine before staging a dramatic comeback against journeyman Bob May in the 2000 event at Valhalla in Louisville. Woods played the last 12 holes in regulation in 7-under, and when May brushed in a 15-foot birdie putt at the 18th, Woods had to make a knee-knocking 6-footer himself to force a 3-hole playoff. "That's why he's Tiger Woods," May said after Woods prevailed in overtime with a birdie and two pars for his third major title of the season—and the third leg of his "Tiger Slam," when he won the 2001 Masters for four in a row.

10. Grip it and rip it. John Daly got into the field in the 1991 tournament as a ninth alternate when Nick Price withdrew because his wife was about to have a baby. Price lent Daly his caddy, Jeff "Squeeky" Medlen, and the two of them pulled off one of the most unlikely upsets in major championship history at Crooked Stick in the Indianapolis suburbs. Daly beat runner-up Bruce Lietzke by three shots and instantly became the darling of galleries worldwide.

9. Beem me up. Playing in only his fourth major, Rich Beem was three shots off the lead going into the final round of the 2002 event at Hazeltine in Minnesota. Playing brilliantly, he opened a 4-shot lead going to the back nine and then held off a furious Tiger Woods rally—four birdies on his last four holes—to win by a shot. Afterward, he said he couldn't have done it without his Pepto-Bismol.

8. Anchors away. Navy recruit Sam Snead was scheduled to report for duty the week after the 1942 event, but he shipped out in style after he beat Army corporal Jim Turnesa 2 and 1 in the 36-hole final at Seaview Country Club in Atlantic City, New

Jersey. Turnesa had a 3-up lead when they stopped for lunch after the opening 18 holes, but Snead tied him after 27 and closed out the match when he holed a 60-foot chip shot on the 35th hole for his first major championship.

7. Sweetest streak of all. In 1945 Byron Nelson won a record 11 straight golf tournaments and 18 for the entire season, also a PGA Tour record. Because of World War II, the PGA Championship was the only major played that year. Nelson defeated Sam Byrd, 4 and 3 at Moraine Country Club in Dayton, Ohio, for the championship, the last of five majors he won in his career. That season, Nelson earned $63,000, mostly in war bonds.

6. Greens giant. Bantam Jerry Barber, all of 5-5 in spiked shoes, may have delivered the greatest display of clutch putting in major championship history when he rolled in putts of 20 feet (birdie), 40 feet (par), and 60 feet (birdie) on the last three holes in the final round at Olympia Fields in Chicago in 1961. He rallied from an early 4-shot deficit and forced an 18-hole playoff the next day against a stunned Don January. Barber shot 67 in the playoff and won by a stroke, becoming not only the shortest but also the oldest (45) PGA Championship winner until Julius Boros prevailed in 1968 at the age of 48.

5. Leapin' Lanny. Gene Littler had a 5-shot lead going to the back nine of the 1977 tournament at Pebble Beach, but four bogeys in a stretch of five holes brought him back to the pack, allowing Lanny Wadkins to tie him for the 72-hole lead. For the first time in major history, a sudden death format was used to settle the issue, and when Wadkins sank a four-foot putt for a par and the win on the third extra hole, he nearly jumped out of his socks.

4. Dandy Sandy. In 1986 Bob Tway had fought back from four shots down on the back nine Sunday and was tied for the lead with Greg Norman when they came to the 72nd hole at Inverness in Toledo, Ohio. Tway's second shot landed in a green-side bunker, but he hit the perfect sand shot on to a lightning-fast green. His ball just kept rolling and rolling, 30 feet and into the hole for a most improbable birdie. When Norman ran his own 25-foot chip to tie ten feet past the hole, Tway had won his first and only major title.

3. Shark bitten again. It was back to Inverness in 1993, and once again Norman felt the agony of defeat when he missed a four-foot putt for par on the second extra playoff hole. Norman had a chance to win in regulation, but his ten-foot birdie putt at the 72nd hole grazed the cup and stayed out. Norman became the second player in history to lose playoffs in all four majors, and Azinger had his first and only major title.

2. Tiger trumped. Tiger Woods had never lost a major championship when he held the outright lead or was tied at the top after 54 holes. That run of 14 straight ended at Hazeltine Golf Club in the Minneapolis suburbs in 2009 when Korean Y. E. Yang, ranked 460th in the world at the start of the season and 110th going into the tournament, overcame a 2-shot deficit going into the last round and beat Woods by three shots. Woods, the No. 1 player in the world, posted an uncharacteristic 75 in the final round, whereas Yang shot 2-under 70 on Sunday and became the first Asian-born player to win a major.

1. Record breaker. In 1973 Jack Nicklaus came to Canterbury Golf Club in Beachwood, Ohio, tied with the great Bob Jones with 13 career major championships each. He left his home state that week with a record-breaking 14th, erasing a mark that had stood for 43 years. Nicklaus posted an ordinary 72 in the first round, but a pair of 68s over the next two days and a 69 on Sunday earned him a 4-shot victory over Bruce Crampton. Over the next 13 years, Nicklaus added four more major titles, for a total of 18, and still remains the all-time leader.

★ ★ ★ ★

"Reverse every natural instinct and do the opposite of what you are inclined to do, and you will probably come very close to having a perfect golf swing."

—Ben Hogan

MEMORABLE INTERVIEWS   ►BY PETER KESSLER

When Peter Kessler does an interview with a golfer, you're going to get much more than club selection and talk about the birdie at 16. Kessler has distinguished himself as one of the top interviewers in golf by getting his subjects to open up and reveal different sides than what the public typically sees. Kessler helped establish the Golf Channel as a viable force during its early days. He has since gone on to host the highly popular radio show *Making the Turn* on the PGA Tour Network.

Kessler recounts his three most memorable interviews.

Gene Sarazen. When the Golf Channel first started, I just looked him up in the phone book in Marco Island. I called and said, "Mr. Sarazen?" He said, "I'm not here and I'm not me," and he hung up. A couple years went by and we finally organized the thing in 1997.

He was 95. He let me be his grandson for an hour. That was the most memorable thing. He told so many stories. He told one about taking the train in to New York City in 1920. He would have been 18. There was a platform where the Ziegfeld Follies girls got on to go into town for rehearsals. He started to flirt with this blonde. She wouldn't give him, in his vernacular, "a tumble." Sixty years goes by, and it's 1980. This woman comes up to him and says, "Do you remember me?" He said, "I looked her over. I didn't recognize her." She said, "You used to flirt with me on the train tracks 60 years ago and my name is Mrs. Bob Hope."

We used to argue all the time about the sand wedge. I told him, "You didn't invent the sand wedge. Bobby Jones used the sand wedge in 1930. You invented yours in 1932. You couldn't remember from morning to night whether it was because when you flew with Howard Hughes and the flaps went down so the plane went up or how a duck's wings work when they land gently on water."

He said, "Now you listen to me. There was a morning paper and there was an afternoon paper. For the morning paper, I told them about Howard Hughes and in the afternoon I gave them an exclusive about ducks landing on the water. That's the way it worked in those days."

Then he said, "Jones's club was illegal, so don't start with me."

Johnny Miller. This interview was a stunner. We did a show in the spring of '95, shortly after the Golf Channel got started. We were talking about some of the tragedies that happened in his family. Particularly, we talked about the passing of his older brother, who drowned in an accident in the Pacific when Johnny was a young boy.

It's very little known. When I uncovered that in my homework, I was stunned because I hadn't heard it or read it before. He talked about it openly and freely. His dad put the mat in the basement for Johnny to hit golf balls as a way to divert his energy away from that tragic loss.

Johnny is sitting there openly weeping about his brother, about his father, about falling in love with golf. I take a phone call, thinking that I'm going to let the audience participate in this very personal moment. And the caller says, "How do you transfer your weight to your left side?"

Without missing a beat, Johnny said, "You don't actually think about transferring your weight. You try to keep your hands as low as possible after the strike and your weight will have transferred all by itself."

I sat there, and I couldn't believe the speed with which he was immediately able to change gears. He was brilliant. He could go from sobbing to this fascinating answer I had never heard before. It was so elegantly stated. And I found myself moving my hands low, feeling my weight transfer.

Jack Nicklaus. At the end of 1996 we went to Jack's house. When we got there, Jack was grilling swordfish steaks. We sit down to do the show. Everything is just great. The second segment starts and it's great.

Then I start to ask Jack a question, and he says, "Peter, Peter. I've been sitting here watching you look very uncomfortable." For the only time I could remember, all of the sudden I didn't have control of the show. Then two guys, one that worked for the Golf Channel and one that worked for him, grabbed me and held down my arms. I didn't know what's going on.

Jack says, "We don't wear ties at the Nicklaus house. Do you know what we do to people who wear ties?" Then he reached under the cushion of the couch and pulls out some scissors. He leaned forward and cut off the tie.

It was such a great moment. It felt like such a personal moment. In a funny way, I took it as kind of a compliment.

The postscript to the story: That coat and tie were given to me by a men's store in Orlando as the beginning of promoting their clothing. The next day I brought the jacket back in. They said, "Where's the tie?"

I said, "The guest cut it off."

They said, "We know. We want to put it on our wall."

I said, "How are you going to get it off my wall?"

We still have the tie in the house. Jack signed it for me. That's a great memory.

★ ★ ★ ★

"It's so bad I could putt off a tabletop and still leave the ball halfway down the leg."

—J. C. Snead, on his putting

THINGS WE DETEST ABOUT GOLF

With the good comes the bad. There are some things about playing and watching golf that simply drive us crazy. They can't be tolerated. There are thousands of them. Here are a few.

10. Rain on your $500 round. You've planned for months for that special round at Pebble Beach or Pinehurst or Bandon Dunes. And then you wake up, and it's raining sideways. Still, you forge ahead, plunk down your big money, and get soaked. You want sun and warmth for that once-in-a-lifetime round. Unless of course you're in Scotland and Ireland. Then you want wind and rain so you could brag to your friends about how you played in miserable conditions.

9. Expensive golf balls. The fact that a golf ball can cost $4 is bad enough. I almost feel like the ball is mocking me. It's even worse when you then dump three straight Pro V1s into the water in a futile attempt to reach the green. Perhaps it is the golf gods' way of saying, "You don't deserve to be playing that ball."

8. Don't sign here. Tiger Woods took a lot of heat for not signing autographs, but he's not the only one. I've seen plenty of pros blow by kids, including my own, without reaching for their Sharpie. No class.

7. Brutal pin placements. In order to preserve par, PGA Tour set-up crews have to revert to placing the pins in often ridiculous positions on the greens. That's fine for the pros, but, I've found that many greenskeepers have mimicked the practice and do the same thing at your local courses. Too often the pins are either tucked or pitched on a slope that would tax a top pro, let alone a 15-handicapper. Hey, Mr. Greenskeeper, Tiger Woods isn't coming out today.

6. Pushy Marshals. Let's say this upfront: The vast majority of marshals at golf tournaments are wonderful. The events couldn't go on without them. However, we've all run into marshals who, when given authority, suddenly become Barney Fife. They order you all over the place and, more often than not, complicate the situation. Also, you've got to love the marshals who yell "quiet please" just as the player is about to pull back the club.

5. Chris Berman at the U.S. Open. Chris Berman handling early-round coverage on ESPN is an incredibly bad idea. I like Berman, and his bombastic style is perfect for football. But please keep him away from golf. He sounds totally out of place on the telecast. I imagine opera fans would feel the same way if he came out as the lead tenor. Usually, I turn down the sound when Berman comes on. Not a pleasing alternative.

4. False promises. Surely you've seen all those infomercials on the Golf Channel for gadgets or swing videos that will either add 50 yards to your drive or knock 10 strokes off your game in two weeks. I have, and many wasted dollars later, I can say they don't live up to their promises. There are no shortcuts in golf. Only hard work.

3. The scorecard rule. There are people and computers tracking every stat in golf, and yet players still get disqualified for signing for the wrong scorecard. The legendary case was Roberto DeVincenzo in the 1968 Masters, but I'll never forget what happened to Mark Roe in the 2003 British Open. The journeyman European pro pulled into contention on Saturday after a round of 67. Everyone saw it on television. Wonderful story. However, minutes later he was disqualified because of an incorrect scorecard. Roe was crushed. In the era of modern technology, it's time to scuttle the scorecard rule.

2. Slow pros. Nothing is hurting professional golf at all levels more than the snail-like pace of play. There were matches at the 2009 Solheim Cup that took more than six hours to complete. Five hours or more is the standard for a threesome pairing. Does anyone think that's exciting? Here's a recommendation: Golf's top executives need to spend more time in the galleries watching the excruciating slow play. Once they see how truly boring it is, they might to do more to resolve the problem.

1. "You the man" dude. Every tournament has one. The guy—make that idiot—who thinks it is hilarious to yell out "You the man" or "It's in the hole" the split-second the ball leaves the player's clubface. It is beyond annoying. Those guys are definitely not "the man."

If you live in North Korea, you believe Kim Jong-il shot the best round of golf ever. He once posted a 34 for 18 holes on a 7,700-yard course, a tidy 38-under. His round included five aces. Yeah, sure, of course. Nobody in North Korea was going to question the Supreme Leader.

Fortunately for golf, there have been other great rounds that are based more in reality. The most memorable occurred when the pressure and conditions were at their toughest. Here are a few of the best rounds ever.

10. Allan Robertson, St. Andrews. Barely breaking 80 would be considered a terrible round for today's pros. Back in the 1850s, such a round was reason to close shop and head to the pubs to celebrate. Robertson was considered one of the fathers of golf in the 1800s. In 1858 he shot a 79 at St. Andrews, becoming the first player to break 80 on the Old Course. The round made history back then, and shouldn't be forgotten now.

9. Annika Sorenstam's 59. It was fitting that Annika Sorenstam became the first woman to break 60 during a tournament round. She did it during the 2001 Standard Ping. She opened her second round with eight straight birdies and was 10-under through 11 holes. She actually had a chance to shoot a 58, but her birdie putt missed on 18. So she had to "settle" for a 59.

8. Al Geiberger's 59. Geiberger did something that Ben Hogan, Jack Nicklaus, Arnold Palmer, Byron Nelson, and all the other greats before him never accomplished: He became the first player to shoot a 59 during the second round of the Memphis Classic. He sealed the deal with a 10-footer for birdie on the last hole. The feat earned him the treasured nickname, "Mr. 59."

7. Greg Norman, 1993 British Open. "The Shark" was better known for his infamous collapses. However, it all came together for him during the final round of the Open at Royal St. George's. Starting the day one shot behind Nick Faldo, he went out and shot a 64 to win his second Claret Jug. It was the lowest final round in Open history, and the best moment of Norman's career.

6. Davis Love III, 2003 Players Championship. I'm including this round because it probably was the best I've seen in person. On a chilly, windy day, Love, wearing a rain suit, shot a 64 at TPC Sawgrass during the final round to win the Players Championship. A 64 in calm conditions is a terrific score on Pete Dye's course, but to do it facing extreme challenges from Mother Nature makes it off the charts. Said playing partner Fred Couples: "It's the best round of golf I've ever seen."

5. Ben Hogan, 1951 U.S. Open. This list wouldn't be complete without an entry from Mr. Hogan. He shot many great rounds in his career, but the one that stands out was the final round at Oakland Hills. The course was a brutal test, but Hogan closed with a 67 to win his second straight U.S. Open. It only was the second sub-70 round for the tournament. Afterward, Hogan uttered his immortal line: "I'm glad I brought this course, this monster, to its knees."

4. David Duval's 59. It wasn't a major, and the Palm Springs courses aren't regarded as the toughest tests in golf. Still, it would be foolish to diminish what Duval did during the final round of the Bob Hope Chrysler Classic. Trailing by seven shots at the beginning of the round, Duval started on fire and never stopped. His birdie putt at 18 gave him the 59 and a 1-stroke victory. Arguably, it was the greatest finishing round in a nonmajor.

3. Arnold Palmer, 1960 U.S. Open. What Palmer did during the final 18 at Cherry Hills will go down as his finest hour. Trailing by seven shots, Palmer promptly drove the first green, a 346-yard par 4. He made birdie and kept on charging, shooting a 30 on the front nine. A 65 gave him his only U.S. Open title. "Arnie's Army" never looked better.

2. Jack Nicklaus, 1986 Masters. If you had to pick the most memorable round in golf history, I'd say nine out of ten people would select Nicklaus's final round 65 to win the 1986 Masters. His 30 on the back nine was a wonderful final blast from the game's greatest player. For as long as they play golf, they will be talking about that day at Augusta.

1. Johnny Miller, 1973 U.S. Open. To shoot a 63 at any course takes considerable skill, but to do it at Oakmont in the final round of a U.S. Open? Well, that has to be the best ever in my book. The day before, Miller shot a 76 to put him six shots behind going into the final round. However, he made an adjustment on the practice tee, opening his stance a bit. The end result was magic on Sunday. Miller went out in 32 and then played even better on the back with a 31. He hit every green, and his average birdie putt was nine feet. The 63 gave Miller the U.S. Open title and a cherished spot in history.

Tiger Woods was the game's top star going into 2000, but his legend had yet to take hold. He went into the year holding only two major titles. However, he picked up steam at the end of 1999, winning his last four events. The momentum then turned into an explosion as Woods, at the age of 24, recorded a season for the ages: nine victories and three straight majors. The year included a victory that should go down as the best performance of all time.

Here's a look back at Tiger 2000.

7. Sportsman of the Year. In 1996, when Woods won his third straight U.S. Amateur and then captured two victories quickly after turning pro, *Sports Illustrated* named him "Sportsman of the Year." Too early, I thought. What was *SI* going to do when Woods really did something special? The magazine never had an athlete win Sportsman more than once. Sure enough, when Woods dominated golf in 2000, it had only one choice for the coveted prize. Woods became the first two-time Sportsman, an honor never bestowed to athletes such as Jack Nicklaus, Wayne Gretzky, and Michael Jordan.

6. Six in a row. Woods came into the season with four straight victories and quickly stretched it to five with a playoff victory over Ernie Els at the Mercedes Championship. The streak, though, looked like it would end at the AT&T National Pro-Am at Pebble Beach. He trailed by seven shots in the final round. Woods, however, put on a dramatic charge, holing a wedge for eagle on 15. A final round 64 gave him his sixth straight victory. He joined Byron Nelson and Ben Hogan as the only other players to have a streak of six tournaments or longer. It ended the following week when Woods finished tied for second in the Buick Invitational.

5. Highlight shots. Woods hit many great shots that year, including that wedge at Pebble Beach. Two others, though, also stand out. At the Canadian Open, he used a 6-iron from 218 yards in a bunker. He knocked the shot over water to a tucked pin, stunning the announcers and galleries. Naturally, he went on to win the tournament.

During his victory at the WGC-NEC Invitational, Woods's biggest obstacle was darkness. Holding an 11-shot lead, Woods went into the night to avoid having to come back the following morning. Without being able to see the flag on 18, he knocked his approach to a foot. Fans flicked lighters to show their approval.

4. Stat man. His scoring average of 68.17 broke the mark Byron Nelson (68.33) set in 1945, the year of his 11-tournament streak. He was 1.46 shots better than his nearest competitor, which translates to six shots a tournament. He went an incredible 47 rounds without having a round over par. In all, he led the PGA Tour in 22 statistical categories, including earnings of $9.18 million. The next highest was Phil Mickelson at $4.5 million.

3. St. Andrews show. Woods just overpowered the home of golf. His final score of 19-under lapped the field. An 8-shot victory meant he won two consecutive majors by a combined 23 shots. He also became the youngest player to win the career Grand Slam. At a course made famous by Bobby Jones and Jack Nicklaus, Woods wrote his own piece of history.

2. Dramatics at Valhalla. Woods changed the script and played it close for the PGA Championship at Valhalla. This time, he was the pursuer, as he had to chase down unlikely leader Bob May. Woods eventually forced a playoff. Then in one of the signature moments of his career, he followed, pointing, a birdie putt as it dropped in the cup. Naturally, Woods prevailed, joining Ben Hogan as the only other player to win three majors in one season.

1. Perfection at Pebble. It doesn't get any better. Quite simply, what Woods did in the U.S. Open at Pebble Beach was the best performance in the history of golf. He won the tournament at 12-under, becoming the first player to win an Open in double-digits under par. His record margin of 15 shots suggested Woods was playing another course. Pebble didn't play easy that week, as the next lowest score was 3-over. Woods, though, didn't make a bogey over the final 26 holes.

Said Jack Nicklaus, who played in his final Open that year: "I knew he was good. I think he is better than I thought he was."

★ ★ ★ ★

"I don't like watching golf on TV. I can't stand whispering."

—David Brenner

TIGER AND MARRIAGE

When Tiger Woods got engaged to Elin Nordegren in 2003, I did a story in the *Chicago Tribune* asking the experts to analyze the impact marriage would have on his game. I asked the question: Does taking on a bride equate to more birdies or bogeys?

Now that we know the rest of the story, the old quotes are amusing to say the least. Here's what they said back then, but now with an updated perspective. Enjoy.

6. Juggling. Michael Aisenberg, a sports psychologist in suburban Chicago, provided this gem: "This is one more ball he has to juggle, and he's already juggling quite a few."

To say the least.

5. Relationships, plural. Deborah Graham, a golf psychologist based in San Antonio, discussed the time commitment that comes with being married.

"Tiger always has seemed to be balanced. When he's practicing, he's practicing, and when he's off, he's off. But he needs to find a way to fit this relationship into it."

Make that relationships.

4. Peace of mind. Again, here is Aisenberg talking about the tranquility that comes with a successful marriage.

"What is helpful emotionally off the course could be helpful to him on the course. If he's happy, he's relaxing. It's a soothing experience. He could win twice as many tournaments."

Now we know why Woods felt so "relaxed," helping him to win so many tournaments.

3. Caveman. Not! CBS golf analyst David Feherty weighed in on Woods's supposed mundane life away from the course.

"He lives in a cave, only coming out to play. You never see him in the tabloids. You never see a picture of him with his shirt off. We don't know anything about him. For all we know, he could be a short, fat, bald white guy."

Now Woods lives in tabloids and we've seen pictures of him with his shirt off in *Vanity Fair*. No, David, he's definitely not a short, fat, bald white guy.

2. Et tu, Jack? Even Jack Nicklaus bought into the notion Woods would settle down in marriage. Jack discussed how marriage to Barbara made his life complete.

"Golf wasn't the only thing in my life. And I don't think it will be the only thing in Tiger's life either."

It turns out Jack was right in ways he never could have imagined.

1. Sounded good at the time. Finally, I ran a quote from Tiger in which he discusses what lie ahead of him in marriage.

"Some guys get married, they start families, and that becomes the most important thing in their life for a little bit. Then they get back to golf and refocus again. For those guys, it ebbs and flows. But I've stayed dedicated to the game. I know things change in everyone's life, and I'm sure there'll be changes in mine too. Injuries, other things come along . . . But that's also where the mental toughness comes in, if you're going to keep it."

Well, there certainly have been "injuries" and "other things [did] come along" for Tiger. If only he knew back then . . .

★ ★ ★ ★

"Don't play too much golf. Two rounds a day are plenty."

—Harry Vardon

Tiger Woods seemed to have the perfect life: immense wealth, beautiful wife, children, fame, and adulation. Then it all changed on Thanksgiving night, 2009, when Woods crashed his car. Suddenly, he became a tabloid target and his carefully crafted image disappeared overnight. The story took on a life of its own.

However, did the damage have to be that bad? If certain elements were handled differently and some things didn't happen, could the firestorm have been avoided, or at least minimized?

Just asking, what if? . . .

10. Woods played in a different era. Judging from the public backlash, you would think Woods was the first athlete who cheated on his wife by having multiple affairs. Hello?! It's been going on since forever. Babe Ruth and Mickey Mantle were notorious womanizers. We learned more about Magic Johnson and Michael Jordan than they wanted us to know. However, Woods had the poor timing of being exposed in the Internet, TMZ, blog era, when everything and anything is fair game. This dynamic helped generate the perfect storm. Meanwhile, many other cheating athletes were counting their lucky stars.

9. Woods was never treated by Dr. Galea. Another element was added during the frenzy of the scandal when it was reported that Woods had been treated by Dr. Antony Galea, who was under investigation for steroids. Woods had received treatments from the doctor in the aftermath of his knee injury. With Woods's credibility blown apart, the link immediately triggered speculation that he had used PEDs. Woods's agent Mark Steinberg tried to stem the initial *New York Times* story with an e-mail to a reporter, saying, "Give the kid a break." Yeah, right. Woods was no kid, and nobody was going to give him a break.

8. Woods had a better relationship with the media. Woods always has had little use for the media and was notorious for limiting access. Arrogance is a good word. Longtime beat reporters hardly knew him. So he had nothing in the media bank when the scandal exploded. Perhaps if he had been a nicer guy and made himself more available, he might have been portrayed in a more sympathetic light. But that wasn't the case, as nobody felt the desire to rush to his defense. What goes around comes around, right?

7. Woods sponsors stayed with him. Companies don't like to be associated with scandal. So it wasn't a big surprise that some of Woods's biggest sponsors, like Accenture, were quick to sever ties with him once the news hit. The defections added another layer to the story, diminishing his image even more.

6. Woods hadn't talked about family at the Australian Open. While playing in the Australian Open in November 2009, he gave an interview in which he talked about the importance of his family. He said his priorities were "family first, golf second." About his wife, Elin, he said, "(She has been) great, actually, the best thing that ever happened." A few weeks later those words came back to bite him big time in the butt when everything hit the fan.

5. Woods played better in his return. Everyone expected Woods to turn the story around when he returned to the course. He would win tournaments and make everyone remember why they loved him in the first place. It didn't happen. After somehow finishing fourth in the Masters with no swing, it completely unraveled when he missed the cut at Quail Hallow and had to withdraw from the Players Championship. Then his swing coach Hank Haney quit on him, perhaps a case of jumping before he got pushed. As a result, the impact of the scandal lingered on and on.

4. Woods decided against live TV for his mea culpa. After going into exile for nearly three months, it was disclosed that Woods was finally going to speak. However, it wasn't the press conference everyone envisioned. Instead, it would be an open confessional to family, friends, and associates. With unprecedented live coverage on all the networks, Woods spoke for 13 minutes, during which he admitted he made many, many mistakes. The whole thing seemed awkward and staged, and he was ripped for not taking any questions. He probably would have been better off doing it in private.

3. Woods confessed sooner. When it comes to damage control, a basic PR principle is to get out in front of the story. Silence leads to the story spinning out of control. Shortly after the scandal hit, PR experts said Woods needed to face the cameras, make his confessions, and minimize the damage. Instead, with the exception of a couple statements on his Web site, Woods disappeared and wasn't seen for months. All it did was add layers upon layers of more speculation and innuendo, taking the story to almost unimaginable levels.

2. Woods hadn't gotten in the car that night. The Thanksgiving night car accident was the proverbial throwing the match in gasoline. Prior to that point, a

National Enquirer story about Woods having an affair, which came out a few days earlier, hadn't gotten any traction in the mainstream media. You wonder if Woods had never had that crash, would the tabloids have rushed in manic pursuit? Would several of his lowlife bimbos have gone public in a shameless attempt to cash in on their flings with Tiger? Is there a chance the whole thing could have blown over with minimal damage? We'll never know.

1. Woods kept his zipper up. Do you think?

★ ★ ★ ★

"I don't know if you're ever finished trying to improve. As soon as you feel like you are finished, then I guessed you are finished, because you've already put a limit on your ability and what you can attain. I don't think that's right."

—Tiger Woods

GOLF IS A SPORT

The age-old debate over whether golf is a sport really gets me riled up. I've had the debate many times with AOL Fanhouse columnist Greg Couch. I decided to bring our debate to these pages. Keep in mind, Couch is a tennis buff. Name me four players beyond the Williams sisters, Federer, and Nadal. Nuff said?

Anyway, let the debate begin.

8. Fat linemen. If you're going to discount golf as a sport because players like John Daly (the fat version), Tim Herron, and Craig Stadler don't have chiseled bodies, then I'll present to you the image of the 340-pound offensive lineman with 60 pounds of flab hanging over his gut. Technically, all they do is stand up and try to get in somebody's way. Carl Lewis, they're not. I know there's much more involved in being a lineman, especially with footwork. Hey, fat guys can be athletes, too. Don't diss golfers just because they like cheeseburgers and beer in mass quantities.

7. Stationary sports. Golf also takes a hit because there isn't any running involved. Following that logic, are we to assume that track and field events such as shot put and javelin aren't sports? What about diving? All you've got to do is fall forward. And really, is a pitcher moving any more than a golfer?

6. Endurance. If you think playing golf is a leisurely activity, try walking 18 holes on a hilly course on a humid 93-degree day. Then do it for six straight days, including practice rounds and pro-ams. The pros do it routinely during the summer. Just like other sports, the endurance factor is huge in golf. If you can't handle the hills and heat, you'll be a goner. I'm guessing 95 percent of those fat linemen wouldn't make it through nine holes.

5. It's difficult. If golf isn't a sport, then how come the best athletes in the world can't master it? Jerry Rice might have been the best football player ever, yet he shot a round in the 90s when he tried to tee it up on the Nationwide Tour. Michael Jordan only dreams of being a professional golfer. Yes, golf is a hard sport.

4. Steroids. Sadly, if you can take steroids to improve your performance, then you're a sport. Golf falls under that category. Golf was way behind the curve on this, but officials finally did institute testing for performance enhancing drugs. Just like sports such as baseball and football, golf reacted to curb a potential problem.

3. Physical toll. Golf actually is a dangerous sport for players at the highest level. The golf swing is a highly unnatural move, and years of pounding usually finds most players on the operating table at some point. Tiger Woods already has had four knee surgeries. Bill Glasson has had more than 20 surgeries on his knees, elbows, and back. If you're not getting operated on, chances are your back feels as if you've been in 40 accidents. That's in a week, not a life. Play the sport of golf at your own risk.

2. Strength, flexibility, coordination. Like every other sport, you need strength, flexibility, and superb hand-eye coordination to play golf. Even when John Daly was fat, he had incredible flexibility that allowed him to wrap the club around his neck. Just ask Tiger Woods if it helps to be strong in golf. His success had a bevy of other players following him to the weight room. The ball may be stationary, but to get it to draw over that tree or to make it land like a feather to that tight pin over a bunker, you need hand-eye coordination that is off the charts. Strength, flexibility, coordination: Yep, sounds like a sport to me.

1. Competitive edge. Just like the other sports, the mental aspect is huge in golf. The player who can think his way around the course, who can handle and overcome adversity, who can stare down an opponent, who can will the putt in the hole with everything on the line, always will reign supreme in golf. Michael Jordan had it in his sport. Tiger Woods has it in his sport.

So yes, Greg, golf most definitely is a sport. Now don't get me started on tennis.

★ ★ ★ ★

"I play in the low 80s. If it's any hotter than that, I won't play."

—Joe E. Lewis

GOLF ISN'T A SPORT

▶BY GREG COUCH

Greg Couch currently is a columnist for AOL Fanhouse. Previously, he worked at the *Chicago Sun-Times*, where his assignments included covering the golf beat. Always provocative, Couch's view on golf is likely to anger many readers of this book. Although we thought about printing his phone number and address, we decided it probably wasn't a good idea. Here is Greg's list.

8. Maid service. In what sport does an athlete not even carry his equipment into battle? The caddy carries clubs and cleans shoes. If you're dragging along a built-in maid service—not a sport.

7. An objective observer. The U.S. Supreme Court ruled that golf is not a sport. Basically, when Casey Martin wanted a cart to accommodate his disability, the activity's governing bodies cried that it would give him an advantage, as others had to walk. The court ruled that walking is not integral to the game. Basically.

6. Walking is aerobic. Yes, minimally. But it's not challenging. A finely tuned athlete could not possibly have difficulty walking five miles. Not to mention that golfers take a break after every shot. That's 70 breaks. I know there are hills on a golf course, too. That almost makes the argument more embarrassing.

Put it this way: Walking five miles for a round of golf in four hours is going, roughly, two feet per second. It is 50 feet from my couch to my fridge, round trip. At golf's "aerobic" pace, I would have 25 seconds to get a beer, come back, and sit down. It only takes 21.

5. Tom Watson. When he almost won the British Open in 2009, it was thrilling. I was there. Imagine a 59-year-old winning a major championship in a sport. No, I can't imagine it, either. Watson nearly buried the golf-is-a-sport argument, a year after old Greg Norman nearly won. No way can a 59-year-old beat the young guys at the highest level of a sport.

Larry Bird is in his early to mid-50s. You think he could play in the NBA today?

4. Tiger Woods. Woods has muscles and is fit. How can you say he isn't an athlete? Good question. And even golf fans who didn't like Woods were glad to have him around just for this argument. Woods might be an athlete, but that's related to golf.

I would say this: If you work in an office, you might find the people in your mailroom who are muscular, too. That's why you pick them for the company softball team. Does that make sorting mail a sport?

3. Beer gut. John Daly is the poster child. Craig Stadler used to be. Too many others to name. Daly used to be fat, but now he isn't. No matter how much golf he played, he couldn't lose the weight. He needed lapband surgery. True, David Letterman once called former baseball pitcher Terry Forster a "fat tub of goo." Sumo wrestlers, offensive linemen aren't fit. You can find examples of anything.

But you cannot play basketball all day and be fat. With golf, you can do it all day long and still need the lapband.

2. Ken Venturi. More than 45 years ago, Ken Venturi got tired while playing golf in the sun at Congressional for the U.S. Open. This is the oldest, most desperate argument among the golf-is-a-sport crowd. His feat in 1964 was incredible.

But getting really tired from walking does not make golf a sport. The tired you get from golf isn't like the tired you get from sports but rather the weary-legged feel you get when your wife drags you shopping all day. Shopping is not a sport.

1. It's just a name. Nothing gets golfers more uppity than when you inform them that their activity isn't a sport. I understand. Activities are knitting, checkers, birdwatching. Golfers don't want to be knitters; they want to be athletes. Yet golf doesn't require any more running than Monopoly does. It offers no more aerobic challenge than mowing the lawn—with a self-propelled mower.

Golf is not a sport. Whatever you call it, though, that doesn't change what's required. It takes coordination, flexibility, some strength—or girth—and the ability to tip the servant carrying your bag, cleaning your shoes, and giving you sandwiches during battle.

Honestly, it's tough. But a sport needs rules, competition, physical skills, and, sorry golf, aerobic challenge.

My theory on the popularity swing from tennis to golf: Tennis was the boom sport in the 1970s, and when the players got old and a little tired, they looked for a place to sit down. Checkers was too sedentary. Their answer: golf.

GOLF WOULD BE BETTER IF . . .

This is our book and we get to make up the rules here. We're dreaming big. Golf would be better if . . .

Beer was calorie-free.

Beer made you play better.

Riding a cart burned 6,000 calories.

Every course looked like Pebble Beach.

Every course felt like Ballybunion.

Every course cost no more than your local muni.

The over-the-move was the key to a successful swing. (I'd have won 10 Masters.)

You got rewarded for hitting a tree.

All balls skipped through the water.

No wait on the first tee at 9 a.m. Saturday.

Every public course looked like Torrey Pines.

Every locker room looked like Seminole's.

You never missed from 18 inches.

Your wife liked to play as much as you do.

Hot dogs were considered health food.

You actually had a clue which way the putt broke.

You actually had a clue how to play out of the bunker.

You got to play one more round with your father.

All of our children enjoyed and honored the game as much as we do.

You got to reach a par 5 in two at least once per round.

The pros played three-and-a-half-hour rounds on Sundays.

Butch Harmon looked at your swing and said, "Perfect."

Each foursome included Ernie Banks. His motto for golf is "Let's play 36."

Each foursome included *SI* swimsuit model Kathy Ireland, an avid golfer.

Pro V1s cost $4.50 per dozen instead of $45.

You had your own personal clubfitter.

You got to wear the Green Jacket for a day.

Ben Hogan said to you, "Nice shot."

Everyone played like they do in Ireland and Scotland: Fast.

The slow group always lets you play through.

At least once per round you got to hit a drive 300 yards.

You actually were able to spin the ball back to the hole.

Golf was indeed better than sex.

★ ★ ★ ★

"I have a tip that can take five strokes off anyone's golf game: it's called an eraser."

—Arnold Palmer

TOP TEN REASONS WHY KIDS SHOULD PLAY GOLF

►BY JOE LOUIS BARROW, JR.

The First Tee is a terrific golf initiative to introduce kids of all backgrounds to the game. The program, though, is about more than swinging the club. Through golf, it is designed to teach kids important life skills and core values that transcend the game. Joe Louis Barrow, Jr., the CEO of the First Tee, lists his reasons why kids should play golf.

10. Enjoy the great outdoors. Young people should play golf because it is an opportunity to spend a few hours in the fresh air. While playing golf, kids can experience all types of plants and wildlife indigenous to their geographic location.

9. Develop lifelong friendships. You never know who you will meet on a golf course, and interaction with others allows young people to develop social skills as they engage with people on the walk between shots.

8. Practice personal responsibility. Sometimes the ball doesn't always bounce your way, but regardless of the outcome, there is no blaming your teammates for what happens. In golf, young people are personally responsible for preparing and performing, and although there are no guarantees you will shoot a low score or win the tournament, you can walk off the last hole knowing you did everything in your control to give yourself the best opportunity for success.

7. Have a safe place to play. The golf course is a safe place and facilitates mentoring relationships in a safe environment.

6. Manage your emotions. Golf often closely parallels real life as one experiences the highs and lows of the game. Through a 3-, 6-, 9-, or 18-hole round of golf, a young person is required to navigate challenges and obstacles that may result in good shots, bad shots, and everything in between. This range of experiences that happens throughout the game rewards a young person's ability to keep each shot in perspective, manage one's emotions, maintain a positive outlook, and focus on the shot at hand.

5. Appreciate diversity. Golf is a game that can be played for a lifetime by anyone regardless of age, gender, ethnicity, size, or skill level. You can even play the game by yourself or with others. When you play with others, you can be paired up with players of varying ability levels.

4. Prepare for business. Golf is a sport that helps prepare kids for careers in business and other professional arenas. Participating in golf activities permits the opportunity to learn social etiquette that can lead to opening doors in business and other opportunities.

3. Learn etiquette. Children should play golf because it is based on characteristics that are missing in our society. Golf places an emphasis on etiquette. In golf there is no judge or referee; instead, players govern themselves and fellow competitors.

2. Spend time with family. Golf is a game that encourages family participation. The most common way young people get started playing golf is through a family member.

1. Wellness for life. With the youth obesity epidemic in our country, golf is a sport that helps young people get off the couch and onto the course. When you play golf, walking the golf course and carrying your bag, a 150-lb. person burns 350 calories per round. One young person said it best when asked what they like most about golf, stating, "It is good for me. I do more walking and less watching TV."

★ ★ ★ ★

"I guess there is nothing that will get your mind off everything like golf. I have never been depressed enough to take up the game, but they say you get so sore at yourself you forget to hate your enemies."

—Will Rogers

TOP PLAYER-CADDY TEAMS

As any good golfer knows, a caddy does more than carry a player's clubs. The caddy is part coach, strategist, security guard, green reader, psychologist, cheerleader, and, more than occasionally, scapegoat. A good caddy definitely can make a difference. Here are some of the most memorable player-caddy teams of all time.

10. Ben Crenshaw and Carl Jackson. For a long time players only could use Augusta National caddies during the Masters. In 1976 a young Crenshaw was paired with Carl Jackson. Even after the club changed the rule allowing players to use their own caddies, Crenshaw kept Jackson on the bag at Augusta. Together, they won two Masters and developed a deep friendship.

Said Crenshaw: "He's a dear man and a dear friend. We've been lucky in that we've seen so much on the golf course, and been through so much. He's a great reason why I've had my two green jackets and a lot of years in contention. He knows this golf course like you can't believe."

9. Nick Faldo and Fannie Sunesson. The 5-6 native of Sweden broke into the boys club by hitting it big with Faldo. She hooked up with Faldo in 1990, and they formed a memorable image as they walked down the fairways. Faldo could be surly and definitely was demanding. But Sunesson was more than up for the challenge.

She once said, "People ask all the time what the difference is being a woman working in a man's world, but I don't know because I've never been a man. How would I know the difference? I'm a woman, but when it comes to my job I'm a caddy. I'm not a woman caddy—I'm a caddy, doing exactly the same things as the guys are doing. I am one of the guys."

8. Fred Couples and Joe LaCava. Laid back Freddie found a soul mate in a caddy when it comes to LaCava. They both are sports nuts who love nothing more than to sit in the recliner and watch a good game on the tube. LaCava has been a staple on Couples's bag for more than two decades. Said Couples in an interview: "You figure it out. I been married twice and can't stay married. But I've been with Joe for 20 friggin' years."

7. Nick Price and Squeeky Medlen. Jeff "Squeeky" Medlen was a fixture on Price's bag during his great run in the 1990s. Obviously, once you heard his voice, you knew why he had his nickname. "Squeeky," though, was a superb caddy. When Nick Price decided to sit out the 1991 PGA Championship, he picked up the bag of unknown player for the week, John Daly, who promptly stunned the world by winning the tournament. Sadly, Medlin died of leukemia in 1997.

6. Francis Ouimet and Eddie Lowery. Ouimet's unlikely victory in the 1913 U.S. Open also had an unlikely caddy in 10-year-old Eddie Lowery. The brash, young kid prodded and encouraged Ouimet during his epic run. He didn't stop there. Lowery went on to become a multimillionaire car dealer in San Francisco, where he helped back the start for a couple young amateurs named Ken Venturi and Harvey Ward.

5. Jack Nicklaus and Angelo Argea. With his distinctive mop of silver hair, Argea began to caddy for Nicklaus in 1963. Together, they won more than 40 tournaments. When Argea died in 2005, Nicklaus said, "Angelo was one of the great all-time characters to be around. He had a lot of personality and was a lot of fun."

4. Lee Trevino and Herman Mitchell. You couldn't miss Mitchell when he was carrying the bag for Trevino. A bear of a man, Mitchell weighed in at more than 300 pounds. Mitchell, though, still was able to get around the course and was on hand for his boss's biggest victories. Trevino once said of Mitchell: "I always know which side a putt will break. It always slopes toward the side of the green Herman's standing."

3. Tom Watson and Bruce Edwards. This was a partnership that went beyond golf. And the golf was pretty good. Edwards was Watson's caddy for 30 years, helping his man earn induction into the Hall of Fame. Their deep bond came to the forefront when Edwards learned he had ALS (Lou Gehrig's disease) in 2003. Despite failing health, Edwards continued to carry the bag for Watson. It's all he ever wanted to do.

Shortly after learning of the disease, Edwards said, "If I go in a year or less, I've had a wonderful life. I've been lucky. I had one of the greatest golfers in the world. I've had a wonderful ride, a lot of wins, a lot of great moments."

2. Phil Mickelson and Jim Mackay. Mickelson will be the first to tell anybody that he couldn't have done it without Mackay. Known affectionately as "Bones," Mackay has been Mickelson's constant companion through thick and sometimes thin. The loyalty is fierce on both sides. Said Mickelson: "I can't verbalize what Bones has meant to me. Besides admiring him as a good person, I respect his grasp of the game. He's right about 80 percent of the time out there to my 20 percent."

1. Tiger Woods and Steve Williams. Williams has a single-minded approach to his job: Doing everything possible to make Woods win. That means he'll stomp on the camera of a fan or snarl at the gallery to keep quiet. If it means many people regard him as a jerk, so be it. There's nothing warm and fuzzy about Williams. Woods wouldn't have it any other way. He has complete confidence in Williams. Together, they are the most successful player-caddy team in golf history.

FLUFF STUFF

►BY MIKE "FLUFF" COWAN

Most people know Mike Cowan as the caddy for Tiger Woods and Jim Furyk. But he also has some game. Cowan, a scratch player, is a full member at the Congressional Country Club in Bethesda, Maryland, the site for the 2011 U.S. Open and the venue often used for Tiger Woods's signature event, the AT&T National.

Cowan got the nickname "Fluff" from his fellow caddies years ago because he bore a slight resemblance to golfer and broadcaster Steve Melnyk, also known as Fluff on the PGA Tour. Cowan caddied for Tiger Woods at the Congressional in the 1997 U.S. Open, and the caddy, not the player, had one of the greatest tournaments of his life. Woods flailed around the six-inch rough for four days and eventually tied for 19th place. But Cowan had a week he'll never forget, for all the obvious reasons.

9. How I met my wife. I had the bag and I was waiting for Tiger to come out from the scoring area when a young woman came up to me and said, "Fluff, would you mind taking a picture with me?" I said, "Sure. Why not?" and then I think I said something smartass like I usually do, and the rest is history. (That woman, Jennifer, was a Washington native and apparently didn't mind the smart-aleck stuff. She eventually married Cowan, and the two have a daughter, Bobbie, and live in Rockville, Maryland.)

8. Where I got good. I grew up in Maine and I started playing when I was eight. I decided to go to college at William Penn University in Iowa. The first time I saw the course my freshman year, the fairways were pretty baked out but the greens were perfect. I started hitting it longer and started progressing from there to where I could shoot some pretty good scores. By my sophomore year, I was the number two man on the golf team, and I played number one my junior and senior year. It was really in my mind back then that maybe I'd like to give professional golf a go and see what happened.

7. No go as a pro. My father was a house painter, and there was no family money available to support a budding golf career. In 1976 I took a job as an assistant golf pro at Martindale Country Club in Auburn, Maine. I didn't last long. The head pro said he couldn't afford to have me around. That same year, one of my golfing buddies came back to Maine after living in California, and we saw that the PGA Tour was making a stop in Hartford. We decided to drive to Connecticut and see if we could pick up a bag and make a little money caddying.

I worked the Monday qualifier for a guy named David Smith. He didn't make it, but I was so green, I didn't know enough to go back to the tournament course to see if I could get another bag for the week. I figured my guy was out, so that was it for me. But Smith asked me if I would caddy for him in the qualifier the next week in Flint, Michigan. It was the middle of the summer, and I had nothing better to do, so I headed to the Midwest with my buddy, Bruce Willette.

6. A big break. We figured we could either caddy or try to qualify ourselves to play in state open tournaments. By the time we got to the Iowa Open, we only had enough money for one entry fee. I'd been playing well, so I entered and Bruce caddied for me. I shot 69 in the final round, earned $285, and that was enough to get us to the next tour stop in Las Vegas.

5. A bigger break. By the end of that season, I was working for a pro named Ed Sabo. He also asked me to work for him the following winter on the tour's West Coast swing. By 1978, when Sabo wasn't playing in an event, I would caddy for Larry Nelson. He was on his way to being a real gun.

I did the Players Championship with him in 1978, my first real splash in the big time. We had a chance to win, finished in the top five, and the whole experience was a great eye-opener for me. I also got to know Peter Jacobsen at that time, and I knew he had an open bag. I was learning the ropes a little and I decided to make a change. I dropped Sabo and picked up Peter's bag. Best move of my life. I was with him for 18 years and almost became a member of his family.

4. Tiger tale. At the 1996 PGA Championship, Jake had to withdraw with a back injury and headed home to heal. He told me he didn't know when he'd be back but wasn't going to play again until he got healthy. I went back home, in Columbus, Ohio, and thought I'd take a little time off. But one day, the telephone rang, and Tiger Woods was calling. He was 20 years old, about to turn professional, and asked if I was available to caddy for him the rest of the year.

I called Jake and he said to me, "It's something you better do. Go do it." I'd seen Tiger play at the British Open at St. Andrews in 1995. We were actually paired with him and Ernie Els, and Peter said to me when we were walking down the first fairway, "This is really something. We're playing with two guys who are going to be the future of golf." He was so right . . . I was seeing things I'd never seen before. The shots the kid was hitting, the length off the tee. It was just blowing my mind. I was also hearing another caddy was going to make a play for his bag. I'm thinking no way, this is my bag if I want it. And I wanted it.

3. Hello Tiger, goodbye Jake. Telling him I was making the switch to Woods was the hardest thing I've ever done in my life. He took it hard, but he was gracious. I took it hard, too. I told him face to face, and I started bawling like a baby. In hindsight, I know now that I did what I had to do. It was a chance to be a small part of Tiger's beginning, and it was more than I could say no to.

2. Say goodbye, Fluff. He won the Masters in 1997, but he decided to make a change two years later. I don't know why and I never will know. This happens all the time—players firing caddies. He never said, "You did this" or "You did that." From a golf aspect, we won only one time in 1998. Maybe he thought we were getting stale. I just said, "The best of luck to you, and thanks for the fun." I have absolutely no ill feelings toward him. I like him. He's a great guy, and he's always been kind to me.

1. One door closes, another opens. I was thinking about going off to play pro golf, maybe on the senior mini-tour circuit. I'd made enough money with Tiger to bankroll myself, but Jimmy Furyk called and asked if I'd take his bag. I knew I'd make more money caddying for him than I would playing myself. That was '99, and we're still at it. He's just a great guy, down to earth, a very real person and a great player. He also lets me caddy. He asks me plenty, and he makes very few mistakes. We do yardage together, we discuss what's going on, and then he'll just pull a club.

One of the biggest compliments I can give any player is that Jim has never blamed me for a bad club. Not once. He'll just say, "Aaah, I didn't hit it right." He won't put it on me. Tiger was never one to blame, either. And Tiger listened, all the time.

★ ★ ★ ★

"Golf is like a love affair. If you don't take it seriously, it's no fun; if you do take it seriously, it breaks your heart."

—Arthur Daley

ANNIKA'S GREATEST HITS: ANNIKA SORENSTAM'S DOZEN GREATEST GOLF MOMENTS

►LS

Annika Sorenstam will go down as one of the greatest female golfers of all time, with 90 worldwide victories—including 72 on the LPGA Tour and ten major championships—on her résumé before she retired from competitive golf in 2008. Ironically, the diminutive Swede with the metronomic swing probably got the most attention over her entire career for a 2003 tournament in Texas in which she missed the cut. More on that in this list of her career highlights.

12. Final triumph. The last LPGA victory of her career came at the 2008 Michelob Ultra tournament at Kingsmill in Williamsburg, Virginia, her 72nd title. Sorenstam had four rounds in the 60s, including a closing 66 to win by seven shots.

11. Eagle eye. Playing in her final U.S. Women's Open in 2008 at Interlachen Country Club in Minnesota, Sorenstam thrilled the crowd at the 18th hole on Sunday by holing out a 199-yard shot from the fairway for an eagle that left her in a tie for 24th place.

10. Hall of Famer. Sorenstam won the 2000 Welch's Circle K Championship, giving her enough career points from tournament wins and player honors to qualify for the World Golf Hall of Fame. Technically, she would have to wait three years to formally fulfill another of the Hall's LPGA requirements (play on the Tour for at least a decade). But her Circle K victory all but ensured that Sorenstam would become the first international female player to earn entry into the World Golf Hall of Fame.

9. En fuego. Sorenstam won five straight events during the 2005 season, tying Nancy Lopez for the all-time LPGA record.

8. Career slam. Sorenstam held off Se Ri Pak down the stretch to claim the 2003 Weetabix Women's British Open by a shot at Royal Lytham and became only the sixth woman to achieve a career grand slam of winning each major women's title at least once.

7. Playoff glory. Sorenstam claimed her tenth and final major championship at the 2006 U.S. Women's Open at the Newport Country Club in Rhode Island. Tied for the lead with Pat Hurst after 72 holes, she prevailed in an 18-hole Monday playoff, shooting 70 to Hurst's 74.

6. Lucky 13. In 2002 she came to the final event of the year, the ADT Championship at Trump International in West Palm Beach, with 12 worldwide victories in 24 starts that season. Sorenstam made it 13 that week, tying the single-season record for tournament wins set by Mickey Wright in 1963.

5. How low. In the second round of the 2001 Standard Ping Register event, Sorenstam shot a 59, becoming the first woman to ever post a score in the 50s while breaking the old record of 61. The round included 13 birdies, no bogeys, and just 25 putts on a 6,459-yard course. She missed one fairway, hit every green in regulation, and her longest par putt was three-and-a-half feet on a day when she also happened to be paired with her sister Charlotta.

4. Three's a charm. Sorenstam opened a 5-shot lead after 54 holes at the McDonalds LPGA Championship in Havre de Grace, Maryland, eventually beating 15-year-old Michelle Wie by three shots to capture her third straight LPGA title.

3. Oh, boy. Sorenstam had always wanted to test herself against the men in an event on the PGA Tour, and she was invited to the 2003 Colonial Invitational, becoming the first female to play in a men's tour event since Babe Zaharias competed at the 1945 Los Angeles Open. Thousands watched her tee off in the first round with a 4-wood that landed in the middle of the first fairway, a shot she later described as the most nerve-wracking of her career. She had rounds of 71 and 74 and missed the cut by four shots, but got a standing ovation at her final hole Friday. "I've climbed as high as I can," she said afterward, "and it was worth every step."

2. Big breakthrough. Sorenstam made the 1995 U.S. Women's Open her first victory on the LPGA Tour. Though Meg Mallon posted a record 54-hole score of 11-under 205 at the Broadmoor in Colorado Springs, the 24-year-old Sorenstam fired a 68 on Sunday to prevail by a shot and avoid a playoff with Mallon, who missed a 15-foot birdie putt by inches on the 72nd hole.

1. Back-to-back. After opening a 3-shot lead over the first 54 holes, Sorenstam came in with a final round 66 to win her second straight U.S. Women's Open title in 1996, beating runner-up Kris Tschetter by six shots at Pine Needles in Southern

Pines, North Carolina. Sorenstam became the first non-American to win back-to-back Open titles, inspiring *Sports Illustrated*'s Michael Bamberger to write that "golf might have identified its next Hogan . . . Sorenstam follows in the tradition of the great Texan whose golf was silent and deadly and at its best at the events that mattered most."

MEMORABLE WOMEN'S MAJORS

The LPGA almost always has taken a backseat to the PGA Tour in terms of crowds, purses, and television ratings. But the women definitely have produced more than their share of bright and shining stars as well as some of the more riveting moments in golf history, particularly in the major championships.

11. Mazda Mallon. Born in the Boston area and raised in Detroit, Meg Mallon was mostly unknown until she came to the Bethesda Country Club in the Washington suburbs for the 1991 Mazda LPGA Championship. Tied for the 54-hole lead with fellow New Englander Pat Bradley and Japan's Ayako Okamoto, Mallon sank a ten-foot birdie putt at the 72nd hole to beat them both by a shot—and win a car, too.

10. Rocky Mountain high. She gave herself the nickname "Birdie" to distinguish herself from all the other South Korean Kims on the LPGA Tour, and the 23-year-old certainly lived up to her name in the 2005 U.S. Women's Open. At Cherry Hills in the Denver suburbs, Kim holed out from a bunker 30 yards from the cup for one last birdie, just enough to hold off two teenage amateurs, 17-year-old Morgan Pressel and 19-year-old Brittany Lang, by two shots.

9. Jewel for Juli. In suffocating Mississippi summer heat and humidity, 38-year-old Juli Inkster, who had been contemplating giving up the tour, blossomed into a dominating champion of the 1999 U.S. Women's Open at Old Waverly Country Club. She ended five shots ahead of runner-up Sherri Turner, and her 16-under par total of 272 shattered the tournament record for lowest score relative to par by six shots. So much for early retirement.

8. Slam dunk. Karrie Webb holed out from 116 yards for an improbable eagle on the 72nd hole at the 2006 Kraft-Nabisco Championship, a stroke of genius that got her into a playoff against Lorena Ochoa, who also eagled the final hole with a clutch 12-foot putt. Webb wasted no time in the playoff, draining a 6-footer for birdie at the 18th to claim her seventh major title, with a final round 65. Of course she took the traditional dive into the pond near the final green shortly thereafter, no doubt employing the Australian crawl.

7. Viva Lorena. Frustrated by constantly being asked when she was going to win her first major championship, Lorena Ochoa went to St. Andrews, the home of golf, to do something about it in the summer of 2007. With an opening round 67, the then–No. 1 ranked player in the world took the lead after nine holes and never looked back, winning by four shots in a week of typical Scottish wind and spitting rain. "This is the most special round of golf I have ever played," said the native of Mexico after her final day 74 in atrocious conditions.

6. Major breakthrough. With three straight birdies in the middle of her final round, Annika Sorenstam opened a 3-shot lead in the 1995 U.S. Women's Open and held on for the first professional victory of her Hall of Fame career. She had to hold off a couple of fast-closing Hall of Famers—Pat Bradley and Betsy King—and won by a stroke over Meg Mallon, who missed a 20-foot birdie putt at the 18th. It was clearly the start of something very big for Sorenstam, who posted a final round 68 that day at the Broadmoor East course in Colorado Springs.

5. Rookie on a roll. It was never really close at the 1978 LPGA Championship contested at the Jack Nicklaus Golf Club in Kings Island, Ohio. Nancy Lopez, in her rookie season, won by six shots over her closest pursuer, Amy Alcott, for the first of her three LPGA major championships, and her only major victories. Lopez, only 21, won nine times that season, including five in a row, and earned Player of the Year honors. Said Hall of Famer Mickey Wright that week: "Never in my life have I seen such control in someone so young."

4. Korean invasion. Playing in her first major championship in her first season on the LPGA Tour, unknown 20-year-old South Korean Se Ri Pak went wire-to-wire to capture the McDonalds LPGA Championship at DuPont Country Club in Wilmington, Delaware. Pak won by three shots, but far more significant, her victories there and at the U.S. Women's Open a month later helped ignite an explosion back home in women's golf that has resulted in more than 40 Korean players now competing on the LPGA Tour and more than 40 on the Futures circuit as well. Ask any of the young Korean players to name their hero growing up, and most will say Hall of Famer Se Ri Pak.

3. Little Patty. Itty-bitty Patty Berg was a giant in women's golf in the 1940s and '50s, winning a record 15 major championships, including the 1946 U.S. Women's Open conducted by the short-lived Women's Professional Golf Association. That was replaced in 1950 by the LPGA, and in 1953 the U.S. Golf Association began running the Open. That first Open in '46 at the Spokane Country Club was decided in a 36-hole match-play format after 36 holes of qualifying by stroke play. Berg won the qualifying medal with rounds of 72 and 73 and beat Betty Jamison, 5 and 4, in the 36-hole final. She collected $19,700 for her efforts.

2. The Wright stuff. In the 1954 Women's Open, 19-year-old amateur Mickey Wright was paired with the great Babe Zaharias and made a huge splash by finishing fourth. Four years later at Forest Lake Country Club in Detroit, she prevailed over another LPGA founder, Louise Suggs, by five shots to win the first of her record four Open titles among her 13 major championships, second only to Berg. Her 82 career victories trail only the 88 posted by Kathy Whitworth. She earned $7,200 from the Scrooges at the USGA, who sliced Open purses dramatically when they took over the event in '53.

1. What a Babe. Perhaps the greatest female athlete of all time, Babe Didrikson Zaharias came to golf later in an athletic life dominated mostly by basketball and track and field. At the suggestion of famed sportswriter Grantland Rice, Zaharias decided to focus on the sport, and she was a quick study. Her victory in the 1954 U.S. Women's Open at Salem Country Club in Peabody, Massachusetts, was among the most inspirational triumphs in sports history. Only months after her first surgery for cancer, Zaharias won the Open by an astounding 12 shots over Betty Hicks, the second greatest margin of victory in tournament annals. Two years later she died from cancer at the age of 45, with 10 career major titles (four as an amateur) and 41 career wins. Her career winnings: $66,237.

BEST PRO TOURNAMENTS OTHER THAN THE MAJORS

The majors get most of the attention, but plenty of other PGA Tour events also are worth the trip. The writers on the beat look forward to attending these nonmajors every year. After all, the great thing about covering golf is that they usually hold these tournaments at really nice places. (Note: Some of the tournaments on this list might have a different name because of sponsorship changes by the time you read this; but you should get the idea.)

10. Phoenix Open. The biggest party in golf. The rowdy atmosphere on the par-3 16th is unlike anything in golf. Crowds are listed at more than 100,000 people per day. It doesn't matter that only 10 percent of them actually watch the golf.

9. AT&T Pebble Beach National Pro-Am. I'll always jump at the opportunity to go out to Pebble Beach. However, this tournament doesn't rank higher for a couple of reasons. Usually, the weather is terrible in February, making delays almost inevitable. Also, though it's fun to laugh at Bill Murray and the other celebs play on TV, you won't be laughing if you have to watch this format as a spectator on the grounds; there's nothing entertaining about rounds approaching six hours. While plodding through an excruciating 18 holes, Tiger Woods once asked me for the time. I said, "You don't want to know." He just threw his head back and groaned.

8. John Deere Classic and BMW Championship. I've got to give a shout out to my hometown events. A location in the Iowa-Illinois Quad Cities area means that John Deere has to try harder. It does, rolling out the red carpet for everybody. Tournament officials can't do enough for you. The "Western" isn't part of the tournament's name anymore, but the Western Golf Association still puts on a first-class event.

7. The Heritage. After the tumult of the Masters, going to Hilton Head is a great way to unwind. Framed by the water and buffeted by the wind, the Harbour Town Links always provides a good test and usually a memorable climax on its postcard 18th hole.

6. Arnold Palmer Invitational. Any tournament that has Arnold Palmer as the host always has an extra dimension. The players often complain about his Bay Hill course, but it usually produces an exciting event.

5. The Memorial. The same holds true for Jack Nicklaus's tournament. One of the highlights is listening to Nicklaus hold court. His Muirfield course also is terrific. I'd love to see a U.S. Open played there, but it'll never happen because Jack won't give up his tournament.

4. Quail Hollow Championship. This relatively new tournament quickly became popular with the players—and with good reason. Quail Hollow is a superb course, which attracts a strong field. From my perspective, it's hard to beat North Carolina in the spring.

3. Torrey Pines. Home to the former Buick Invitational, Torrey Pines has an enticing mix of scenery (a little thing called the Pacific Ocean), location (San Diego always is a favorite spot), and course (worthy of the 2008 U.S. Open). It also is the de facto season opener on the PGA Tour, as Tiger Woods and Phil Mickelson usually make Torrey Pines their first tournament of the year.

2. Players Championship. The so-called "Fifth Major" has a big-time field and feel on a big-time golf course. TPC at Sawgrass probably is the best viewing course in golf, and there's nothing like camping out at 17. The Jacksonville Beach area has many fine restaurants and nearby is the World Golf Hall of Fame. Hard to beat.

1. Tournament of Champions. Maui is my favorite place in the world. Thus, the site of the Tour's official season opener will always be my dream destination. The Plantation Course is a wild ride, featuring elevation changes that produce staggering views. From our perch near the first tee, you could see whales breaching in the distance. Plus, you're in Maui! In January! And the best part from my perspective: We get paid to be there. Yes, it's good to be a golf writer.

★ ★ ★ ★

"The more I practice, the luckier I get."

—Gary Player

NATIONWIDE ON THEIR SIDE

It began in 1990 as the Hogan Tour, a series of 30 events that first year designed to provide regular playing opportunities for up-and-coming young golfers not quite ready for prime time on the PGA Tour. Over the years, it's also been called the Nike Tour (1993–99), the Buy.com Tour (2000–02), and since 2003, the Nationwide Tour. The first season, purses totaled $3 million and offered about $100,000 per event. In 2010, there were 27 events and total purses of $17 million, with players competing for purses ranging from $500,000 to $1 million a week.

Over the years, the developmental tour has been the springboard to success for scores of players now on the PGA Tour. Here's a list of the ten best graduates.

10. Lucas Glover. The Clemson graduate had one victory, earned $258,681 on the Nationwide Tour in 2002 and 2003, and has since gone on to win twice on the PGA Tour, including the 2009 U.S. Open. He's also played on two Presidents Cup teams and has over $11 million in career earnings.

9. Stuart Appleby. The Australian played one season on the Nike Tour in 1995 and had two wins and $144,419 in earnings that year. Over his 14-year PGA Tour career, he's won six times, with over $23 million in earnings, and has played on five Presidents Cup teams.

8. Zach Johnson. The Iowa native played two seasons on the Hogan/Nike tours, in 2000 and 2003, and had one of the best years in history in '03 when he won twice, was second four times and third three times, with 16 top 25s in twenty starts with a then record $495,000 in earnings. He's since won six times on the PGA Tour, including the 2007 Masters, with over $18 million in career earnings, one Ryder Cup, and two Presidents Cup appearances.

7. John Daly. He played the first year of the Hogan Tour in 1990, with one win and prize money of $64,692, and was on the satellite circuit in 1991 when he stunned the world of golf by winning the PGA Championship as a ninth alternate into the field at Crooked Stick, earning an automatic promotion to the PGA Tour. He's won five times, including the 1995 British Open, with over $9 million in career earnings.

6. David Duval. He won twice and earned $212,312 in two seasons (1993–94) on the Nike Tour. Duval became the second developmental tour player to get to No. 1

in the world rankings, a feat accomplished in 1999, when he won four times. He has 13 career victories on the PGA Tour, including the 2001 British Open, with over $18 million in earnings along with two Ryder Cup and three Presidents Cup appearances.

5. Tom Lehman. Contemplating retirement from competitive golf for a career as a teaching pro, he found his A-Game on the Hogan Tour in 1991 when he was Player of the Year, won three times, and was second three times, with 24 top-25 finishes in 27 starts. The Minnesota native became the first Hogan Tour player to become No. 1 in the world rankings after he won the 1996 British Open, the same season he won Player of the Year and the money title on the PGA Tour. After earning $20 million on the PGA Tour, he's now a regular on the Champions Tour. He played on three Ryder Cup and three Presidents Cup teams and is the only developmental tour player to captain a Ryder Cup team.

4. Stewart Cink. The man from Georgia Tech had three wins and earned $251,699 in 1996 and has gone on to earn $28 million on the PGA Tour, with six victories, including the 2009 British Open. He's been as high as No. 5 in the world rankings and played on four Ryder Cup and four Presidents Cup teams.

3. David Toms. Started on the Hogan Tour in 1990, he lost his PGA Tour card and came back to the Nike Tour in 1995 when he won twice, had ten top-ten finishes, and moved up again, this time for good. An LSU graduate, he's won 12 times on the PGA Tour, including the 2001 PGA Championship in a final-day dual against Phil Mickelson and has $32 million in earnings. He also was a member of three Ryder Cup teams.

2. Jim Furyk. The Pennsylvania native took that unorthodox loopy swing and a cross-handed putting style to the Nike Tour in 1993 and won his first event as a professional at the Mississippi Gulf Coast Invitational. He moved up to the PGA Tour the following year and has now amassed 14 wins, including the 2003 U.S. Open. He pushed up to No. 2 in the world rankings in 2006 and has earned $43 million over his career, with appearances on six Ryder Cup teams and five Presidents Cup teams.

1. Ernie Els. The Big Easy was only 21 when he played eight events on the Hogan Tour in 1991 in an effort to get some seasoning and learn how to live on the road. His best finish was a tie for ninth that year, but three years later the South African won the first of his two U.S. Open titles. Els, who also won the 2002 British Open, has always played an international schedule and has earned more than $37 million on the PGA Tour, with 17 victories. He's moved up to No. 2 in the world rankings numerous times and played on six Presidents Cup teams.

THE (SOMETIMES) HONORABLE PENALTY BOX

►LS

Rules are rules and, in golf, are definitely not made to be broken, even if done so inadvertently. Occasionally, only the player knows he did wrong, and the game has a long history of do-the-right-thing behavior best exemplified by the great Bobby Jones. Congratulated by a friend for calling a penalty on himself during a major championship, Jones responded by saying, "you might as well praise me for not robbing banks." Our list of some of the game's most famous penalties includes several that actually brought great honor to the punished player.

11. Shark bites himself. In the 1996 Greater Hartford Open, Greg Norman, the defending champion, was the leader after the first round. But he also noticed the ball he had been using was not on the list of approved, conforming golf balls. He reported the violation and was subsequently disqualified.

10. Early bird (not so) special. In the final round of the 1941 U.S. Open, Porky Oliver was one of six players who decided to tee off slightly earlier than their original tee times in order to avoid an incoming storm. All six were disqualified, and Porky was the biggest loser of all because he was tied for the lead after 72 holes in an event won by Craig Wood.

9. Bad advice. In the second round of the 2007 Honda Classic, Mark Wilson's caddy yelled out the loft of the hybrid club Wilson had just used off the tee to reach the green of a par-3 hole. Wilson suspected that might have been in violation of the rule that prohibits giving advice to a fellow competitor, and a rules official confirmed it, ordering a 2-shot penalty. The good news: Wilson tied for the 72-hole lead and won in a sudden-death playoff.

8. Wait a second. Actually Denis Watson waited longer than that as his ball hung on the lip of the cup at the eighth hole in the first round of the 1985 U.S. Open at Oakland Hills. The ball eventually dropped for a birdie, but because Watson had waited longer than the allowed ten seconds, he was assessed a 1-shot penalty. He tied for second that week, a single shot from forcing a playoff with eventual champion Andy North.

7. Over the limit. Tied for the lead in the 2001 British Open going into the final round at Royal Lytham, Ian Woosnam assessed himself a 2-shot penalty for having 15 clubs in his bag, one more than allowed. He had brought along an extra driver that went undiscovered until after he had played the opening hole, a par 3. Woosie finished tied for third, four shots behind champion David Duval.

6. Lots of lip. That's what Jeff Maggert's ball found as he tried to get out of a fairway bunker in the final round of the 2003 Masters. His shot hit the lip of the hazard and then ricocheted into his chest. That resulted in a 2-shot penalty, a triple bogey on the hole, and knocked Maggert out of the lead. He eventually finished fifth.

5. Sudden death. Brian Davis was locked in a playoff with Jim Furyk at the 2010 Verizon Heritage on Hilton Head Island when he stepped up to hit a shot near a marshy area beside the 18th green. In his takeaway, Davis's club barely ticked a loose reed when trying to execute his shot. Only he knew it, but he immediately raised the issue, and a subsequent television replay confirmed the violation. Davis was penalized a shot for moving a loose impediment, thereby ending the playoff and giving Furyk the win and a $1.025 million check. Davis got $615,000, but earned the respect of every golfer on the planet.

4. DQ-school. J. P. Hayes was still in contention to earn his playing card on the PGA Tour at the 2008 Qualifying Tournament. That is, until his caddy flipped him a new ball out of his golf bag that Hayes put into play for one hole, until he noticed that it was a different model Titleist than the one he had been using. Hayes took a 2-shot penalty but determined after the round that the offending ball also had been a prototype he'd been given several weeks before. Because it was a nonconforming ball, he was disqualified from the tournament, ending his chance to make it to the Big Show that year.

3. Bunker mentality. American Dustin Johnson had no idea he was in one of Whistling Straits's 1,300 bunkers on his 72nd hole at the 2010 PGA Championship. So he grounded his club behind the ball after a wild drive he thought was simply in the rough, trampled down by hundreds of spectators all around. Bad move. Needing a par to win the tournament, Johnson was informed by a rules official on the green that he'd actually been in a bunker when his club touched terra firma, and he was assessed a 2-stroke penalty, thus preventing him from getting into a playoff that was eventually won by German Martin Kaymer.

2. What a stupid. Argentina's Roberto De Vicenzo signed an incorrect scorecard after tying for the 72-hole lead of the 1968 Masters. His playing partner, Tommy Aaron, had marked down a par 4 on the 17th hole instead of a birdie 3 on De Vicenzo's scorecard, and when poor Roberto signed it, with a score one shot higher than his true total, he lost to champion Bob Goalby by a shot. "What a stupid I am," De Vicenzo said that day, arguably the saddest quote in Masters history.

1. Bank job. On a greenside chip from a steep bank during the 1925 U.S. Open, the great Bobby Jones noticed that his ball had moved ever so slightly just before he was about to make contact. Playing with Walter Hagen, who did not see the infraction, Jones nevertheless immediately called the 1-shot penalty on himself, eventually costing him the outright victory. Tied for the lead after 72 holes, he lost the Open in a 36-hole playoff to Willie Macfarlane.

★ ★ ★ ★

"Golf and sex are the only things you can enjoy without being good at them."

—Jimmy DeMaret

TOP TEN AFRICAN AMERICAN PROFESSIONAL GOLFERS YOU PROBABLY NEVER HEARD OF

▶ BY PETE MCDANIEL

Pete McDaniel is an award-winning golf journalist, a longtime editor at *Golf Digest*, and the author of *Uneven Lies: The Heroic Story of African-Americans in Golf*. He also cowrote the screenplay for *Uneven Fairways*, a documentary based on the book that aired on the Golf Channel. He wrote two best sellers, *Training a Tiger: The Official Book on How to Be the Best* with Tiger Woods, and *Training a Tiger: A Father's Guide to Raising a Winner in Both Golf and Life* with the late Earl Woods.

10. John Shippen. As a 16-year-old caddy, he shared the first-round lead of the second U.S. Open (1896) at Shinnecock Hills Golf Club on Long Island. He's also recognized as this country's first professional golfer.

9. James Black. Enlisted as a hustling partner by members of a Charlotte (NC) country club, Black, a preteen at the time, might have been the first black phenom. A legend on the black golf tours, he had a short stint on the PGA Tour in the 1960s.

8. Nathaniel Starks. A stalwart on the black golf tours, he played several years on the PGA Tour in the 1970s, finishing 124th on the money list in 1974.

7. James (Junior) Walker, Jr. One of the best "money" players on the black golf tours, he notched a 30th place finish in the 1965 Westchester Open and 1969 L.A. Open.

6. Bill Wright. Won the U.S. Public Links championship in 1959 and the small college, NAIA individual title a year later. He also played the PGA Tour in the 1960s.

5. George (G. G.) Johnson. Won the 1971 Azalea Open and finished second in four other PGA Tour events.

4. Rafe Botts. Became the second (Charlie Sifford was the first) African American member of the PGA Tour in 1961. He also played on the Senior Tour for a while.

3. Bill Spiller. Quite a player in his heyday (his 68 in the first round of the 1948 L.A. Open tied Ben Hogan for second place). Some credit him with the abolishment of the "Caucasian-only" clause then used to exclude African American players from PGA events.

2. Chuck Thorpe. A member of the PGA Tour in the '70s (best finish was a tie for 10th in the 1973 Houston Open), Chuck was generally considered a much better player than his more famous younger brother Jim.

1. Ted Rhodes. Winner of the more than 150 tournaments on the black tours, he was called the "black Jack Nicklaus" by Charlie Sifford. He was nicknamed "Rags" because of his reputation as a clothes horse.

★ ★ ★ ★

"The worst club in my bag is my brain."

—Chris Perry

OY VEY, CAN THEY PLAY

With a couple of guys (not goys) named Sherman and Shapiro as the coauthors of this future best seller (from our lips to God's ear), how could we in good conscience not include a short list of the finest Jewish golfers who played at the highest levels of the game?

Each of the following splendid six won at least one tournament on the regular or senior tour that is now considered a major championship. By the way, Sherman and Shapiro play at the lowest level of the game, with no kvetching ever allowed.

6. Emilee Klein. The California native won three events during her 11-year LPGA career, but one of them was the 1996 Weetabix Women's British Open. It wasn't considered a women's major until 2001, but we'll still give her credit for it just because she's a nice Jewish girl and mostly because we can. She also played on Curtis Cup and Solheim Cup teams and now coaches the women's golf team at San Diego State.

5. Bruce Fleisher. Though he won the U.S. Amateur title in 1968, he was mostly a nonentity when he played on the PGA Tour, winning only one event, the 1991 New England Classic in a season when he also was named the tour's Comeback Player of the Year. But Fleisher's game truly blossomed when he hit age 50 and got to the Champions Tour, where he's won 18 times, including seven events in 1999 when he was the tour's Rookie of the Year and leading money winner as well as the U.S. Senior Open in 2001.

4. Cristie Kerr. The South Florida native was a highly decorated teenager who joined the LPGA Tour at age 19. She struggled over her first three seasons on the women's tour but has since become one of the game's most consistent players, with 12 LPGA victories and 16 top ten finishes in major events through 2009, including the 2007 U.S. Women's Open championship at Pine Needles in Southern Pines, North Carolina.

3. Morgan Pressel. In 2001, at the age of 12, she became the youngest player ever to qualify for a U.S. Women's Open, and she joined the LPGA Tour at age 17 after a brilliant career as a junior golfer that included the 2005 U.S. Women's Amateur title. That same year, she tied for second in the U.S. Women's Open at Cherry Hills in Denver, eventually beaten when Korean Birdie Kim holed out a shot from the bunker at the 72nd hole. Pressel, the niece of former top-ten tennis player Aaron Krickstein, has won twice on the LPGA Tour, but one of those victories came at the 2007 Kraft-Nabisco. She was 18 at the time, the youngest player ever to win a women's major.

2. Corey Pavin. The California native and UCLA graduate had 15 PGA Tour victories, the most memorable being the 1995 U.S. Open Championship at Shinnecock on Long Island. Pavin also was a gritty player on three U.S. Ryder Cup teams, a key member of the 1991 squad that won at Kiawah Island, and he served as captain of the American team in the 2010 Ryder Cup in Wales. He now plays full time on the senior Champions Tour.

1. Amy Alcott. Another California girl and a highly decorated junior player, Alcott turned pro at age 19 and won her third start on the LPGA Tour, one of 29 victories she amassed over her Hall of Fame career. She also won five major championships, three in the Kraft-Nabisco and the 1980 U.S. Women's Open at Richland Country Club in Nashville. Alcott had 24 top-ten finishes in major events, including second place in the LPGA Championship in 1978 and 1988, the only major title missing on her sterling résumé. She was named to the World Golf Hall of Fame in 1999, the only Jewish player ever enshrined.

★ ★ ★ ★

"No one will ever have golf under his thumb. No round ever will be so good it could not have been better. Perhaps this is why golf is the greatest of games. You're not playing a human adversary; you're playing old man par."

—Bobby Jones

SO CLOSE YET SO FAR AWAY

►LS

It happens almost every year in just about every major championship. An obscure golfer rises out of the pack and soars up the leader board during the first, second, and occasionally even the third round. Some even manage to lead on Sunday, but virtually all of them eventually fall by the wayside, all the while producing some of the most compelling stories in the history of the game. Here's a list of 13 unlucky losers.

13. Jim Simons, 1971 U.S. Open. A 20-year-old amateur from Pittsburgh, Simons opened with rounds of 71-71 and added a third-round 65 to take a 2-shot lead over Jack Nicklaus into the final round at Merion in the Philadelphia suburbs. He was still ahead by a shot going to the back nine Sunday, but bogeys at the 10th and 14th hole and missing makeable birdie putts at 15, 16, and 17 left him needing birdie at the 72nd hole to get into a playoff. Instead, he made double bogey and finished fifth in an event Lee Trevino won in an 18-hole playoff over Jack Nicklaus.

12. Gene Sauers, 1992 PGA Championship. The journeyman professional opened a 2-shot lead over Nick Price going into the final round at Bellerive Country Club in St. Louis. Price shot a steady 2-under 70 in the final round, but Sauers soared to a Sunday 75 and settled for a tie for second place with John Cook, Nick Faldo, and Jim Gallagher, three shots behind Price, who won the first of his three major titles that day.

11. Marty Fleckman, 1967 U.S. Open. A fine amateur player from Houston and a member of three NCAA championship teams at the University of Houston, Fleckman took a 1-shot lead into the last round over Nicklaus, Arnold Palmer, and Billy Casper. Fleckman hit it in the trees on his opening drive Sunday, posted a bogey, and went on to shoot an 80 in an event Nicklaus won with a final round 65 for a new Open record score of 275. Fleckman turned pro the next year and won his first event, the Cajun Classic in Lafayette, Louisiana, but he never won again in 13 years on the PGA Tour.

10. Lu Liang Huan, 1971 British Open. Lee Trevino seemed in total control in the final round when he took a 5-shot lead into the back nine. But the Formosa native Royal Birkdale crowds affectionately called "Mr. Lu" managed to close within a shot when Trevino double bogeyed the 16th. Tipping his trademark pork-pie hat toward the crowd after every shot, Huan eventually lost by a stroke when Trevino

260

birdied the final hole. Mr. Lu's golf career ended four years later when he suffered a back injury in a plane crash.

9. Ed Sneed, 1979 Masters. With a 5-shot lead over Tom Watson and 6 shots clear of Fuzzy Zoeller after 54 holes, Sneed still led by three strokes with three holes to play, but he bogeyed all three, leaving a six-foot putt hanging on the lip on the 18th hole that forced him into a playoff against Zoeller and Watson. Zoeller eventually birdied the 11th hole and won the title; Sneed never contended in a major again.

8. Mike Reid, 1989 PGA Championship. Three shots ahead with three holes to play at Kemper Lakes Golf Club in the Chicago suburbs, Reid hit his drive in the water for a bogey at 16, missed a 30-inch putt for a double bogey at 17, then missed a seven-foot birdie putt at the 18th to lose by a shot to Payne Stewart, who posted a 5-under 31 on the back nine for a Sunday 67. "I cry at supermarket openings," Reid said that day after shedding plenty of tears over his stunning collapse.

7. Brian Watts, 1998 British Open. An American pro who mostly played on the Japanese Tour at the time, Watts hit a stunning 45-foot shot from the sand to within two feet of the cup at the 72nd hole and made the par putt to force a playoff against Mark O'Meara at Royal Birkdale. But then Watts missed a 4-footer for par on the opening hole of a 4-hole playoff and lost by two shots. He never won on the PGA Tour and suffered a series of injuries that ended his career after the 2005 season.

6. Billy Joe Patton, 1954 Masters. A long-hitting 28-year-old amateur who made his living as a lumber salesman, he faded from contention with a third-round 75. Patton got back into the mix when he made a hole-in-one at the sixth hole on Sunday on his way to a front-nine 32 that left him tied for the lead with Ben Hogan going to the back nine. A double bogey at the 13th and a bogey at the 15th, both reachable par 5s, led to a round of 1-under 71, but a shot short of a playoff between Sam Snead and Hogan. Snead shot 70 in the playoff to Hogan's 71 and won. Patton played in a dozen more Masters and finished eighth in 1958 and '59. Years later he said, "even though I didn't win the tournament, the 1954 Masters changed my life."

5. Bob May, 2000 PGA Championship. An obscure pro who had mostly played on the European Tour, the Southern California native went shot-for-shot against Tiger Woods in a memorable Sunday duel at Valhalla in Louisville. Playing the final round with Woods in the last group, May made a 15-foot birdie putt at the 72nd hole, only to watch Woods sink his own 6-footer for birdie to force the first 3-hole aggregate playoff in tournament history. May shot 66 in the final round and made three pars in the playoff, but Woods's 20-foot birdie putt at the first playoff hole ultimately proved decisive. May played several years on the PGA Tour, but now mostly competes on the Nationwide circuit.

4. T. C. Chen, 1985 U.S. Open. With a double eagle on his second hole of the first round, Taiwanese golfer T. C. Chen eventually took a 2-shot lead into the final day and was ahead by 4 after the first four holes. Disaster struck on the 5th hole, however, when a drive into the trees wreaked major havoc. On his fourth shot from deep rough, Chen somehow popped the ball straight up in the air, then inadvertently hit the ball a second time on his follow through. The double hit added a penalty stroke, and Chen made quadruple bogey eight. Chen stayed close but eventually settled for second place, tied with Denis Watson and Dave Barr, a shot behind champion Andy North. Forever more, T. C. Chen was known as Two-Chip Chen.

3. Jason Gore, 2005 U.S. Open. He came into the Open the 818th ranked player in the world, but at the end of three rounds, Gore had become the toast of the tournament at Pinehurst No. 2, trailing two-time Open champion Retief Goosen by only three shots. They played together in the final round and melted down together. Goosen shot 81 and tied for 11th place; Gore posted 84 and tied for 48th. Gore went on to win the 84 Lumber Classic later that season, his only victory on the PGA Tour.

2. Jenny Chuasiriporn, 1998 U.S. Women's Open. A 19-year-old junior at Duke University, the Baltimore amateur made a remarkable 45-foot birdie putt at the 72nd hole at Blackwolf Run in Wisconsin to force an 18-hole playoff the next day against Se Ri Pak. Chuasiriporn made bogey at the 18th hole to send the match into sudden death, and Pak finally won the title with a birdie on the 20th hole of the day. Chuasiriporn played another year of college golf, but she never was able to make it to the LPGA Tour.

1. Mike Donald, 1990 U.S. Open. A Michigan native with one PGA Tour win on his résumé, Donald seemed like a lock to win the Open at Medinah until Hale Irwin knocked in a 60-foot birdie putt at the 72nd hole, leading to an 18-hole playoff the next day. Donald had a 1-shot lead after 17 playoff holes but couldn't get up and down for par from a bunker, missing a 20-foot putt that would have won the Open. In sudden death, Irwin prevailed on the first hole when Donald missed a 30-footer and settled for par, whereas Irwin rammed in a ten-foot birdie putt for the title. Donald never again contended in a major or won on the PGA Tour.

THE ODDS—HOLE-IN-ONE

Golf definitely isn't a fair game. As of this writing, after hitting millions of shots, I'm still searching for my first ace. Meanwhile, my mother-in-law, Judy, who has played maybe 20 times in her life, has a hole-in-one. I don't know whether to laugh or cry.

Recording a hole-in-one definitely means beating the odds. A search through various sources shows your chances of being like my mother-in-law and experiencing a memory for a lifetime.

12,000-1. The odds of an average amateur player making a hole-in-one. In 2000, *Golf Digest* hired a mathematician to calculate the various odds for making an ace. This figure seems fairly consistent with others, including those from insurance companies.

3,000-1. The odds for a tour player making a hole-in-one. They were considerably lower at the 2009 Canadian Open. The tournament featured eight aces. You almost wonder if the sport was basketball, not golf that week.

5,000-1. The odds for a low handicapper making a hole-in-one. Yes, it helps to have a better game. Also, these players usually play more, thus increasing their chances.

150,000-1. The odds of an average player acing a 200-yard hole, according to the *Golf Digest* researcher. It figures. Plenty of average golfers can't hit a fairway from 200 yards, let alone put the ball in the hole from that distance.

26.4 million-1. The odds of an average golfer making two holes-in-one in the same round, according to US Hole in One, a company that provides insurance for contests. If you get two holes-in-one in the same round, just quit. It'll never get any better than that.

156 million-1. The odds of making holes-in-one on consecutive holes, according to US Hole in One. If you make aces on two straight holes, drops your clubs and buy a bunch of lottery tickets now!

488 billion-1. The odds of three golfers from the same foursome making holes-in-one on the same hole, according to US Hole in One. Wonder how the fourth player must feel? Imagine this scenario: The three guys who hit before you record an ace. Talk about pressure.

1 million-1. The odds for recording a double eagle, otherwise known as an albatross. It is the rarest feat in golf because it means holing out from distances usually more than 250 yards. In 2009 there were only four double eagles on the PGA Tour, compared to 36 aces.

Then there's the day Nicholas Thompson enjoyed at the Frys.com Open in 2009. On the par-5 11th, he sank a 3-wood from 261 yards for a double eagle. Then on the par-3 13th, he canned a 7-iron from 199 yards. He played those two holes in 5-under. It doesn't get much better than that.

★ ★ ★ ★

"One of the most fascinating things about golf is how it reflects the cycle of life. No matter what you shoot—the next day you have to go back to the first tee and begin all over again and make yourself into something."

—Peter Jacobsen

SOUND WITH A LITTLE FURY

The sounds of the game are everywhere on a golf course, from the chirping birds in the trees—often manufactured via tape during network telecasts— to the quiet morning hush just before that first swing as the sun comes up at your local muni. It can come from 10-deep galleries at the U.S. Open or your very own throat—YESSSSS!!!!—when that 40-footer drops into the hole. We offer some of our favorite golf-related sounds, some with fury surely to follow.

A Nicklaus roar at Augusta National, unlike any other.

The **marching feet of Arnie's Army** in his prime.

"Ole, Ole, Ole" from the European side and fans, following a Ryder Cup victory.

KER-POW!!! when John Daly's driver connects with a ball about to fly 365.

The **ker-plunk of a splashed 8-iron** into the pond short of the green.

The **thwaaack of a ball** smacking flush into a tree trunk.

The **agonizing "ooooooh" from thousands** all around when a tee shot finds water at the 17th island green at Sawgrass.

The **ping** of a well-struck 3-iron.

The **chunk** when you hit more earth than ball.

The **click-click-click of press cameras** all around as the late Byron Nelson teed off as an honorary Masters starter.

"You suck Tiger Woods, Goddammit!!," from the mouth of Tiger Woods after a poor shot at the 6th hole Saturday in the 2010 Masters, five days after he said he planned to control his temper following a five-month layoff.

The **thumping thud of a towering wedge shot** landing on a soft green stiff to the pin.

The **reverberating soft rattle** as your ball goes over the edge and bounces down to the bottom of the cup.

The **clank of a perfectly struck shot that hits the flagstick from the fairway**, then skitters off the green.

"Hey-lo," Lorena Ochoa's lovely hello, her gracious first word at every one of her news conferences.

A buzz, getting louder now, ever louder by the inch as Tiger's 60-footer tracks inexorably toward the hole, followed by **a sonic boom** when it disappears.

The **click of ball hitting the asphalt cart path,** adding 50 yards to that tee shot.

"Champion Golfer of the Year" from the chairman of the Royal and Ancient when he hands the Claret Jug to the British Open winner on the 18th green.

"Play well," from one opponent to another on the first tee.

"SHOTTTT!!!," from one admiring pro to another after a well-executed play.

"FORE!!!" (left or right), one sound you never want to hear, along with **"You da man"** and **"You're still away."**

★ ★ ★ ★

"Golf is an awkward set of bodily contortions designed to produce a graceful result."

—Tommy Armour

RÉSUMÉ GAPS

There are several golf legends that have a notable hole or two on their golf résumés. They are forever dogged by never being able to win a particular major. It kept them from joining that exclusive club of career Grand Slam winners.

Here's a list of what's missing from the best of the best.

10. Walter Hagen. Many historians will quibble with Hagen being included in this list. The Haig won 11 majors from 1914–29. However, none came in the Masters. Of course, the famed tournament didn't debut until 1934. He wound up playing in six Masters, with his best finish being an 11th-place in 1936. To be fair, Hagen was past his prime in the '30s. If the Masters existed earlier during his peak years, it's a good bet he would have won at least one Green Jacket, if not more. However, the record shows that Hagen did play in the Masters and didn't win. Hence, he is on this list.

9. Byron Nelson. Lord Byron has a similar scenario as Hagen. He won five majors: two Masters, two PGAs, and one U.S. Open. Nelson, though, never won a British Open. Of course, back then most players didn't make the trip over the pond. Nelson played in only one British Open, finishing fifth in 1937. You'd think Nelson would have won a Claret Jug if he played the tournament on a regular basis. But he didn't, and as a result, he only won three-fourths of the career Grand Slam.

8. Raymond Floyd. Floyd won four majors, but he never was able to get over the top in the British Open. His best chance came in 1978 when he charged hard with a closing round 68 at St. Andrews. However, it wasn't good enough, as he finished in a tie for second, two shots behind Jack Nicklaus.

7. Nick Faldo and Seve Ballesteros. The two superstars are entered as a double combination because they both had similar careers. Each found glory at the British Open (three titles each) and Masters (three for Faldo, two for Ballesteros). But their bids for the career Grand Slam were denied by coming up short in the U.S. Open and PGA Championship. Faldo finished second at the 1988 U.S. Open and 1992 PGA. Ballesteros never did better than third at the 1987 U.S. Open and fifth in the 1984 PGA.

6. Tom Watson. Watson was the dominant golfer of his generation, winning eight majors. An impressive record to be sure, but thanks to the PGA Championship, he failed to join the career Grand Slam club. His best effort was a second at the 1978 PGA. He led the tournament after each of the first three rounds, but he stumbled with a 73 on Sunday. He eventually lost in a playoff to John Mahaffey.

5. Arnold Palmer. His storyline almost is identical to Watson's. The King won seven majors during his run, but none of them came at the PGA Championship. Three times he knocked on the door, only to finish second in 1964, 1968, and 1970.

4. Lee Trevino. "The Merry Mex" won six majors, but he never had a chance to finish off the career Grand Slam because of the Masters. For starters, the course didn't fit his game, which favored a fade. He called it a "stupid course." The golfer who came from humble beginnings also felt out of place with the blueblood atmosphere at Augusta National. He even went as far as to not enter the 1970–71 tournaments. Trevino did return, but with his negative mindset about the place, he never finished higher than 10th.

3. Kathy Whitworth. The final three entries on the list have a common void. They each won a slew of tournaments but never claimed the U.S. Open. Whitworth holds the LPGA record with 88 victories. She won six majors, including three LPGA Championships. However, the U.S. Open eluded her grasp. Her best finish was a second in 1971.

2. Nancy Lopez. Lopez had so many terrific moments in a career that saw her win 48 titles. However, one of the most lasting images of her will be from a tournament she didn't win. At the age of 40, she made one last valiant bid to win the 1997 U.S. Open. She had finished second on three previous occasions. The Open was the tournament Lopez wanted the most, and with the crowd pulling for her, she needed to make a putt for birdie on 18 to force a playoff with Alison Nicholas. The 15-footer slid just past the hole. Lopez broke into tears, knowing she would never win the U.S. Open.

1. Sam Snead. "The Slammer" is credited with winning 82 PGA Tour titles. His seven major victories include three Masters and three PGA Championships. Yet incredibly, Snead never won a U.S. Open. Four times he came in second. At the 1939 Open, he came into the 18th hole needing a par to win. Instead, he made a triple bogey 8. Snead's inability to win the U.S. Open was always held against him. He once said, "When they say that I couldn't win the big one, I ask: What do you call all those others? What's big and what's small?"

ED'S FAVORITE MEMORIES

The first golf tournament I ever covered was the 1997 Masters, Tiger Woods's first Green Jacket. Nothing like starting with one of the most historic golf moments of all time. I would go on to cover many more of Woods's victories—an up-close look at greatness. Yet for me, the lasting memories of covering golf seem to center around the people I met and the unique experiences of being around the game. Here are a few.

8. Lord Byron. When it comes to royalty in golf, they don't come much bigger than Lord Byron. Byron Nelson's epic winning streak included a title at the Chicago Victory Open at Calumet Country Club. The club got Nelson to accept an invitation to return nearly 60 years later. Gracious as always, he held a session with the media. For more than 30 minutes, he told stories and talked about his swing and the game. It was a special day.

7. Victory march. I followed Tiger Woods many times during his career, but the one that always stands out for me is the final round of the 2005 British Open. I walked all 18 holes with him that day at St. Andrews. You could sense that we were witnessing history as Woods pulled away from the field on this hallowed ground for golf. One shot stood out. At 16, we packed ourselves in on the tee box. I could have grabbed one of the markers if I wanted to cause a scene. It was a short par 4, and José Maria Olazabal went first, using an iron. Then it was Woods's turn. He also used an iron, but when it hit the ground, there was a distinct thud. The sound was completely different. It was the sound of perfection.

6. Overcoming adversity. Casey Martin truly was an inspiring figure in golf. However, his struggle took on a whole new dimension for me when I got to play a round with him during a media day prior to a Nationwide Tour event. He was nearing the end of his playing days, and we played on a cold wintery day on what passes for spring in May in Chicago. You could see how painful it was for him to walk on that ailing leg. Even though he rode in a cart, he still had to walk up and down some hills around tees and greens. Yet he never complained, and he hit the ball as pure as I'd ever seen. It made you wonder just how good he could have been on a healthy leg.

5. Make my day. After Tiger Woods won his sixth straight tournament at the 2001 AT&T at Pebble Beach, I saw Clint Eastwood at the side of the green. I went up to him for a quote. He didn't have much to say, but he quickly found me useful. As the autograph seekers came up to him, he used me as a shield, saying, "Can't right now. Doing an interview." When we got to his Mercedes, perhaps feeling guilty, he asked if I needed a ride. I passed, as I only had to walk a few more feet. To this day, my biggest regret is that I didn't get in that car with Clint Eastwood. I should have made him drive me all around Monterrey.

4. Presidential. I had heard George H. W. Bush was at the 1997 Ryder Cup at Valderrama in Spain. Lo and behold, there he was, sitting on the side of a hill off the 17th green. He was chatting with a couple of photographers, so I went over to him. I figured: When would I get another chance to talk to a former president? The next group was on 14, and Bush wasn't in any hurry to go anywhere. Joined by London writer John Hopkins, we talked with the former president for 45 minutes. The subject was mostly golf, although I did ask how my paper, the *Chicago Tribune*, treated him as president. "Well, I can't think of anything bad, so it must have been Okay," he said.

3. A diss from Oprah. As I said, the 1997 Masters was my first tournament on the beat. I tried to be cocky and wrote in bold print that Woods, then 21, "wouldn't tame Augusta." As Maxwell Smart would say, "Missed it by that much." Woods went on to win by 12 strokes, shooting a record score. I wrote a mea culpa, but that didn't stop people from piling on—including Oprah. A few days after the event, Woods came to Chicago to do her show. The media was invited to watch the taping in the control room. Just prior to the show, Oprah came barging in, asking, "Where's that reporter who said Tiger wouldn't win?" Then on the show, she told Tiger that there was "a reporter eating crow" back there. Well, at least I got some national publicity.

2. The first Masters. There were so many things that stood out from my first trip to Augusta National in 1997. The sense of history being made was overwhelming. Woods's gallery included Ernie Banks. They don't any bigger in Chicago than "Mr. Cub." Banks was one of my heroes growing up. And there he was, like everyone else following this 21-year-old golfer. I approached Ernie and found out he is a huge golf fan. In fact, whenever I see him now, he always asks me about who I liked in an upcoming major.

It was fitting that I ran into Ernie on this day. He played in the same era as Jackie Robinson. Ernie knew Tiger's victory would inspire countless people, the same way Robinson once inspired him.

1. A special birdie. This one truly is personal. I've always said if the over-the-top move was the key to a good golf swing, they'd be writing about me. Yet for one brief moment, I got to experience what it is like to feel like a pro on the most famous course in the world. In 1999 I had a chance to play Augusta National the day after Olazabal's victory. The adrenalin was pumping so much that I barely got the ball up in the air for the first three holes. Eventually, I settled down, and we arrived at the par-3 12th.

There was a three-group back-up, but we didn't care. We enjoyed being on one of the most famous holes in golf. Finally, it was our turn. Even though the hole only played 155 yards, I noticed everyone had been coming up short. That famed, swirling wind. So I went with a 5-iron. I hit it as pure as any golf shot I ever hit. The ball drew over the bunker (I'm a lefty) and landed four feet from the pin. The Sunday pin!

Stunned and numb, I felt my caddy grab my club and hand me my putter. I don't know if there is a better feeling in golf than walking over the Hogan Bridge with a putter in your hand. Then it did get better when I sank the putt for a birdie. The sense of exhilaration was unlike anything I ever felt in sports.

It turned out that on the previous day, the best players in the world made only four birdies on that hole with that pin. To those people who say I didn't face the same pressure as the pros, I counter with, "Yeah, but they didn't have to do it with my swing."

★ ★ ★ ★

"Golf is not just an exercise; it's an adventure, a romance . . . a Shakespeare play in which disaster and comedy are intertwined."

—Harold Segall

LEN'S FAVORITE MEMORIES

As a kid growing up on Long Island in the 1960s, I first was introduced to golf as a 14-year-old caddy at the Woodcrest Country Club on Long Island. It was $5 a bag, no tips, a free soda and hotdog for lunch, and if you were lucky, you broke even in the daily blackjack game back in the caddy shack. More than thirty years later, I started covering golf for the *Washington Post* in 1991, a dream assignment that's produced all manner of grand memories and goose-bump moments. Here's one man's top ten.

10. Living statue. Covering my first Byron Nelson Classic at the Las Colinas Resort in the Dallas suburbs in the mid-1990s, one morning I stopped for a moment to admire the statue of Byron Nelson in the courtyard of the golf complex. As I was admiring the sculpture, a tall fellow in a porkpie hat walked into my line of sight, and when I looked up, there was Lord Byron himself, in the flesh, on his way to the pro shop. He said nothing. I said nothing. But talk about life imitating art.

9. Beem me up. It was the Sunday of the 1999 Kemper Open at the old TPC at Avenel in the Washington suburbs, and I was watching eventual up-from-nowhere winner Rich Beem play the eighth hole when CBS analyst David Feherty walked over and went into a classic riff. "Len, Len, I've just picked up air traffic control at Dulles Airport in my headset," he gushed. "They wanted to know my position and height. I told 'em I'm 5-foot-11 and standing in the middle of the 8th fairway at the TPC at Avenel." Okay, maybe you had to be there. But I was, laughing out loud.

8. What happens in Vegas. I went out to the 1996 Las Vegas Invitational to research a feature story on a widely heralded young golfer named Tiger Woods who had recently turned pro. Woods just happened to win for the first time on the PGA Tour that week, beating Davis Love III in a playoff, and I'm pretty sure I was the only national newspaper writer on hand to witness his historic triumph. My most vivid memory was the victory ceremony, when a gaggle of shapely Vegas showgirls wearing the bare minimum surrounded the seemingly bashful 21-year-old Woods as he held up his oversized champion's check and smiled for the cameras. Knowing what we all know now, I bet he had a great night, too.

7. A last salute. At the 2000 U.S. Open at Pebble Beach, less than eight months after his tragic death in a bizarre plane crash, more than 40 of Payne Stewart's fellow players also gathered not far from the 18th green for an emotional 35-minute ceremony that began at 7 a.m. and ended with what was described as a "21-tee salute." With hundreds of somber spectators looking on, two waves of golfers, on the command "ready, aim, fire," struck golf balls off the 18th fairway over the stone wall and into the Stillwater Cove in a moving gesture to honor the man who had won his second U.S. Open championship only a year earlier in Pinehurst, North Carolina. The sound of silence as all those shots soared into the morning mist was interrupted only by the voice of a kayaker paddling down below: "We love you Payne."

6. Wild thing. The very first PGA Championship I ever covered was the very best PGA Championship I ever covered. It was 1991, at Crooked Stick in the Indianapolis suburbs, and an obscure 25-year-old rookie who had been the ninth alternate into the field went from being a total unknown to a global superstar in the space of four days. John Daly gripped it and ripped it and won by three shots that week. His performance was stunning, but I still remember his then girlfriend and future wife, Bettye Fulford, telling several of us in an interview behind the 18th hole on Sunday that her main man was a wonderful fellow in addition to being a fabulous golfer. Then came the kicker: if she could just get him to cut back on the Jack Daniels . . .

5. Roars unlike any other. Jack Nicklaus was 58 at the time, with no great expectations at the 1998 Masters. But there he was on the front nine Sunday, making birdie after birdie and evoking sonic-boom roars every time his ball found the bottom of the cup. I'd never heard sounds like that nor ever seen the sight of hundreds of spectators literally dashing from all corners of the golf course to join an ever-expanding monster gallery to witness Nicklaus's last great run in a major. He eventually cooled off on the back nine, but his final round 68 left him tied for sixth place, the oldest golfer ever to finish in the top ten of the tournament he won for the last time a dozen years before. Amazing.

4. Goodbye Arnold. Arnold Palmer had just posted an 81 in the second round of the 1994 U.S. Open at Oakmont, his final appearance in America's national championship. Not long after he signed his card, he came to the media center for a news conference that was anything but. The great Dan Jenkins, writing in *Golf Digest* a few weeks later, described the scene far better than I ever could: "On Friday," he wrote, "Arnold Palmer conducted the most memorable non-press conference after playing in his final Open. He uttered 20 difficult words in about five minutes but was so overcome with emotion he was forced to excuse himself. There weren't many dry eyes in the audience, either, and suddenly, for one of the few times in their cynical lives, the press inhabitants spontaneously gave this most cooperative athlete they would ever know a standing ovation."

3. Toughest tee shot ever. That would have been Annika Sorenstam's opening shot at the 2003 Colonial Invitational, when she became the first female since Babe Zaharias in 1945 to play in a PGA Tour event. I was in the middle of thousands of spectators gathered around the tenth tee (she started her first round on the back nine at Colonial) and lined six-deep down the fairway to watch her historic first round begin, and she did not disappoint. She launched a 4-wood smack down the middle and did a mock swoon of relief not long after she made perfect contact. Sorenstam played well but missed the cut that week and has said many times since that she will never forget the support she received from the massive galleries that day in Ft. Worth. She's also admitted she had never been more nervous in her life than in the moments before she walloped that first pressure-packed drive. She was not alone.

2. *Comedie Francaise*. Jean Van de Velde came to the 487-yard 18th hole at Carnoustie with a 3-shot lead in the 1999 British Open, needing only a double bogey to win. Instead, the Frenchman made a triple bogey seven that left him in a three-man playoff with Justin Leonard and eventual winner Paul Lawrie. The playoff began in rain, and several of us were on the course huddled under umbrellas watching the extra session. Davis Love III had also come out in a show of support for his friend and fellow American Leonard, and at one point, I asked him how he might have played the 18th hole with a 3-shot cushion. A 7-iron, 7-iron, wedge, and three putts was the short answer, and anything but the driver off the tee that Vande de Velde had chosen on his way to the greatest disaster in major championship history. *C'est la vie.*

1. Masters for the ages. On Sunday of the final round of the 1997 Masters, I was standing next to Lee Elder, the first African American golfer to play in the Masters, about thirty yards from the first tee. We were waiting for Tiger Woods to finish up on the practice putting green and make his way through a funnel of fans to begin his historic final round as the first man of color to win the tournament, with a record score and margin of victory to boot. As Woods was being introduced, I could see the tears welling in Elder's eyes as he took it all in. Then I turned around and gazed back to the nearby clubhouse. The second-floor balcony overlooking the course was lined not so much with Augusta National members but mostly with the men and women who served their meals, mixed their drinks, washed their dishes, shined their shoes, and cleaned their rooms, virtually all of them African American as well. I also felt a shiver down my spine standing there on that memorable afternoon, and I still get goose bumps typing these very words.

THE ALL-TIME TOP TWENTY
LPGA GOLFERS

So many qualified players, so maddening having to keep more than a few well-known names out. You could probably make a case that players like Judy Rankin, Laura Davies, Cristie Kerr, Dottie Pepper, and Meg Mallon, among others, belong in the top twenty, but who would you leave out? And of course, comparing players of different eras is never easy, but in one man's opinion, these are the best of the best.

20. Se Ri Pak. She was singularly responsible for spawning the dramatic influx of South Korean players into the professional ranks. Her victories in the 1998 LPGA Championship and U.S. Women's Open led to hundreds of Korean girls taking up the game. She was inducted into the Hall of Fame in 2007 and had five major titles.

19. Lorena Ochoa. The Mexican star had a meteoric rise and then gave it all up to marry and start a family in 2010, even as she was ranked the No. 1 player in the world, a position she held for three years. Ochoa won two majors and 27 other LPGA events and will always be remembered for her magically humble personality and world-class grace and dignity.

18. Carol Mann. The 6-foot-3 star won 38 LPGA Tour events over a brilliant career, including two major titles. She also finished in the top ten on the money list nine times between 1965 and 1975 and was among the more vocal players in helping form LPGA policy over the years.

17. Beth Daniel. The South Carolina native won 33 times on the LPGA Tour during the Nancy Lopez era, including four major titles. In 1990 she had seven victories, and when she won her last event in 2003, at age 46 years and eight months, she became the oldest champion of a tour event in history, a triumph that ended a seven-year winless drought.

16. Juli Inkster. Inkster was still an active player on the LPGA Tour at age 50, trying to add to her 31 wins and seven major titles. She also became an inspiration to many young women who watched her raise her two daughters while still pursuing her playing career. Inkster was a highly decorated amateur as well, winning three U.S. Women's Amateur championships.

15. Amy Alcott. At age 19, in her third start on the LPGA circuit she won the first of her 29 victories, among them five major championships. In 1991, after winning her third straight Nabisco Dinah Shore (now the Kraft-Nabisco), she began what is now a tradition of the winner jumping into the water hazard at the 18th hole. It was her final career victory.

14. Sandra Haynie. The Texas native won 42 events, including four majors, and was in the top ten on the money list every year from 1963 to 1975. She did it again in 1982 in a year when she had five runner-up finishes and continued playing full time through the 1989 season.

13. Betsy Rawls. The South Carolina star joined the LPGA in 1951, its second season as an official organization, and went on to win 55 times, with eight major titles. In 1996 she was presented the Bob Jones Award, given by the USGA to honor her great sportsmanship, and after retiring, she became a widely respected tournament director, including the LPGA Championship in Wilmington, Delaware.

12. Pat Bradley. A Massachusetts native, she won 31 events and four majors, and she had one of the greatest seasons in history in 1986 when she won three of the four majors—the Kraft-Nabisco, U.S. Women's Open, and du Maurier Championship. That season she also was fifth in the U.S. Women's Open. What's more, she was the third woman in history, joining Louise Suggs and Mickey Wright, to win a career grand slam of all the majors.

11. Patty Sheehan. Born and raised in Middlebury, Vermont, Sheehan joined the LPGA in 1980 and was named Rookie of the Year that season. She went on to win 35 titles and six major championships. She was the tour's Player of the Year in 1983 and was one of several athletes named *Sports Illustrated*'s Sportsman of the Year in 1987.

10. Louise Suggs. An LPGA founder, the Georgia native was a highly decorated amateur player in the 1940s. She turned pro in 1948 and went on to win 55 tournaments, including 11 majors, and was a charter member of the LPGA Hall of Fame. The tour's Rookie of the Year award bears her name, and in 2007 she also won the Bob Jones Award.

9. Karrie Webb. The Australian made a huge splash in her rookie season on the tour in 1996 when she won the second event she played, the Health South Classic. Considered her nation's greatest all-time female golfer, Webb has won 36 times on the LPGA Tour, with four majors. In 1995 she also won the Women's British Open, at the time not considered a major.

8. Betsy King. From 1984 to 1989, King won 20 tournaments, more than any other player in the world over the same span. She has 34 tour wins, with six majors; has been named Player of the Year three times; won the scoring title twice; and led the money list three times. She also won at least one event a year for ten straight seasons, from 1984 to '94, with a six-win season in 1989.

7. Patty Berg. After winning 29 amateur titles, Berg turned professional in 1940 and began to pile up even more victories, with 60 tournament titles, fourth on the all-time list, and a record 15 major championships. Berg was a founding member of the LPGA and won the inaugural U.S. Women's Open in 1946. Berg also served as the LPGA's first president.

6. JoAnne Carner. From 1956 to 1968, JoAnne Gunderson (her maiden name) was the dominant amateur in the country before turning professional at the age of 30. She was known as The Great Gundy back then, and eventually she won 46 LPGA titles and five majors. Also known affectionately as Big Mama, she played competitively into her early 60s and became the oldest ever to make an LPGA cut in 2004 at the age of 65.

5. Babe Didrikson Zaharias. A versatile athlete who excelled in golf, basketball, and track and field, she didn't start playing golf until her mid-20s. But she was a dominant player in the 1940s and early 1950s, both in the amateur and pro ranks, and competed in several men's events as well. Her greatest year was 1950, when she won all three women's majors—the U.S. Open, Titleholders, and Western Open. She also was an LPGA founder and one of the most popular athletes, male or female, in American sports history.

4. Nancy Lopez. As an 18-year-old amateur, she tied for second in the 1975 U.S. Women's Open and then took the LPGA by storm in 1978, her first full season on the tour. She won nine events that year, including five straight. She was named both Rookie of the Year and Player of the Year as well as the Associated Press's Female Athlete of the Year. Lopez won eight more events the following season and 48 LPGA tournaments, with five majors. She may well be the most popular player in the tour's history and remains a great ambassador for the sport.

3. Kathy Whitworth. The first woman to earn $1 million in career purses, a feat accomplished in 1981, she won a record 88 tournaments, more than any other player, male or female, in golf history. Between 1966 and 1973, she was Player of the Year seven times, and starting in 1962, she won the low scoring average a record seven times. Between 1965 and 1969 she won 45 times, including ten wins in 1968.

2. Mickey Wright. A native of San Diego, she won 82 LPGA events, second only to Whitworth, with 13 major titles, second only to Berg. In one stretch, she won at least one event for 14 straight seasons from 1956 to 1969. Wright was coached by Harvey Penick, who also developed Tom Kite and Ben Crenshaw, and Ben Hogan once said he'd never seen a better golf swing. She also is the only LPGA player in history to hold four major titles at the same time. In 2009 *Golf* magazine rated her the No. 1 female player of all time.

1. Annika Sorenstam. We've decided to make the Swedish star our No. 1 simply because she faced deeper fields than Wright had to contend with as the women's game went global over the span of her career. She won 72 tournaments, with ten major titles, and another 18 international wins to her credit. She earned $22 million, more than any player in history, before retiring at age 37 to marry and start a family. She was the tour's Player of the Year a record eight times and remains the only female ever to shoot the holy grail score of 59. She also made history by becoming the first female since 1945 to play in a PGA Tour event at the 2003 Colonial. Though she missed the cut, her performance under extreme pressure drew raves from around the world, and it was not long after that "Annika" became an international brand.

★ ★ ★ ★

"If you think it's hard to meet new people, try picking up the wrong golf ball."

—Jack Lemmon

TOP TWENTY MEN PLAYERS OF ALL TIME

You're talking a lot of history when you start ranking the top 20 men players of all time. In Scotland, they'll tell you they don't come any better than Young Tom Morris, who won four straight Open Championships (British Opens). Does Young Tom make the list? Of course. I don't want to offend the Scots, some of my favorite people in the world. However, when you're only talking about 20 golfers, you're excluding plenty of good golfers. My apologies. It's just one man's opinion, and here's mine.

20. Greg Norman. You could make the argument that Norman shouldn't be on this list. What about Hale Irwin, Raymond Floyd, Julius Boros, and countless others? Norman's career (20 PGA Tour victories and two majors) was defined more by his heartbreaks than victories. But unlike the other players, there's no denying that for a long period Norman was the top player of his era. Norman made sure things were never dull.

19. Cary Middlecoff. He started his adult life as a dentist and didn't turn pro until he was 26 in 1947. It turned out to be a good move. He wound up winning 40 PGA Tour titles, including three majors.

18. Young Tom Morris. The native of St. Andrews was golf's first true superstar. He won his first British Open in 1868 at the age of 17 and then won three more in a row. He recorded the first ace and first double eagle in Open history. Tragically, he died on Christmas day in 1875 at the age of 24. Golf fans visit his grave and that of his father, Old Tom Morris, at St. Andrews.

17. Seve Ballesteros. The Spaniard was golf's ultimate thrill show. Time after time, fans watched in awe as Seve escaped from trouble with shots that came from one of golf's most creative minds. He won five majors, including three British Opens. He also transformed the Ryder Cup, making it one of the top events in golf.

16. Nick Faldo. Faldo enjoyed a stellar career, leading the charge of great European golfers in the 1980s. He won six majors (three Masters and three British Opens). Methodical and steady and often surly as a player, Faldo since has let the fun side of his personality shine as the lead analyst for CBS and Golf Channel. It's been a remarkable transformation to watch.

15. Phil Mickelson. For a while, it looked as if "Lefty" would top the list as the best player never to win a major. However, he finally broke through in winning the 2004 Masters. When he won his third Green Jacket in 2010, he firmly cemented his status as one of the all-time greats.

14. Lee Trevino. Everyone loved the "Merry Mex." His humble origins, coupled with a funky homemade swing, made him an unlikely success story in golf. But there he was, going to toe-to-toe with Nicklaus and Palmer, winning his share of the hardware: 29 PGA Tour titles and six majors.

13. Billy Casper. Perhaps the most underrated golfer in history. Despite winning 51 tournaments, his name rarely comes up in best player conversations. Yes, Casper's record was hurt by winning only three majors. However, two of them were U.S. Open and the other was a Masters. He had plenty of game and shouldn't be overlooked.

12. Harry Vardon. Vardon was the most important player as the game started to capture people's attention at the turn of the century. The British golfer won a record six British Opens and the 1900 U.S. Open. He also popularized the Vardon Grip, or overlapping grip.

11. Gene Sarazen. "The Squire" was a brilliant player, winning 39 PGA Tour titles and seven majors. Even though he is credited with inventing the sand wedge, he will be most remembered for a shot with his 4-wood. His 235-yard double eagle during the final round of the 1935 Masters is the most famous shot in golf history. It put the Masters on the map.

10. Gary Player. It's incredible to think of what Player accomplished, considering he did it during an era prior to high-speed travel. Nobody logged more miles than the native of South Africa. His work ethic and wonderful approach allowed him to win nine majors and post more than 100 victories worldwide. "The Big 3" of Nicklaus and Palmer wouldn't have the same without Player.

9. Tom Watson. He proved to be a worthy rival for Nicklaus, often getting the best of him. Watson won 39 PGA Tour events and eight majors. But he likely will be best remembered for the one that got away: his epic near-miss in winning the 2009 British

Open at the age of 59. Any golfer who can almost win a major pushing 60 has to be a top-ten player in my book.

8. Byron Nelson. He is perhaps the Joe DiMaggio of golf. He had a relatively short career, retiring to his ranch at the age of 34. But he left a lifetime of memories. Like DiMaggio's 56-game hitting streak, Nelson's 11-tournament winning streak in 1945 never will be broken.

7. Walter Hagen. Only two modern-day players, Nicklaus and Woods, won more majors than Hagen, who bagged 11. And his peak years were before the Masters was created. Hagen was perhaps the game's ultimate showman. He didn't just win. He won with style.

6. Sam Snead. "Slammin' Sammy" won young and he won old, winning an event at the age of 52. The reason was simple: Snead had the best swing in golf. It propelled him to a PGA Tour record of 82 victories and seven majors.

5. Bobby Jones. He was the first player to take golf to another level in the United States. His dominance during the '20s and then his Grand Slam in 1930 put him in the team picture with Babe Ruth, Jack Dempsey, and Red Grange as the iconic athletes of that era. He retired at the age of 28 and then played as an amateur. Who knows what he would have accomplished if he had a long career as a pro?

4. Arnold Palmer. No player was more responsible for elevating the popularity of golf than "The King." He won 62 PGA Tour titles and seven majors. But he didn't just win. He seized tournaments with a go-for-broke approach that led to the creation of "Arnie's Army." Millions enlisted and remain loyal to this day.

3. Ben Hogan. Although the two players ahead of him on this list have better records, there's never been another golfer who had his mystique. Mention the name "Hogan," and you think of perfection achieved through incredibly hard work and dedication to the craft. If you asked who is the one player you'd most want to emulate, I'd bet more than 80 percent of golfers would say Hogan.

2. Tiger Woods. Regardless of how his career plays out, Woods will be remembered for feats that defied the bounds of reality of golf. Winning a Masters by 12 shots? Winning a U.S. Open by 15 shots? Are you kidding me? He's the only player in the history of golf to hold all four major titles at the same time. And there are countless other marks. Who knows? Woods still could end up at the top of this list when it is all said and done.

1. Jack Nicklaus. His 18 majors remains the gold standard in golf. Until somebody tops that magic number, Nicklaus will hold on to the top spot. What further sets apart Nicklaus from the rest is that he dominated in era that featured perhaps the best collection of golfers of all time, as evidenced by this list. Nicklaus had to beat players like Palmer, Player, Trevino, and Watson. No small feat there. All hail "The Golden Bear."

★ ★ ★ ★

"They say golf is like life, but don't believe them. Golf is more complicated than that."

—Gardner Dickinson

Photography Credits: